The Bookshops of London

The Bookshops of London

Martha Redding Pease

Salem House Publishers
Topsfield, Massachusetts

© 1981 Martha Redding Pease
Additional research by Penny Gillespie

First published in the United States by
Salem House Publishers
462 Boston Street
Topsfield, MA 01983
Revised edition 1984, reprint 1985
Third edition 1987

Pease, Martha Redding
  The bookshops of London.

  Includes indexes.
  1. Booksellers and bookselling—England—London—
  Directories. 2. Antiquarian booksellers—England—
  London—Directories. I. Title.
  Z330.6.L6P4   1987   070.5′025′421   87-4494

  ISBN 0–88162–294–X (pbk.)

The publishers have made every effort to ensure that the information contained in this book is correct. They cannot, however, accept responsibility for any errors or inaccuracies contained herein.

Typeset by Rapidset and Design Ltd, London WC1
Printed and bound in Great Britain by
Richard Clay (The Chaucer Press) Ltd, Bungay, Suffolk

To David with love and thanks

Contents

Acknowledgements

My sincere thanks go to all the London booksellers who tolerated my incessant questioning. I am grateful, also, to my publishers for their confidence in the book, and for the work of my in-house editor. Most of all, I want to thank my parents without whom I would never have ventured this far.

Introduction

'If a book is worth reading,' said Ruskin, 'it is worth buying', but first it must be found. For the busy professionals in the City who can't locate that hard-to-find reference book, for students, who need a source for second-hand textbooks, for the sci-fi fanatics who have looked all over for issue number 34 of *Weird Fantasy*, for visitors who want to explore part of London's rich literary heritage, indeed, for anyone who wants to find a particular book, or merely wants to browse looking for nothing in particular — this book is for you. This is a guide to London's bookshops, the first comprehensive account of one of London's greatest resources.

When William Caxton set up his printing press in Westminster in 1476, he also became London's first retail bookseller and heralded an age and tradition of English pre-eminence in bookselling which we still enjoy to this day. Now there are over 500 bookshops in London, each of which, in its very existence, testifies to the continuing English delight in the written word. And though a book from the press of Caxton is virtually priceless, a wealth of affordable and fascinating literature can be found in the bookshops of today, from paperback reprints of Caxton's titles to books on technologies never dreamed of even a hundred years ago.

Within the last century booksellers have benefited incalculably from sophisticated distribution and supply networks, modern methods of printing which have increased the available range and number of books, and a growing book-buying public. Shops have sprung up all over London, from the northernmost suburbs of Southgate and Mill Hill to the southern reaches of Wimbledon, Dulwich and Crystal Palace.

The face of London bookselling today is a far cry, literally, from the booksellers of Caxton's era when all but Caxton were huddled in the churchyard of St Paul's. In fact, the ravages of fire, war and progress nearly destroyed all traces of one of the world's most active book centres. From the fifteenth through the eighteenth centuries, hundreds of English and Continental printers and booksellers teemed in the areas of Little Britain around Smithfield market, Cornhill and Lombard Streets, Paternoster Row,

Chancery Lane, St Paul's and even on the old London Bridge. Until the late eighteenth century, the City harboured the combination printers, publishers and booksellers from the dictatorial control of the nobility and the dominion of university presses. Sadly, only two antiquarian booksellers are left within the square mile of the City, along with a handful of general bookshops and a few speciality shops.

In the last century Charing Cross Road became the locus of quality London bookselling and today, still lining the road from Trafalgar Square to Oxford Street, are some of London's leading bookshops: Foyles, Zwemmer, Collet's and Waterstone's – a major new force in London bookselling, with five branches throughout the centre. Other retailers have also caught on to the fact that bookselling doesn't have to be a dingy, dusty trade, and none more so than Dillon's, whose expansion and modernisation has set a high standard for others to emulate.

Along the narrow side-streets of Charing Cross Road are newer specialized bookshops in fields like science fiction, photography and Greek studies. Kensington, Chelsea, Mayfair, Marylebone and Bloomsbury, too, have their booksellers dating back many decades, like Maggs Bros, Sotheran and Andrew Block. But many of London's newest shops have avoided the sky-rocketing rents and rates of Central London and set up shop in established residential and small business areas all over town.

New energy and direction have been given to modern bookselling in London with these recently established, often smaller and sometimes specialized shops outside Central London where the personalities of the neighbourhoods are reflected in the make-up of a bookshop's stock. The Kilburn Bookshop, for example, has special sections of books on Ireland, the Caribbean, Africa and radical politics which give an immediate sense of the special racial and political mix in the neighbourhood. Islington has a women's cooperative running Sisterwrite, a complete feminist bookshop where working-class, professional and home-bound women from all over North London can come to find the best in recent feminist fiction and non-fiction. In East London two shops — the Tower Hamlets Arts Project and Centerprise — not only sell books, but publish local authors, organize discussion groups and make a continual effort to improve the quality of life for people in their neighbourhoods, while South London is seeing the slow, but encouraging, rise in the number of quality second-hand booksellers such as Stone Trough in Camberwell and Chener Books in Grove Vale, as well as their own community bookshops such as the Bookplace in Peckham and Sabarr Books in Brixton.

The myriad specialities of the shops in London have been long in developing, linked directly to the cessation of censorship and the ever-expanding range of subjects in which the public demands books. In the first 200 years of bookselling, titles rarely deviated from religious and classical subjects; indeed, in 1520, the bestselling authors were Erasmus and Luther. Caxton sowed the seeds of popular literature in the fifteenth century by printing and selling books in English (rather than Latin), books that might delight the literate nobility rather than instruct the grave divines. Jacob Tonson, a printer and bookseller in eighteenth-century London, finished opening the doors of the literary world to the general public when he published Rowe's edition of Shakespeare in 1709. Today we have access to all the corners of human knowledge, from the life cycle of red ants to previously heretical political philosophies.

Not only do we have choice in the books we buy, but we also have convenience. Our word 'book' derives from the German 'buch' meaning beech, as in beech wood. Early handwritten manuscripts (the precursors of our Penguins) were protected with beech wood covers, which were cumbersome to say the least. Wisecracking Erasmus said of the bound manuscript of Thomas Aquinas's *Secunda Secundae*, 'No man could carry it about, much less get it into his head'. The advent of paperbacks have made bookselling and book-buying easy, high-speed and high-volume activities, as books can be produced quickly, in large numbers and not take the place of furniture in our homes.

So between the old and the new worlds of book production sit hundreds of bookshops in London. This book brings them together in an easy-to-use format with descriptive, rather than judgemental, information about each shop. Here are all of London's bookshops, from the shop selling 10p second-hand thrillers to the shop with priceless incunabula. 'Where is human nature so weak,' asked Henry Ward Beecher, 'as in a bookshop?' At least one of the shops listed in the pages below should prove his point.

How to Use the Guide

As the form and content of books have evolved through eight centuries, so have the language and structure of the business of bookselling. With specialized publishing and retailing, specialized terminology is used in the trade, and this often filters down to the consumer. I have used many 'bookseller's' terms in this book, so a few definitions are appropriate here.

In-print versus out-of-print books
A book is 'in-print' if it is currently available from the publisher's stock. Out-of-print books are no longer printed by the publisher, nor are they usually available through normal channels of stock ordering. Titles which have recently gone out-of-print can sometimes still be found on the shelves of a shop which carries in-print books.

New or current titles
Any book which is in print is a 'new' or 'current' book. Current titles include books being published for the first time, new editions of previously published works and 'back list' titles such as classics of English literature and reference books which are continually published over the course of many years and are always kept in stock.

Remaindered and end-of-run books
When a publisher declares a title out-of-print a sizeable stock of the end of the printer's run of a book may still be sitting in a warehouse. The publisher makes these unsold, soon to be out-of-print books available to booksellers and the public at significantly reduced prices, as 'remainders'. Remaindered books are usually restricted to hardcover titles, as it is cheaper to shred out-of-print paperbacks than go to the expense of distributing them.

Second-hand books
Out-of-print and remaindered titles, books which have been sold and resold, antiquarian and rare books, and 'review copies' of

newly published titles (see below), all of these kinds of books are classed as second-hand. Within this classification fall valuable modern first editions, the rarest of incunabula and the tattiest of used paperbacks.

Antiquarian and rare books
It seems that no one in the book trade can agree on a definition of antiquarian books. For my purposes I have classified 'antiquarian' books as those which were published before 1850. The further distinction of 'rare' books denotes antiquarian and second-hand books which are particularly valuable because of their scarcity, condition, associations and/or content. An antiquarian book does not necessarily have to be rare, and a 'rare' book could just as easily be a modern first edition as a finely bound volume of the King James Bible.

First editions
The term 'first edition' describes the first print run of a particular title. Throughout this book I have referred, also, to first editions of sought-after writers' works in the twentieth century as 'modern first editions'. To most bibliophiles, these are valuable and collectable books, be they paperback Penguins or hardcover titles.

Review copies
With the publication of a new title, publishers send copies of the book to newspaper, magazine and TV reviewers and to people working in the book trade. Many second-hand book dealers have access to these review copies and sell them as 'brand new' at bargain prices.

Reprints
Theoretically any book that is issued in either paperback or hardcover is a reprint. In reality, reprints usually refer to scholarly works which are in great enough demand by academics, librarians and researchers to warrant a small print run by the publisher.

Mail order
Many shops will post books to customers provided the client pays postage fees. Mail order does not always mean that a shop produces a mail order list or catalogue from which books can be ordered.

Special order
Usually on a basis which is limited to the range of publishers from which the shop orders, individual books which are not on the

shelves can be specially ordered by the shop. A deposit is most often required before the shop orders the books.

Search service
Antiquarian and second-hand bookshops often provide an active search service for customers looking for hard-to-find books. The shop will place advertisements in a variety of trade and professional magazines to locate one or several volumes. Depending on the shop, there may or may not be a fee.

Wants list
Several antiquarian and second-hand bookshops are willing to accept customers' 'wants lists' for out-of-print, antiquarian and valuable books which the client has not been able to locate. Wants lists differ from a search service in that the bookseller simply keeps an eye out, so to speak, for titles on wants lists he or she has received. No guarantees are given that the particular book will be found (through either a search service or a wants list), but it is not unusual for a bookseller to contact a client many years after a wants list has been received with news of the desired title.

Book exchanges
In recent years second-hand paperback 'book exchanges' have cropped up all over the city. These shops give a 50 per cent credit on books bought at the shop and returned for exchange towards more books from the same shop. Most of these shops carry low-price paperback science fiction, fantasy, romance, war and western novels as well as second hand magazines and comics (which are not sold on the basis of 50 per cent return and exchange).

In this book you will find general, speciality, and antiquarian and second-hand bookshops which have a retail outlet in a numbered postal code in London. Every shop is in these pages with the exception of the combination newsagents and booksellers, unless the book portion of the business is in some way specialized (as in the case of Witherby & Co.). Students of the history of bookselling may groan at this omission arguing that the patent medicines, sewing machines and sundries which Victorian bookshops often sold to augment their incomes did not exclude them from the bona fide ranks of their contemporary booksellers. Indeed, today almost every high street newsagent has a limited selection of the newest paperback fiction, and chain shops like Menzies and Lavells often have extensive ranges of paperback and hardback fiction and non-fiction. Their numbers, however, are almost endless, though their contribution to making books accessible is not to be discounted.

This guide is divided geographically according to London's postal codes. Within each postal code are subdivisions listing (1) general bookshops (2) speciality bookshops and (3) antiquarian and second-hand bookshops. Shops considered as 'speciality bookshops' do not always deal exclusively with books in their speciality. Often they will have a general stock of titles but the strength and distinction of their stock is in a particular subject area which determines their classification.

Shops which sell antiquarian, second-hand and new books have been listed under the heading in which the larger portion of their stock falls. For example, Sotheran is considered an antiquarian bookshop though they sell new books as well. Some second-hand and antiquarian bookshops specialize in only one subject, but these shops are listed in the second-hand and antiquarian section rather than the speciality section.

The first index provides an overview of London's bookshops. Bookshops are grouped here by speciality. Thus, all the general bookshops will be listed together, as well as all the religious bookshops and all the shops specializing in children's books. Shops, of course, may well fit under several headings, so Sotheran will be indexed under the categories of 'Antiquarian', 'Second-hand', and 'New', and in certain speciality areas such as 'Bibles', 'Literature', 'Illustrated Books' and 'Natural History'.

A complete alphabetical listing of all of the shops in this book can be found in the second index, with their postal codes noted as well as the page on which they can be found in the text.

Note

It is inevitable in a guide of this sort that in the period between final preparation of copy and the appearance of the finished book changes will have occurred; some shops will have moved, others closed down altogether; more cheerfully, others will have opened. Especially in the second-hand areas, shops so often depending on the cheaper end-of-lease properties, it is difficult to keep track of these shiftings. The publishers will be glad to receive details of any such moves and new appearances, both from proprietors and customers, so that the guide can be made as useful as possible in each printing. An increasing number of booksellers are working from home with the regular issue of catalogues, such is the difficulty of meeting the rate bills of a shop; where the proprietor is willing to meet customers at fairly regular times it might prove worthwhile to be listed in a guide essentially devoted to bookshops – again the publishers would be happy to hear from such bookdealers.

It is clear, meanwhile, that there is sufficient enthusiasm among both dealers and customers to combat those planners and developers who would be happier with a bookless capital.

London WC

General Bookshops

Adelaide Book Centre   *(Charing Cross)*
9 Adelaide Street
The Strand WC2
836-6502

M–Sun 10:00a.m.–10:00p.m.

Africa / archaeology / Australia / biography / Britain / building construction / business / child care / children's books / classics / communications / cookery / DIY / drama / economics / education / essays / fiction / foreign literature / gardening / historical biography / history / humour / language teaching / law / literature / London / maritime history / Middle East / military history / modern first editions / music / mysticism / mythology / naval history / New Zealand / North America / occult / philosophy / plays / poetry / politics / population / psychology / racial issues / religion / royal family / sex in society / Shakespeare / sociology / sports / stamp collecting / textbooks / theatre / transport / travel / zoology

Situated in a partial pedestrian precinct off the north side of the Strand, near Charing Cross Station, the shop is on two floors, selling new books on the ground floor and second-hand books in the basement. The owner is also the proprietor of the Greenwich Book Place and this shop carries an extensive range of titles similar to that at Greenwich, with particular emphasis on the humanities and social sciences. There is a small section of antiquarian books and special sections of Dover and Penguin books. The shelves are well organized – each subdivision within a category is clearly marked – so it is fairly easy to find a particular subject. Old and modern prints, and a variety of watercolours, deck the walls and a framing service is also available.

Non-book material: cards, prints, watercolours
Services: mail order, special order, framing service
Catalogue: occasional selected lists

Book Bargains   *(Covent Garden)*
124 Long Acre WC2
836-0625

M–Sat 10:00–midnight   Sun 2:00–6:00

This is a remainder bookshop selling among other subjects, travel, art, photography, performing arts, natural history.

Services: mail order
Catalogue: twice yearly

Book Inn   *(Leicester Square)*
17 Charing Cross Road WC2
839-2712

M–Sat 9:30–11:00p.m.   Sun 11:00–10:00

art / biography / children's books / cookery / crafts / dictionaries / fiction / military history / natural science / science fiction / travel guides

This is a general bookshop selling new and remaindered titles, with a particularly large selection of science fiction books.

Non-book material: cards, London and UK maps, stationery

Books Etc.   *(Tottenham Court Road)*
120 Charing Cross Road WC2
379-6838

M–Sat 9:30–8:00

antiques / art / biography / children's books / classics / computers / crafts / crime / DIY / fiction / film / gardening / health / history / humour / literary criticism / literature / music / natural history / philosophy / photography / plays / poetry / politics / psychology / reference / religion / science fiction / sports / thrillers / travel guides

This large general bookshop was the first of the Books Etc. chain to open. It stocks more paperbacks than hardbacks but recent new books are given a fair amount of space and are well displayed. There is a particularly good choice of paperback fiction, sci-fi and crime upstairs, and you will find, among other things, an expanded section of music, film, photography and art books in the basement.

Non-book material: cards, wrapping-paper, stationery, calendars and diaries
Services: special order

The Booksmith   *(Tottenham Court Road)*
148 Charing Cross Road WC2
836-3032

M–Sat 9:00–8:00

Just next to Centre Point is The Booksmith which carries bargain priced hardcover and paperback books in a range of subjects (the stock changes frequently). Full-price paperback fiction and non-fiction are also available.

Catalogue: regular book lists available through Bibliophile Book Club

Collet's International Bookshop   *(Leicester Square)*
129-131 Charing Cross Road WC2
734-0782

M–F 10:00–6:30   Sat 10:00–6:00

black studies / cinema / cookery / development / economics / education and EFL / feminism / fiction / gay books / health / history / Ireland / literary criticism / literature / Marxism / media / North America / philosophy / politics / psychology / race / reference / rights / Russian and Eastern European literature / Russian language-teaching / sociology / Soviet and Eastern studies / Third World / travel

Collet's is the leading specialist bookseller of Russian and Eastern European titles in this country, even though only 25% of the total floor space is occupied by these sections. As distributor for the national Soviet publisher, Progress Publishing, Collet's maintains an extensive stock of Russian language texts (including fiction, politics, classics), as well as Russian and Soviet works in translation. Another speciality of the shop is language-teaching aids for learning Eastern European languages. The staff are very knowledgeable and will help you to track down titles from behind the Iron Curtain. Some second-hand Russian books are also stocked.

For the most part Collet's is a general bookshop in the Charing Cross mould and now incorporates Collet's London Bookshop which used to be in a separate building. In the general section there is an impressive social sciences department, a good range of feminist and gay literature, a selection of art books, travel, etc., and also some new hardback fiction. Two other strings to its bow are a vast selection of left-wing newspapers and periodicals from all over the world and a specialist folk record department.

Non-book material: badges, cards, language-teaching cassettes and records, Melodia (Soviet label), posters, records, T-shirts, wrapping-paper
Services: mail order, special order
Catalogue: selected catalogues
Publications: the Collet's imprint appears on selected Eastern European titles

Dillon's the Bookstore   *(Goodge Street/Euston Square)*
1 Malet Street WC1
636-1577

M–F 9:00–5:30   Tue 10:00–5:30   Sat 9:30–5:30

basement:
art materials / Athena / biology / chemistry / computing / electronics / engineering / geography / mathematics / medicine / physics / stationery / transport / travel maps

ground:
bargain books / biography / children's / fiction / leisure / literature / magazines / newspapers / Penguin

first:
art / classics / history and politics / languages / music and records / philosophy / reference

second:
economics / education / law / management / psychology / religion / second-hand / sociology / Third World

third:
book tokens / cash office / reception

Dillon's lays claim to the title 'Europe's finest bookstore' and one can well see why. With over five miles of shelving, highly informed staff and a strikingly modern yet elegant design, it is an exciting place to search for and buy books. The main entrance is on Malet Street and once inside a wooden staircase sweeps up and away beckoning the customers to come and explore, while to right and left of the marble-floored hallway are similarly enticing shelves and in-store displays. To dispell confusion there is a display board showing each subject and its appropriate floor – the list runs to over four hundred categories. There is also a customer lift in case you feel exhausted before you have even begun.

The literature department is excellent and beyond this, with its own entrance on Gower Street, is a comprehensive paperback collection including several shelves of Penguin books. The social sciences, too, are covered in depth and looking for just the right map in the travel department is greatly facilitated by the special drawers which slide easily in and out. Dillon's has always had a good music department and this now includes separate areas devoted entirely to extensive choices of cassettes, compact discs and records. The language department has a proud boast, which is that the staff between them can offer eight languages. Each department has separate enquiry desks and cash tills – these are clearly labelled, so there is no excuse for getting it wrong.

This shop has everything going for it, except for the fact that it is somewhat off the beaten track for the general public, being originally conceived as a university bookshop for the University of London, which is on its doorstep. It was founded by Una Dillon in 1946 and reopened by Princess Anne in 1986.

Non-book material: art materials, Athena stationery and card shop, audio-visual language-teaching aids, cassettes, compact discs, computers and software, records
Services: special order

Foyles   *(Leicester Square/Tottenham Court Road)*
119 Charing Cross Road WC1
437-5660   439-8501 (mail order only)

M–Sat 9:00–6:00   Th 9:00–7:00

basement:
bargains / dentistry / medicine / nursing / veterinary services

ground floor:
autobiography / BBC / beauty / biography / catering / children's

books / cookery / dictionaries / English literature / fiction / language teaching / linguistics / literary criticism / literature / Penguin / poetry / travel classics

first floor:
astronomy / education / geography / management / mathematics / photography / physics / technology / transport

second floor:
anthropology / antiques / archaeology / architecture / art / classics / crafts / foreign literature / gardening / history / military history / natural history / politics / rare books / sports / zoology

third floor:
astrology / ballet / cinema / commerce / drama / economics / law / media / music / philosophy / plays / psychology / records / religion / scores / sheet music / sociology / theatre history / theology / videos

Foyles continues to stock an exceptionally broad range of titles in each of the subject areas outlined above, some of which have become shelved by publisher rather than the more conventional, useful way by alphabet or subject. So if you are looking for a particular title, make sure you know who publishes it.

Unfortunately Foyles is one of the most disorganized bookshops in London with books bursting from the shelves, piled on the floor and haphazardly ordered. Because the staff does not seem to cull the shelves regularly, recently out-of-print titles are often mingling next to new books which are often at less than the list-price. If you are willing to hunt you may well find the book you want – somewhere. Should you be lucky enough to locate what you want, the next obstacle is paying for the book. Foyles has an absurd system, redolent of a Moscow department store, of wrapping your book and giving you a receipt for the merchandise which you can then take across the floor to the usually long queue in front of the cage-like cashier's box. There you finally get to pay before returning to the wrapping desk to claim your purchase.

My experience with Foyles suggests the staff are as baffled and frustrated by the chaos of the shelves as most of the customers. The sales people are ill-informed, but part of this is possibly due to the lack of training at the start of their tenure at the shop and the fact that many of them are foreign students on short-term contracts.

There must be many customers who now turn to Waterstone's next door for efficiency and enthusiasm. By the way – a word of warning: do not think you can escape the experience that is Foyles by telephoning them. They are permanently engaged.

Non-book material: art gallery, records, stationery, videos
Services: mail order, special order

The Good Book Guide   *(Tottenham Court Road)*
(Braithwaite & Taylor)
91 Great Russell Street WC1
580-8466   24 hr order service 720-8182

M–Sat 10:00–6:00   Sun 12:00–6:00

arts / bestsellers / biography / business / children's / discovery /
fiction / food and drink / history and war / human society / humour /
natural world / practical activities / reference / sports and fitness /
travel and adventure / world affairs

The Good Book Guide has a very pleasant atmosphere. This is
created by the carefully selected titles on sale here and the
effective way they are displayed together with the design of the
shop. It has a cosy fire and a postbox set into the wall for
customers to post their orders and there is a children's corner with
a painted mural. Books stocked are those featured by Braithwaite
& Taylor in their catalogue of the same name. They pride
themselves on their excellent international mail order system and
gift service through which you can send books, tokens and gift
subscriptions anywhere in the world. The guide itself appears six
times yearly and there is a special Children's Guide and a
Business Guide.

Services: see above
Catalogue: see above

Greenwich Book Company   *(Covent Garden)*
37 Neal Street WC2
240-3319

M–F 10:00–7:00   Sat 10:00–6:00

biography / classics / cookery / fiction / gardening / health /
humour / plays / poetry / psychology / reference / sport / travel /
women's books

Neal Street is an attractive pedestrian area near Covent Garden. It
is crammed with fascinating little shops amongst which you will

find this general bookshop, which also sells some remainder books. They stock a good selection of paperback fiction, poetry and plays and they do have some new hardback fiction and biography.

Services: special order

Hatchards   *(Charing Cross/Covent Garden)*
390 Strand WC2
379-6264

M–Sat 9:30–6:00

ground: hardbacks
antiques / architecture / art / biography / cookery / gardening / literature / natural history / performing arts / photography / reference / sport / travel

basement: paperbacks
biography / children's / classics / fiction / humour / reference / science fiction

This branch of Hatchards is smaller than the King's Road or Piccadilly branches, but retains the same style with carpeting throughout and well lit books easy to identify against the dark wooden shelving. The staff are friendly and know their subjects well.

Services: mail order, special order
Catalogue: Spring and Autumn catalogues, monthly reviews gardening and art catalogues

Kings Bookshop   *(Russell Square)*
17a Rugby Street WC1
405-4551

M–F 9:45–5:30

autobiography / biography / children's books / cookery / fiction / travel

This is a very small general neighbourhood bookshop, with a selective stock of mainly UK publishers' titles. Because of the nearby children's hospital the shop stocks books for children under age 10.

Services: special order (any subject)

Lovejoys   *(Leicester Square)*
99a Charing Cross Road WC2
437-1988

M–Sat 10:00a.m.–10:30p.m.

It is rather strange that a sex shop should penetrate the book market; perhaps it is so that customers can go to the basement, where the licensed adult material is stocked, without feeling guilty or perhaps it is for licensing purposes. Be that as it may, the bookshop on the ground floor is quite respectable, selling new paperbacks and remainders in the areas of fiction, crime, horror, science fiction and general subjects.

Non-book material: licensed adult material in the basement, weekly events magazines

The Penguin Bookshop   *(Covent Garden)*
10 The Market
Covent Garden WC2
379-7650

M–Sat 10:00–8:00

art / biography / business and economics / classics / cooking / crime / drama / education / feminism / fiction / film, TV / games, sports / history / humour / language / literary criticism / literature / music / natural history / philosophy / poetry / politics / psychology / reference / religion / science, mathematics / science fiction / sociology / travel guides

This is a general bookshop right in the centre of the market, which despite the shop's name is not devoted exclusively to Penguin books, although all Penguin titles are here. Certain hardbacks are stocked as well. They manage to cram an awful lot into really quite a small space, have interesting window displays and also frequently host busy signing sessions which tend to spill out enticingly onto the pedestrian area of the market.

Non-book material: literary magazines, postcards
Services: mail order, Penguin monthly stocklist, special order

Pipeline Bookshop   *(Holborn)*
87 High Holborn WC1
242-5454

M–Sat 9:00–6:00

astrology / biography / children's / classics / cookery / crime /
drama / fictional film / gardening / health / history / humour /
music / occult / philosophy / photography / politics / psychology /
reference / religion / science fiction / sociology / sport / travel /
women's studies

This is a general bookshop on two floors and is owned by the book
wholesalers of the same name. This means that customer orders
can usually be fulfilled within 24 hours. The shop is efficiently run
and the staff very knowledgeable.

Non-book material: cards, wrapping-paper
Services: special order

St Martin's Lane Bookshop   *(Leicester Square)*
36a St Martin's Lane WC2
836-5110

M–Sat 10:00–8:00

There are two floors of bargain books in a variety of subject areas
at this shop which is part of Booksmith's mail order section.
Indeed its stock is almost the same as that to be found at the
Booksmith chain. It, too, has a basic range of full-price
paperbacks.

Catalogue: regular lists are available through Bibliophile Book
Club

W.H. Smith   *(Holborn/Kingsway)*
11 Kingsway WC2
836-5951

M–F 8:30–5:30   Tue 9:30–5:30

This branch of W.H. Smith is on the corner at the south end of Kingsway and has a reasonable-sized book department carrying a range of general titles in both hard and paper covers. They have a good section of reference books and dictionaries.

Non-book material: stationery, cards, records, news, etc.
Services: post-a-book, special order, tokens
Catalogue: *Bookcase* review of books twice yearly

Souvenir Press Ltd   *(Tottenham Court Road)*
43 Great Russell Street WC1
580-9307

M–F 9:30–5:30

biography / childcare / children's books / cookery / crafts / education / fiction / gardening / guides and maps / health / history / hobbies / non-fiction / reference / sport / travel

This is a small shop with a few new titles on display in what is basically the Souvenir Press publishing office.

Non-book material: maps
Catalogue: publisher's catalogue bi-annually
Publications: Souvenir Press is a general book publisher

Templar Books   *(Chancery Lane)*
76a Chancery Lane WC2
405-3189

M–F 9:00–6:00

art / biography / classics / fiction / law / literature / natural history / non-fiction / reference / travel guides

Current hardcover and paperback titles are stocked in this general bookshop, including paperback series of Pan, Penguin, Pelican, and Fontana. Some remainders are sold.

Non-book material: cards, wrapping-paper
Services: mail order, special order

Vermilion Books   *(Holborn)*
57 Red Lion Street WC1
242–5822

M–F 10:30–6:00

applied art / architecture / biography / cinema / collecting / criminology / dance / drama / education / games / gastronomy / history / literature / military history and affairs / music / occult / ornithology / poetry / politics / sculpture / sport / theatre / transport / travel

This is a general bookshop selling new books at reduced prices and some second-hand titles, with an emphasis on the subjects of literature, ornithology, military history, cinema and theatre. Despite the moderate sized display space, the shop has an excellent range of titles and is well worth a visit. Almost any recent paperback can be found here at a third off normal price.

Services: wants lists accepted

Waterstone and Davies   *(Holborn/Russell Square)*
62-64 Southampton Row WC1
831-9019

M–F 9:00–6:30

ground floor:
bestsellers / children's books / classics / cookery and food / fiction / London / travel

basement:
art / atlases / biography / crafts / current events / DIY / drama / economics / Faber / gardening / history / military and naval / performing arts / philosophy / poetry / politics / psychology / reference / religion / sociology / sports and games / women's studies

Keeping hours suited to the local business customers, this, the smallest of the Waterstone's group, maintains an excellent stock with sections also useful for the local student population. An earlier population, continuing to grow in print, is well represented by a section devoted to the Bloomsbury Group. The shop is close to Faber and Faber's offices in Queen's Square and has developed a section containing almost all the firm's books (and it can obtain anything from the Harlow warehouse within twenty-four hours); the back-list contains numerous fascinating titles some of which one might have thought to be long out-of-print.

Non-book material: cards, maps, literary magazines
Services: mail order, special order, school supply, a Waterstone's credit card which can be used in the shop and by telephone

Waterstone's   *(Tottenham Court Road)*
121-125 Charing Cross Road WC2
434-4291

M–F 9:30–7:30   Sat 10:30–7:30

basement:
classics / literary criticism / poetry

ground floor:
best-sellers / humour / reference / travel

first floor:
antiques / architecture / art / children's / cookery and food / drama / gardening / music / natural history / performing arts

second floor:
biography / business / computer science / current affairs / economics / feminism / foreign languages / health / history / management / military / psychology / social sciences / sport

third floor:
astrology / occult / philosophy / record department specializing in classical and spoken word titles / religion

This is a lively and efficient bookshop well advertised by its invariably interesting and attractive window displays. With some irony it bought one of Foyle's buildings and has shown that it can provide a far more rapid, knowledgeable and enthusiastic service – the staff gives the impression of really working in a bookshop rather than their neighbours' one of listlessly filling in time. Like the other shops in the Waterstone's group this branch concentrates on the humanities but it does have a substantial section about computer science as well. The emphasis is more on academic topics than at the other branches but a wide general stock is maintained, religion, philosophy and new fiction being especially strong areas. Notable, too, is the expanding section of second-hand art books – out-of-print and rare – for which a search service is also provided.

Non-book material: cards; cassettes and records; magazines such as the *Fiction Magazine*, the *Literary Review*, the *London Review of Books* and the *Times Literary Supplement*; maps; posters
Services: mail order, prompt special order, a Waterstone's credit card which can be used in all branches and by telephone

Speciality Bookshops

Africa Book Centre   *(Covent Garden/Leicester Square)*
38 King Street WC2
240-6649

M–Sat 9:30–5:30

architecture / art / bibliography / economics / education / fiction /
geography / health care / history / politics / religion / sociology

This is a bookroom on the ground floor of the Africa Centre,
specializing in titles concerning Black Africa, the Carribean, the
Third World and Black Britain. Some of the books, but not all, are
for sale, being part of publishers' exhibitions.

Non-book material: African records, tapes, videos

The Albanian Shop   *(Covent Garden)*
3 Betterton Street WC2
836-0976

M 10:00–3:00   Tue–Sat 10:00–6:00

Situated in the same premises as the Gramophone Exchange this
shop has an almost complete stock of English-language
publications from the foreign-language press in Tirana, as well as
some titles in Albanian. The books in English, of which there are a
surprising number, cover current affairs in Albania and abroad,
history, archaeology, art, literature, music and travel. Some
recent Albanian illustrated periodicals in English are kept in
stock.

Non-book material: cards, maps, posters, records, handicrafts
Services: mail order, special order

Al Hoda   *(Leicester Square)*
76-78 Charing Cross Road WC2
240-8381

M–Sat 9:30–6:00

art and culture / biography / children's books / cookery / economics / dictionaries / Farsi / Hadith / history / Islamic sciences / jurisprudence / literature / mysticism / philosophy and ethics / Quran / reference / science / theology

Al Hoda is given over entirely to the broad concerns of Islam and the Middle East. The educational section is strong, backed by records and cassettes, as is the children's with books both in England and Arabic. This is a small, new, but most friendly and enterprising bookshop.

Non-book material: Arab, Middle Eastern and Third World periodicals, children's educational games and jigsaws
Services: catalogue (six-monthly), mail order (in preparation), special order

The Alternative Bookshop   *(Covent Garden)*
3 Langley Court WC2
240-1804

M–Sat 11:00–6:00

Conservatism / defence / economics / foreign affairs / history / Liberalism / philosophy / USSR / Zionism

The Alternative Bookshop sells new, second-hand and remaindered titles. It is concerned with individual liberties, libertarian ideals, a free market economy and an open society. Books and periodicals on subjects within this political and economic context form the majority of the shop's stock, with most of the titles relating to British society.

Non-book material: journals
Services: mail order, special order in field, search service, libertarian meeting centre
Catalogue: selected lists, second-hand catalogues, monthly review

The Art Book Company   *(Covent Garden)*
18 Endell Street WC2
838-7907

M–F 9:30–5:30

advertising / airbrush / architecture / art education / ceramics / cinema / crafts / design / fashion / fine art / furniture / graphic design(ers) / graphic design annuals / musuem collections / photography: technical and illustrated / photography annuals: UK and foreign

This relatively small shop, now incorporating the old Bloomsbury branch, on Endell Street focuses on design and graphics. Most of the books are illustrated and their stock of graphic design annuals is particularly large. Periodicals on design and graphics are also available, with monographs and *catalogues raisonnés*.

Services: mail order, special order, microfilm service for periodicals
Catalogues: lists on a variety of topics (e.g., architectural history)
Publications: under the imprint of The Art Book Company, a few titles have been published, e.g. *Tubular Steel Furniture*

Arts Bibliographic   *(Tottenham Court Road)*
37 Great Russell Street WC1
636-5320

M–Fri 10:00–6:00

architecture / art criticism, history and theory / craft / design / fine art (20th-century) / graphics / photography

Here is an unusual cross-section of new books on all aspects of the visual arts. Leading UK, US and Continental art magazines and journals are also sold, with (mainly new) exhibition catalogues.

Non-book materials: calendars, diaries, audio-arts tapes, arts magazines
Services: mail order, special order, travelling display van to libraries
Catalogue: catalogue and supplements

Atlantis   *(Tottenham Court Road)*
49a Museum Street WC1
405-2120

M–Sat 11:00–5:30

alchemy / astrology / Aleister Crowley / divining / dream interpretation / Egyptology / flying saucers / folklore / freemasonry / healing / magic / occult / palmistry / practical magic and witchcraft / psychic worlds / qabalah / spiritualism / symbolism / tarot and Ching / western mysteries / witchcraft

Atlantis sells new and second-hand books on withcraft, magic, the occult and related fields, and most of the titles focus on these phenomena in the Western world. The stock of occult books is the most comprehensive of any shop in London. For the would-be practitioner, Atlantis has a large section of 'how to' books on witchcraft, divining and dowsing, among other subjects.

Non-book material: crystal balls, tarot cards
Services: mail order, special order, wants lists accepted, credit cards
Publications: Neptune Press publishes books on magic and witchcraft

Australian Gift Shop   *(Charing Cross)*
Western Australia House
115 Strand WC2
836-2292

M–F 9:00–5:30   Sat 9:00–1:00

aborigines / children's books / culture and lifestyle / emigration / history / illustrated books / poetry / travel guides / wildlife

This is a complete gift shop, with the sunny atmosphere of Australia surrounding both the staff and their stock. The books in the shop are imported from Australia, all are current titles, and cover all aspects of Australian society.

Non-book material: Australian-made gifts, including Vegemite (a form of Marmite) and other foods
Services: mail order, dollar gift vouchers for Australia

The Biography Bookshop   *(Covent Garden)*
49 The Market
Covent Garden WC2
240-0621

M–Sat 10:00–6:00

This bookshop, on the Jubilee Market side of Covent Garden, stocks biographies only – both new and second-hand – hence the wide range and depth of its stock. It is also building a reputation for finding out-of-print titles in its field. The bookshop is in fact part of Biografia Ltd – a large company who publish and sell books, videos and films in the area of biography.

Services: mail order, special order
Catalogue: comprehensive list of stock
Publications: see above

The Bookroom—Coo Press Ltd   *(Russell Square)*
19 Doughty Street WC1
242-0565

M–F 10:30–6:00

annuals / catalogues of photography collections / collections of individual photographers' works (US, UK, France, Japan, Russia, China, Middle East) / history / period albums / yearbooks

This shop in a listed Queen Anne house is tucked out of the way, but although the display space is small, there are lovely new (and a few remaindered) books on photography, particularly from the Far East and the US. Indeed, it has perhaps the widest selection of photography books in the UK. The emphasis is on the artistic, cultural and historical aspects of photography, as well as the technial elements. A selection of major international photography magazines is sold. There are many photographic studios in the area and so the shop is able to meet speedily both professional and amateur needs.

Non-book material: portfolios of reproductions
Services: mail order, special order, library and college supply
Catalogue: occasional lists
Publications: the affiliated firm Coo Press Ltd publishes *Creative Camera International Yearbook* and *Creative Camera Magazine*

Books for a Change   *(Leicester Square)*
52 Charing Cross Road WC2
836-2315

M–Sat 10:00–7:00

ecology / fiction / Third World authors / Third World development

This bookshop specializes in three main subject areas: the threat of war, both conventional and nuclear; polution, wasteful consumption of scarce resources and environmental destruction; and hunger and disease in the Third World. The directors of the shop include representatives of CND Publications, Friends of the Earth, War on Want and the United Nations Association.

As you enter there is a notice in the door warning 'you are now in a nuclear and smokefree zone'. There is a small section of second-hand books too and plenty of campaigning magazines to choose from including *Green Line, Links, Sanity,* and *Central America Report*. They also stock all Minority Rights Group publications.

Non-book material: badges, posters, stickers, magazines
Services: mail order, special order
Catalogue: frequently updated lists

Boswell Books and Prints   *(Tottenham Court Road)*
44 Great Russell Street WC1
580-7200

M–F 10:00–12:30   2:30–5:30   Sat 11:00–4:00

The largest selection of Japanese prints in London is complemented by a collection of books on Japan and China, antiquarian, second-hand and new. The book stock also covers an antiquarian collection of nineteenth-century English literature, modern first editions and a natural history section. In 1987 the bookshop will be extended when a Japanese prints gallery opens on the first floor.

Non-book material: Japanese prints
Services: mail order

Books from India (UK) Ltd/ Hindi Book Centre

(Tottenham Court Road)

45 Museum Street WC1
405-7226 / 405-3784

M–F 10:00–5:30   Sat 10:00–5:00

art / biography / classics / cookery / crafts / dictionaries / education / fiction / health administration / history / homeopathy / language teaching / law / lifestyle / literature / medicine / philosophy / politics / religion / sociology

The owner of this shop is a journalist and BBC commentator whose vision of 'India' is shaped by social, cultural and political realities, rather than geographically defined borders. There are books on all aspects of Afghanistan, Bangladesh, Nepal, Ceylon, Bokara, Burma and more, in English, Hindi, Urdu, Punjabi, Gujarati and Bengali. The Centre also is engaged in publishing books, information sheets, catalogues and pamphlets on India. Out-of-print books are kept in stock, as are scholarly journals, and occasionally they have remainders.

Non-book material: cards, cassettes, paper, posters, prints, records
Services: mail order, special order, search service, library and school supply worldwide
Catalogue: various lists (forty, at present) in specialized areas
Publications: Books from India (UK) Ltd publishes books on all aspects of India

British Crafts Centre

(Covent Garden)

43 Earlham Street
Covent Garden WC2
836-6993

M–F 10:00–5:30   Sat 11:00–5:00

There is a small section of books downstairs amidst the beautiful displays of pottery and crafts. They cover ceramics, textiles, wood and furniture, glass, metal and jewellery, paper, book-binding, calligraphy and general craft.

Services: mail order

British Institute of Management   *(Holborn)*
Africa House
64-78 Kingsway WC2
405-3456

M–F 9:30–5:00

This is a very small shop specializing in books and booklets on subjects of interest to top level managers in the UK. It sells only its own publications. Employee financial participation, recruiting, report writing, problems in the workplace and international business are a few of the areas covered, and the shop does a yearly list of new titles of particular interest to managers.

Non-book material: check-lists for managers, pamphlets, reports
Services: mail order
Catalogue: annual list of BIM publications
Publications: BIM publishes the monthly *Management News*

British Museum Shop   *(Tottenham Court Road)*
The British Museum
Great Russell Street WC1
636-1555

M–Sat 10:00–4:45   Sun 2:30–5:45

anthropology / archaeology / art / BM guides / coins and medals / Egyptian antiquities / Greek and Roman antiquities / history / horology / Oriential antiquities / pre-history / Romano-British antiquities / Western Asiatic art

The large, brightly-lit bookshop is immediately on your left as you enter the museum. It has a comprehensive stock of titles in the above disciplines with particularly strong sections on archaeology, numismatics, Rome, Greece and Egypt. There is also an extraordinary range of postcards featuring BM subjects.

Non-book material: gifts, replicas, jewellery, postcards, posters
Services: mail order, gift tokens, book tokens
Catalogue: replica and jewellery catalogue, list of BM titles
Publications: British Museum Publications produces books related to the museum's collections

Building Bookshop Ltd   *(Goodge Street)*
26 Store Street WC1
637-3151

M–F 9:30–5:15   Sat 10:00–1:00

accountancy / acoustics / architecture / building technology / DIY
and home improvement / earthworks / energy / engineering (civil
and structural) / gardening / home building and maintenance /
joinery / land and property / law / management / mathematics /
municipal engineering / plant / plumbing / roads / site
organization / surveying (land, quantity, structural) / technical
drawing / town planning / wiring

This shop in the front of the Building Centre stocks books for
adventurous do-it-yourselfers and titles useful to the building
trade. A variety of trade, professional and consumer magazines
and journals in the field are also available.

Non-book material: cards, prints, surveyors' tapes
Services: mail order, special order in field
Catalogue: annual complete list, new titles list three times yearly

Butterworth's Bookshop   *(Temple/Chancery Lane)*
9-12 Bell Yard WC2
405-6900

M–F 9:00–5:30

This modern, quiet, well-organized shop is one of London's
leading legal booksellers and publishers. Butterworth's stock
covers all aspects of law and taxation in the UK, as well as some
international legal subjects. Their customers are primarily
members of the legal profession or students of law. All books are
new, with Butterworth's titles comprising approximately 25% of
the stock.

Services: mail order, special order, LEXIS service for transferring
books to computer programs
Catalogue: available by subscription annually with monthly
updates in the form of *The Butterworth's Bulletin*
Publications: Butterworth's publishes books in the field of law,
medicine, service and technology

Chapman's Professional Bookshop   *(Covent Garden)*
20 Endell Street WC2
240-5011

M–F 9:00–6:00

accounting / business / business law / commerce / management / office administration / statistics / taxation

The field of accounting is the speciality of this business bookshop where current titles from the UK and US are stocked. Students and professionals will find that most of the titles are relevant to business in the UK, although there are some that deal with commerce within the EEC. The *Accountant* journal is also stocked, as are all of the Gee & Co. publications.

Non-book material: see above
Services: mail order, special order
Catalogue: Gee and Co. Publishers' list with books in accounting and management

Robert Chris Bookseller   *(Leicester Square)*
8 Cecil Court WC2
836-6700

M–Sat 11:00–5:30

acupressure / acupuncture / allergies / childcare and pregnancy / first aid / healing / herbalism / massage and relaxation / nutrition / osteopathy / radionics / recipe books / shiatsu / special diets / women's health / yoga

This ground-floor shop contains a comprehensive number of books about the idea of positive health and non-suppressive therapies. The emphasis is on diet, nutrition and health. The staff is friendly and knowledgeable, happy to explain the various subjects displayed. The section on women's health is especially good, as are those on specific conditions such as heart disease and arthritis. The shop is devoted to the idea of taking responsibility for one's health, a condition not often heeded by many booksellers used to wheezing in the dust.

Non-book material: photographs; pictures; pressed flowers; pendulums; posters; yoga and meditation cassettes; agent for bio-feedback and Kirlian photography-machines
Services: library supply, mail order
Catalogue: specialized book lists available

The Cinema Bookshop   *(Tottenham Court Road)*
13 Great Russell Street WC1
637-0206

M–Sat 10:30–5:30

avant-garde film / biography / censorship / cinema annuals / criticism / film guides / gangsters / genres / history / music / musicals / pre-cinema / reference / technical / theory / TV

This is, to my knowledge, one of only two bookshops in London specializing in the literature of film. Selling mostly new but also a large number of out-of-print titles, The Cinema Bookshop has a large stock of books about films and the people who make them. I was a bit disappointed to find that books of biography and history far outnumber those of criticism and film theory but it does none the less keep all that are in print and for those interested in the world of film, the shop is a delight. The shop also boasts a large stock of still photos from films of the past, comprising an archive which is a fine resource for students, writers and others wishing to hold a bit of the glamour.

Non-book material: film ephemera, magazines, posters
Services: mail order, special order

City Lit Bookshop   *(Holborn)*
16 Stukeley Street
Drury Lane WC2
242-9872

M–F 11:30–7:45

art / biography / classics / drama / economics / feminism / fiction / film / Greek classics / history / languages / literary criticism / literature / mathematics / music / Penguin / philosophy / poetry / politics / psychology / reference / religion – East and West / sociology

This small shop in the foyer of the City Lit caters to the students of the college, but the shop also keeps a solid stock of recent titles in areas other than college course subjects, including contemporary fiction and feminism. It has a small second-hand section.

Non-book material: stationery, language cassettes, literary magazines.
Services: special order

Central Books   *(Chancery Lane)*
37 Gray's Inn Road WC1
242-6166

M–F 10:00–6:00   Sat 10:00–2:00

Africa / art / biography / British Labour movement / children's books / civil rights / cookery / drama / economics / education / feminism / fiction / film / Ireland / literary criticism / London / Marxist classics / media / Middle East / minorities and race relations / peace movement / poetry / politics / Russian fiction / socialism / sociology / Soviet Union / Third World

The ideological slant of most titles is progressive and leftist, even in the general areas of fiction, literary criticism, art, etc., as well as in the imported Eastern European books in translation.

The British Labour movement and related socialist subjects are the specialities of the shop, and a second-hand section in the field is now flourishing. Also interesting is the selection of Soviet children's books and the wide range of Eastern European, Continental and Third World political newspapers and pamphlets.

Non-book materials: badges, posters, postcards, T-shirts
Services: mail order, special order
Catalogue: a variety of lists on specialized subjects

The Coliseum Shop   *(Charing Cross)*
31 St Martin's Lane, WC2
240-0270

M–Sat 10:00–7:30

The Coliseum is the home of the English National Opera and this shop is right next to it, just off Trafalgar Square. Much of its stock consists naturally of records and cassettes, programmes, etc., though they do also sell a fair selection of opera and music titles. The shop usually has interesting window displays and the inside of the shop is invariably festooned with T-shirts on suitably operatic themes.

Non-book material: records, cassettes, compact discs, videos
Services: mail order
Catalogue: Christmas catalogue

Collet's Chinese Gallery and Bookshop

(Tottenham Court Road)

40 Great Russell Street WC1
580-7538

M–Sat 9:45–5:45   gallery 10:30–5:30

ground floor:
acupuncture and medicine / Buddhism / Chinese pottery / civilization / cookery / dictionaries / Japan / language teaching / literary criticism / literature / philosophy / politics / post-revolutionary history / pre-revolutionary history / travel guides / Zen

basement:
Chinese book department: books in Chinese on pre-modern aspects of China, classics, philosophy

Amid a variety of gifts and Oriental art are books on all aspects of China and, to a lesser extent, Japan. Most of the books are in English, although titles are imported from China, the US and the Continent. There are a few remaindered books, as well as a selection of magazines and journals about China. The shop has a special section of publications from the Percival David Foundation of Chinese Art.

Non-book material: artists' materials for Chinese brush painting; gifts; original art and sculpture; woodblock reproductions of painting albums, antiques, and embroidery; coins
Services: mail order
Catalogue: specialized lists (e.g. acupuncture, Chinese art)
Publications: Collet's publishes books on Chinese language teaching

Collet's Penguin Bookshop

(Leicester Square)

64-66 Charing Cross Road WC2
836-6306

M–F 10:00–6:30   Sat 10:00–6:00

buildings of England / classics / cookery / crime / economics / educational / English Library / fiction / linguisties / new titles / Pelican / philosophy / plays / poetry / politics / reference / sexual politics / sociology / travel

This branch of Collet's sells only new (and a good range of second-hand) Penguins and Pelicans.

Services: mail order, special order (Penguin and Pelican only)

J. B. Cramer & Co. Ltd.   *(Leicester Square)*
99 St Martin's Lane WC2
240-1612

M–F 10:00–6:00

biography / conducting / history / humour / jazz / libretti / madrigals / musical education / musical instruments / musicals / opera and operetta / teaching / vocal methods

Cramer specializes in new books on all aspects of music, from classical (a particularly strong section) to contemporary composers and works. Sheet music comprises a large portion of the stock and major music periodicals are available. There is sometimes a small section of reduced-price books at the front of the shop.

Non-book material: sheet music, song books
Services: mail order, special order
Catalogue: occasional list of available sheet music
Publications: J.B. Cramer & Co. Ltd publishes a large list of sheet music and has recently acquired two other firms' lists.

Dance Books Ltd   *(Leicester Square)*
9 Cecil Court WC2
836-2314

M–Sat 11:00–7:00

With new, and some antiquarian, books on all aspects of ballet and modern dance, Dance Books Ltd has a particularly strong section of titles on dance education. They also carry books on choreography, technique, dance history and biography, as well as the major UK and US dance and arts journals.

Non-book material: calendars, posters, records, still photographs of dancers and dance scenes
Services: mail order, special order, search service in field

Catalogue: selected annual list and list of new books
Publications: Dance Books Ltd, with sixty books in print, is the largest publisher of dance books in the country. It has books on all areas of dance including criticism, education and scene painting.

Dillon's Arts Bookshop   *(Covent Garden)*
8 Long Acre WC2
836-1359

M–Sat 10:00–8:00   Sun 12:00–8:00

visual arts:
antiques / architecture / drawing / exhibition catalogues / general fiction / literary criticism / painting / poetry / photography

performing arts:
ballet / cinema / drama / music: popular and classical / opera / play-texts / theatrical techniques

Dillon's Arts Bookshop is the sister shop to the excellent Dillon's the Bookstore. It is divided into two sections: one housing books on the visual arts, and the other (in the rear of the shop, with a separate entrance in Garrick Street) concentrating on the performing arts. The shop keeps a wide range of art journals and magazines and some overseas publications. They also have an excellent selection of cards and some high-quality remaindered art books. Further expansion of the sales area is planned for 1987.

Non-book material: glass picture frames, greetings cards, postcards, posters, wrapping-paper
Services: mail order, special order

Dorling Kindersley Ltd   *(Covent Garden)*
9 Henrietta Street WC2
240-5151/5

M–F 9:30–5:30

computers / cookery / crafts / health / knitting / photography

A showroom for the publisher's offices, stocking their range of illustrated reference books. The shop also sells publications by the Ebury Press, Michael Joseph and Macdonald.

Catalogue: comprehensive catalogue available
Publications: Dorling Kindersley publications

The Economists' Bookshop   *(Holborn/Temple)*
Portugal Street/Clare Market WC2
405-5531

M–F 9:30–6:00 W 10:30–6:00 Sat 10:00–1:30 (closed Sat in
summer and out of term)

anthropology / biography / computer studies / development
studies / economic history / economics / geography / history /
labour and management / law / left-wing publications /
philosophy / politics / psychology / reference / socialism / sociology /
statistics

Run by *The Economist* and the London School of Economics, this
bookshop not only has an excellent range of economics titles, but
new books in all areas of social sciences. The publishers are UK
and US, texts are in English and all the paperback series are
stocked (e.g., Granada, Pan, Fontana, Penguin and Pelican).
Social science and political journals are carried, as are specialized
pamphlet publications. There is an adjoining second-hand
bookshop (see separate entry).

Services: mail order, special order, institutional and library
supply
Catalogue: social science selection guide six times yearly

Falkiner Fine Papers Ltd   *(Covent Garden)*
117 Long Acre WC2
240-2339

M–Sat 9:30–5:30

This is really, as its name suggests, an art shop dealing in
calligraphy, lettering, typography, bookbinding, papermaking,
marbling and printmaking. It does however stock magazines,
periodicals, limited edition publications and a few books from the
UK and abroad on related subjects.

Non-book material: see above
Services: mail order
Catalogue: list available on each subject

Fine Books Oriental Limited   *(Tottenham Court Road)*
46 Great Russell Street WC1
636-6068

M–F 9:30–5:00

Central Asia / China / Indian sub-continent / Japan / Middle East / South-East Asia

This well-known Oriental specialist shop, the largest of its kind in Europe, sells books on all aspects of these countries – from architecture and crime to religion and travel. All, including the antiquarian works which form about a quarter of the shop, are at reasonable prices. (A card inside each book contains full bibliographical details.) Some are in the original languages, and Japan is the largest section. From government reports of 19th-century sanitary conditions to religious studies, this excellent, friendly shop contains a wide range of fascinating books.

Non-book material: early photographs, learned periodicals and journals
Services: mail order, special order, 24-hour answering machine
Catalogue: specialized catalogues regularly issued

Flinders Australian Bookshop   *(Euston)*
45 Burton Street WC1
388-6080

M–F 10:00–6:00   Sat by appointment only

Flinders has an amazingly large and varied collection of new, rare and second-hand books about Australia. From the flora and fauna to biographies, history, art and fiction, it's all here. There are well over 500 Penguins too, as the owner is an agent for Penguin Australia. Apparently life in the shop can be quite hectic with frequent urgent demands from the BBC, Australia House, or local advertising agencies for books on specific Australian topics or requests for the loan of a couple of yards of books to give an authentic background to a play or advert

Non-book material: stationery, cards, posters
Services: mail order, special order, search service

Forbidden Planet   *(Tottenham Court Road)*
23 Denmark Street WC2
836-4179   mail orders 980-9711

M–Sat 10:00–6:00   Th 10:00–7:00

anthologies / collections / fantasy / fiction / film and TV / illustrated books / science fiction / sorcery

Forbidden Planet is making it in the competitive world of science fiction bookshops, with current sci fi and fantasy books from the UK and US, and a large selection of new and second-hand (many are collectors' items) comics and sci fi magazines. The shop is owned by a major UK distributor of sci fi books, so they do have quick access to recently published titles. Sci fi artists' portfolios and illustrated books on fantasy and sci fi are also featured.

Non-book material: artists' portfolios, badges, posters
Services: mail order

Note: There is a Forbidden Planet II at:
58 St Giles High Street WC2
379-6042

M–Sat 10:00–6:00   Th 10:00–7:00

They have more film and TV books and stills.

Four Provinces Bookshop   *(Chancery Lane)*
244-246 Gray's Inn Road WC1
833-3022

M by appointment   Tue–F 11:00–5:45   Sat 11:00–4:30

art / children's books / cookery / fiction / history / language / literature / music / politics / reference / travel

This shop covers a wide range of subjects related to Ireland, its history, politics, language and culture. They have a selection of novels in Gaelic, courses in the Gaelic language and a collection of Irish socialist writings. There is also a section for Irish journals and periodicals, so both the specialist and the general interests are catered for here. Pamphlets of the Dublin Historical Association are available and although most of the stock is new there is a small second-hand collection.

Non-book material: badges, bookmarks, calendars
Services: mail order, educational supply
Catalogue: catalogue available on request

Gay's The Word   *(Russell Square)*
66 Marchmont Street WC1
278-7654

M–Sat 11:00–7:00   Sun 2:00–6:00

art / biography / black studies / feminism / fiction / gay, lesbian /
plays / poetry / politics / US imports

Gay's The Word stocks new, out-of-print and second-hand books
on gay and feminist issues. New books cover the range of
political, social and economic issues, as well as classic gay and
feminist literature, while the second-hand section holds rare,
hard-to-find gay and feminist classics. The shop also has a good
section of new titles from the US and a selection of gay and
feminist journals from the UK and abroad.

In addition to book selling, the shop is kept busy hosting
various discussion groups – lesbian, gay, black and men's groups
are those currently running – and there is a coffee bar at the shop
as well. The staff are cordial, accessible and knowledgeable.

Non-book material: badges, posters
Services: mail order, special order
Catalogue: complete list of new books with some second-hand
titles included
Publications: a two-monthly newsletter, *Gay's the Word Newsletter*

The General Store   *(Covent Garden)*
111 Long Acre Covent Garden WC2
836-5051

M–Sat 10:00–midnight   Sun 12:00–8:00

In the basement of this fascinating store are a few shelves of books
on cookery and a wide selection of humorous paperbacks.

Catalogue: General Store catalogue

Note: There is another branch in The Trocadero, Piccadilly.

Geographers   *(Chancery Lane)*
44 Gray's Inn Road WC1
242-9246 and 405-7322

M–F 9:00–5:00

These are the people who publish the A-Z Guides to London and in this small shop they also stock a range of maps, guides and atlases. There is a very selective range of travel books.

Services: mail order
Catalogue: lists Geographers publications
Publications: Geographers maps, guides and atlases

Stanley Gibbons   *(Covent Garden)*
399 The Strand WC2
836-8444   ext. 223

M 10:00–5:30   Tue–F 9:00–5:30   Sat 10:00–1:00

Stanley Gibbons is the world's largest stamp shop, selling stamps and stamp albums. It also carries many new and old books of interest to the philatelist.

Non-book material: stamps, stamp collecting accessories
Services: mail order, special order
Catalogue: general catalogue is available which includes books
Publications: stamp and other collecting books are published by Stanley Gibbons

The Golden Cockerel Bookshop   *(Holborn)*
25 Sicilian Avenue WC2
405-7979

M–F 9:30–5:30 (sometimes to 6:30)

Africana / architecture / art / biography / drama / film / history / literature and criticism / music / natural history / philosophy / politics / sociology / theology

The Golden Cockerel Bookshop sells books published by the Associated University Presses, whose members include such publishers as the Folger Shakespeare Library, University of

Delaware Press, the Philadelphia Art Alliance Press, Fairleigh Dickinson UP and Cornwall Books. All their books, whose emphasis is on the humanities, are kept in stock. Although currently available books include such unlikely titles as *Lapsing Out: Embodiments of Death and Rebirth in the Last Writings of D.H. Lawrence* and *The Moon's Dominion: Narrative Dichotomy on Female Dominance in the first five Novels of D.H. Lawrence*, there are certainly enough interesting books here, many of which do not get sufficient prominence in other shops, to make a visit to The Golden Cockerel Bookshop well worthwhile.

Services: mail order, special order
Catalogue: currently available titles

The Gramophone Exchange   *(Covent Garden)*
3 Betterton Street WC2
836-0976

M 10:00–3:00   Tue, Th, Sat 10:00–6:00

A small section of second-hand books about the gramophone and records, as well as titles on other aspects of music, can be found here.

Non-book material: second-hand records (including rare 78s)
Services: mail order

Grower Books   *(Russell Square)*
50 Doughty Street WC1
405-7135

M–F 9:00–12:00 1:00–4:30

amateur growing and horticulture / commercial growing / crop information / environment / glasshouse / harvesting / husbandry / marketing / open air growing / preparation / vegetables

While the premises on Doughty Street are not really those of a bookshop, individuals looking for new books about commercial growing and horticulture can stop by Grower Books for a browse. The titles are from the UK and US, including Ministry of Agriculture and Royal Horticultural Society publications, and provide a comprehensive source of information to the commercial grower and amateur.

Services: mail order, special order
Catalogue: complete list continually updated
Publications: Grower Books publishes titles on horticulture

Guanghwa *(Leicester Square)*
7-9 Newport Place WC2
437-3737

M–Sat 10:30–7:00   Sun 11:00–7:00

acupuncture / art / biography / children's books / cookery / cultural history / Eastern healing arts / Engels / fiction / health / history / language teaching / Lenin / lifestyle / Marx / medicine / poetry / politics / sciences / shipping / tales and legends / war and revolution

In the heart of Chinatown, this is a large gift and book shop specializing in China. Most of the titles are imported from China and Hong Kong, in Chinese, but there are an increasing number of English-language books especially in the area of language teaching. The level of the books starts at titles for children and reaches up to scholarly and academic texts on specialized subjects. A wide range of literary, cultural, sports and science magazines is also available at the shop.

Non-book material: gifts imported from China, prints
Services: mail order, special order
Catalogue: regular lists of new and specialized titles

The Hellenic Book Service *(Leicester Square/ Tottenham Court Road)*
122 Charing Cross Road WC2
836-7071

M–Sat 9:00–6:00

archaeology / architecture / art / Byzantium / cookery / costumes / Crete / Cyprus / dictionaries / fiction / history (modern and ancient) / language teaching / literature / magic / medicine / mythology / natural history / poetry (modern and ancient) / philosophy / politics / theatre / theology / travel accounts and guides / Turkey

Said to have one of the world's largest ranges of new, second-hand and antiquarian books in Greek and about Greece, this shop is certainly a rich source for students, actravellers, writers and anyone interested in Greece. The mother and daughter who own and run the shop are extremely knowledgable about their books and the people who write them, and are energetic in locating new and out-of-print titles in Greek and English. Books in both modern and ancient Greek are stocked in subjects ranging from children's stories to the academic texts in archaeology and mythology. Also available is a selection of Greek newspapers, magazines and journals.

Non-book material: antiquarian prints, icons, language teaching cassettes and records, old and modern maps, postcards
Services: mail order, special order (in any field), search service

HMSO Bookshop   *(Holborn/Chancery Lane)*
49 High Holborn WC2
211-5656

M–F 8:15–5:15

Acts of Parliament / agriculture / art / building design and construction / careers / computers / ecology / economics / education / energy / environment / finance / Hansard parliamentary debates / health and medicine / historical monuments / history / housing and planning / industrial training/relations/society / law / management / metrification / natural history / Ordnance Survey maps / reference / road and traffic / social services / statistics / trade and commerce

HMSO is the source for government publications in the UK, most of their titles originating in some governmental department. HMSO is the international agent for the UN, EEC and OECD publications.

Non-book material: Imperial War Museum posters, Ordnance Survey maps
Services: mail order, special order
Catalogue: complete annual catalogue, selected listing in specialized areas

Housing Centre Bookshop *(Goodge Street)*
33 Alfred Place WC1
637-4202

M–F 10:00–5:00

This is a very small but compact space in the Housing Centre Trust building. The shop deals with publications on social and legal aspects of housing and urban planning as well as finance, management and administration. Though its holdings are not large, it can get any British housing publication and has access to many overseas publications in the field; its emphasis is on those aspects rather than design or planning.

Services: mail order, special order
Catalogue: selected list of new housing publications, updated frequently
Publications: The Housing Centre Trust publish a bi-monthly magazine, *Housing Review*, as well as books on housing issues

Intermediate Technology Bookshop *(Leicester Square/*
9 King Street WC2   *Covent Garden)*
836-9434

M–F 9:30–5:30   Sat 11:00–6:00

agriculture / alternative energy / building / disseminating information / education and teaching guides / fiction / health / politics / sanitation / small industries / suitable technologies / Third World development

This small shop (which is part of a consulting and research group) carries a broad range of development books specializing in, as its name suggests, intermediate technology. Particularly interesting is the literature on getting information about alternative energy sources, sanitation systems or building techniques to large groups of people, say a village population in India.

Non-book material: charity Christmas cards, recycled paper, solar energy kits, leaflets, pamphlets and journals on projects and studies in intermediate technology throughout the world
Services: mail order
Catalogue: general list annually, updated regularly
Publications: a list of courses in the UK about intermediate technology is published by the Intermediate Technology group, as well as a quarterly journal, *Appreciate Technology*

Jewish Memorial Council Bookshop   *(Euston)*
Woburn House
Upper Woburn Place WC1
387-3081

M–Th 10:00–5:30   F 10:00–2:00   winter 10:00–4:00   summer Sun 10:30–12:45

Bible and Talmud / biography / comparative religion / culture and civilization / fiction / history / holidays / literature / music / philosophy / scholarly texts

Judaism is, of course, the focus of the Jewish Memorial Council Bookshop. Most of the books here are in English; there are, however, some Hebrew texts imported from Isreal, including recent literature, and all the books are new. A few related journals and newspapers are kept as well. Once a year a book fair is held, at which publishers from around the UK speak about new titles from the UK, US and Israel.

Non-book material: religious requisites
Services: mail order, special order
Catalogue: general catalogue

Knightsbridge Books   *(Goodge Street)*
32 Store Street WC1
636-1252

M–F 9:00–5:30

Africa / anthropology / art / crafts / culture and lifestyle / Far East / fiction / history / Indian subcontinent / literature / Middle East / poetry / politics / religion

New books about the Far and Middle East, Africa and India are the specialities of this shop. Most of the titles are scholarly and specialized, many are lavishly illustrated and a few are imported from the Continent and beyond.

   The shop will be moving in 1987, so it is best to telephone to find out its new address.

Services: mail order, special order
Catalogue: lists on Africa, Far East, Near and Middle East

Law Notes Lending Library   *(Chancery Lane)*
25-26 Chancery Lane WC2
405-0780

M–F 9:30–5:00

Both new and second-hand books on all aspects of British law, together with some international and EEC law, are sold at this combined bookshop and lending library. Major law journals are available here, as are the book series produced by the leading legal publishers.

Services: mail order, special order
Catalogue: selected list produced annually
Publications: *Law Notes* is a monthly publication from the Law Notes Lending Library Ltd

H.K. Lewis & Co. Ltd   *(Warren Street/Euston Square)*
136 Gower Street WC1
387-4282

M–F 9:00–5:30   Sat 9:00–1:00

ground floor: medical books
anaesthesia / anatomy / bacteriology / biochemistry / biography / cardiology / dentistry / diabetes / diagnosis / dictionaries / endocrinology / first aid and home nursing / forensic medicine / haematology / hospitals / immunology / industrial medicine / infectious diseases / medical history / medical statistics / medicine / memoirs / midwifery / neurology / nursing / obstetrics, gynaecology / ophthalmology / orthopaedics / paediatrics / pharmacology / pharmacy / physiology / physiotheraphy / psychiatry / psychoanalysis / psychology / sex / surgery / therapeutics / toxicology

first floor: natural sciences
aeronautics / agriculture / animal behaviour / applied mechanics / aquatic biology / astronomy / biology / botany / building construction / computer science / ecology / electrical engineering / electronic engineering / entomology / forestry / fuel technology / general and inorganic chemistry / genetics / geology / heat engineering / hydraulics / industrial chemistry / industrial management / materials science / mathematics / metallurgy / microscopy / organic chemistry / ornithology / physical chemistry / physics / plant pathology / refrigeration / sanitary engineering / statistics / surveying / veterinary science / zoology

Located across the street from University College Hospital, H.K. Lewis is one of London's largest medical and scientific booksellers. New books, periodicals and journals are stocked and the shop also houses a rather large second-hand book department.

Services: mail order, special order, wants lists accepted
Catalogue: weekly new book lists, regular specialized catalogues
Publications: H.K. Lewis publishes medical books

Luzac & Co. Ltd   *(Tottenham Court Road)*
46 Great Russel Street WC1
636-1462

M–F 9:30–5:00

Arabic literature / art: Chinese, Islamic, Japanese / Buddhism / business / central Asia / complementary medicine / crafts / dance / drama / Far East / health / history / India / Islam / language teaching / literature / magic / Middle East / Mughal Empire / mythology / occult / photography / Quran / religion / spiritualism / Sufism / textiles / theatre / Turkey

Established in 1740, Luzac specializes in current titles on the Middle and Far East, with texts and studies of Buddhism a particular strength in its stock. Literature in translation, illustrated art books and titles on comparative religion are also good sections, and the extremely helpful staff are able to assist scholars, students and business people in locating new and out-of-print titles on the Middle and Far East.

Non-book material: language cassettes
Services: mail order
Catalogue: specialized list for the Buddhist Society, quarterly selected lists
Publications: Luzac & Co. Ltd publishes books about the Middle and Far East, especially in the field of art

McCarta Ltd   *(King's Cross)*
122 King's Cross Road WC1
278-8278

M–Sat 9:30–5:30 (times may vary)

59

This shop specializes in maps and guides to Europe and the world, from large-scale walking maps and town-plans to more general maps of countries.

Coverage of France is particularly extensive, the shop being agents for the French Official Survey (IGN) and many other cartographic companies. The extremely diverse stock includes bilingual guides to the French waterways and the Topo guides published by the French Ramblers Association. Various wine-maps are also available.

Non-book material: see above
Services: mail order, special order
Catalogue: lists by country available

Motor Books   *(Leicester Square)*
33 & 34 St Martin's Court WC2
36 St Martin's Court WC2
836-5376/6728/3800

M–F 9:30–5:30   Sat 10:30–5:00

At numbers 33 and 34 St Martin's Court Motor Books specializes in new books on motoring, railways and steam powered vehicles (including manufacturer's repair manuals) while at number 36 books on military, naval and aviation subjects are featured. The shops import titles from abroad, so a few of the books are in languages other than English. The bias in these shops is towards material which is technical and informative (e.g., a history of aviation with detailed specifications of aircraft) and there is a wide range of DIY material, from books on boat building to assembling explosives. The shops stock a number of current magazines in their respective areas of speciality.

Non-book material: videos (historical transport only)
Services: mail order, special order
Catalogue: annual, specialized catalogues

The Museum Bookshop   *(Tottenham Court Road)*
36 Great Russell Street WC1
580-4086

M–F 10:00–5:30   Sat 11:00–5:30

Africa / America / applied art / archaeology / civilisation /
Egyptology / Islamic studies / Israel / Middle East / pre-history /
Roman classics

With a speciality in archaeology (including British) and classical
studies, this lovely shop sells both new and antiquarian books in
the general area of the humanities. Current and back issues of
archaeological journals are also available.

Non-book material: maps of the classical world, prints
Services: mail order, special order, search service in speciality
Catalogue: selected book lists six times yearly

Mysteries   *(Tottenham Court Road)*
9 Monmouth Street WC2
240-3688

M–Sat 10:00–6:00

alternative medicine / comparative religions / divination / dreams /
healing techniques / mythology / ritual magic

This bookshop specializes in all areas of spiritual and occult
studies, under the blanket term of New Age Learning. It is a part
of the New Age Centre, which is a busy nucleus for psychic and
spiritual studies in London.

Non-book material: candles, crystals, decorations, jewellery,
music – cassettes and records of New Age music – meditation and
spiritual instruction, oils
Services: mail order, courses organized in astrology, meditation,
ritual and tarot, supply for trade
Catalogue: catalogue available on request

National Portrait Gallery Bookshop   *(Leicester Square)*
2 St Martin's Place WC2
930-1552

M–F 10:00–4:50   Sat 10:00–6:00   Sun 2:00–5:50

art history / biographies of artists and their sitters / British history /
children's / classics / photography / the Royal Family

A large shop, as museum bookshops go, in which most of the books have some relationship to the artists, and their subjects, in the adjacent gallery. Remaindered books are often on sale on the bargain tables in the shop.

Non-book material: badges, bags, calendars, diaries, medallions, miniatures, postcards, posters, prints and slides.
Services: mail order
Catalogue: National Portrait Gallery publications list, slide collection catalogue, postcard catalogue
Publications: the National Portrait Gallery publishes books about 'the British face' in art

Neal Street East   *(Covent Garden)*
5 Neal Street WC2
240-0135/6

M–Sat 10:00–7:00   Sun 11:00–6:00

architecture / art / calligraphy / carpets and textiles / cookery / eastern health and acupuncture / literature / philosophy / poetry / sociology / travel and topography / yoga / Zen

This large store specializes in everything to do with the Orient. It has three floors incorporating fashion, a bazaar, an antiques and ethnic gallery, a café and, last but not least, a bookshop. This is on the right-hand side of the ground floor and contains many titles of fiction and non-fiction on the Orient.

Non-book material: newspapers and magazines, and see above

Nihon Token   *(Tottenham Court Road)*
23 Museum Street WC1
580-6511

M–Sat 10:00–5:00

This is a Japanese antiques shop with a small selection of books about Japanese antiques, history, cookery and the martial arts. There is also a small collection of 18th- and 19th-century wood-block books.

Services: special order

Publications: Nihon Token have published part of a 19th-century study of Japanese Mon (family badges) and a highly specialized book on Japanese laquers

Odyssey Bookshop   *(Holborn)*
30 Lamb's Conduit Street WC1
405-6735

M–F 10:30–6:00   Sat 11:30–4:00

alternative therapies / astrology / earth mysteries / humanistic and transpersonal psychology / mythology / natural healing / New Age thought / western and eastern mystery traditions / whole food and vegetarian cookery / yoga and meditation

This small bookshop deals solely in holistic books for mind, body and spirit. This includes books for self-development and subjects such as astrology and natural healing.

Non-book material: homeopathic, bach flower and aromatherapy remedies
Services: mail order, special order
Catalogue: some lists available

Paperchase   *(Goodge Street)*
213 Tottenham Court Road WC1
580-8496

M–Sat 9:00–6:00   Th 9:30–7:00

African art / American art / applied art / architecture / British art / children's illustrated story and craft books / crafts / DIY / fine art / Italian art / London art and architecture / modern art / natural history / photography / primitive art / reference

The first floor of this large and wonderfully frivolous shop has a book department with a particularly good selection of colourfully illustrated children's books. There are also books on the fine and applied arts.

Non-book material: stationery, paper gift items, toys on first floor, art room on second floor
Services: mail order, special order

Parks Bookshop   *(Holborn)*
244 High Holborn WC1
831-9501/2

M–F 9:00–6:00   Sat 9:00–1:00 (9:00–5:00 Sept–Nov)

accountancy / banking / economics / investment / law / management / marketing / reference / tax: VAT

This bright, neat shop has been opened close to Holborn station to meet the needs of those professions that do not find themselves dealt with sufficiently quickly by more general shops, the owners feeling that such shops 'tend to have a somewhat antiquated image'. Parks, with books in both hardback and paperback, certainly is vigorous in its stock of books for the accountant, businessman, banker and lawyer – both practitioner and student – and expert in its staff. It has up-to-date stock from such bodies as the Institute of Chartered Accountants, Institute of Bankers, Institute of Personnel Management and HMSO as well as home-study material from such publishers as Holborn Law Tutors, Brierley Price Prior and Emile Woolf.

Services: special order, prompt mail order
Catalogue: specialized lists, annual catalogue

The Photographer's Gallery Bookshop   *(Leicester Square)*
8 Great Newport Street WC2
240-5511

Tue–Sat 11:00–7:00

essays and criticism / history of photography / individual photographers / international photography / monographs / photojournalism / technical aspects

This bookshop, situated within one of the gallery's exhibition areas, stocks new, out-of-print and remaindered books about photography. The majority of the books are current titles on photography and related visual and performing arts. Also available is a selection of international magazines, yearbooks and journals. For anyone interested in the subject, a visit to the gallery followed by a browse in the bookshop is an absolute must.

Non-book material: calendars, cards, catalogues, gallery exhibitions, magazines, postcards, posters
Services: mail order, special order, 10% discount to museums and colleges
Catalogue: complete title list

Arthur Probsthain   *(Tottenham Court Road)*
41 Great Russell Street WC1
636-1096

M–F 9:30–5:30   Sat 10:30–4:00

Arabic / art / China / civilization / history / India / Islam / Japan / language teaching / literature / Middle East / religion / South-East Asia

The Arthur Probsthain bookshop is a long-established shop specializing in books on all aspects of the Middle and Far East. Most of the books are new, although there is a large second-hand stock and there are also a few remainders on sale. The shop's clientele tends to have academic or specialized interests as well, so that 'students' of the Orient will be well served here. A range of journals, in a variety of languages, is available.

Non-book material: cards, posters
Services: mail order, special order – all fields
Catalogue: specialized lists on a number of subjects, occasional second-hand list
Publications: Arthur Probsthain Oriental Series has published scholarly translations of Oriental writing

The Professional Bookshop   *(Temple)*
(Professional Books Ltd)
234 The Strand WC2
583-1031

M–F 8:30–6:00

This bookshop can be found in the heart of London's legal territory, conveniently positioned for barristers in need of a quick reference before entering the High Court. They specialize in law and business and the books are aimed at students and practitioners.

65

Services: mail order
Catalogue: annual catalogue for law books
Publications: Professional Books Ltd publish their own legal titles

Psychic News Bookshop   *(Covent Garden/Leicester Square)*
20 Earlham Street WC2
240-3032

M–F 9:00–5:00

psychic worlds / religion / spiritual healing / spiritual nature / supernatural

This is London's only bookshop dealing solely with literature about the psychic and spiritualism. Most of the books are new, though there are a few second-hand titles and an occasional remaindered book. The speciality of the shop is quite narrowly defined and does not include books on the occult, mysticism, magic and witchcraft.

Non-book material: meditation tapes
Services: mail order, special order
Catalogue: one comprehensive list yearly
Publications: The Psychic Press publishes the newspaper *Psychic News* and a few books on psychic worlds

The Puffin Shop   *(Covent Garden)*
1 The Piazza
Covent Garden WC2
379-6465

M–Sat 10:00–8:00

basement: children's books / games / soft toys / stationery

ground floor: bargain books / London guides / new adult fiction

first floor: child care / cookery / education / GCSE and A-level texts / reference

The Puffin Shop is a paradise for children and great fun for adults too. It occupies an enviable site overlooking Covent Garden Piazza where there always seems to be something going on – from clowns and breakdancers to opera singers and mime artistes. The long-suffering staff prefer the quieter acts, I'm reliably informed!

As for the interior, the choice of books is great and they are well signposted, with frequent instore displays. The shop also hosts regular events such as signing sessions, readings, parties and competitions.

Non-book material: as above plus cards and wrapping-paper
Services: special order
Catalogue: Puffin's own catalogue

Ray's Jazz Shop   *(Covent Garden)*
180 Shaftesbury Avenue WC2
240-3969

M–Sat 10:00–6:30

This specialist jazz shop has both new and second-hand titles about musicians, composers, instruments and the history of jazz. It covers everything from Blues and early jazz to contemporary improvised music.

Non-book material: cassettes, records, compact discs, 78rpm records
Services: mail order
Catalogue: lists available on request

Salvationist Publishing and Supplies Ltd *(King's Cross)*
117-121 Judd Street WC1
387-1656/5621

M–F 8:45–4:30   W 8:45–9:30   Sat 9:30–12:30

Most of the books here are Salvation Army publications and the range includes biographies and autobiographies of Salvationists, histories of the Salvationists, bibles and hymn books.

Non-book material: calendars, diaries, souvenirs
Services: mail order

Ian Shipley (Books) Ltd   *(Leicester Square)*
70 Charing Cross Road WC2
836-4872

M–Sat 10:00–6:00

aesthetics and writings on art / architecture / art / design / exhibition catalogues / furniture / graphics / illustration / interior design / Japan and the Orient / photography / typography

This shop specializing in the visual arts has become one of the better art bookshops in London. The wide stock of new and out-of-print titles includes books in English and foreign languages, from India to China to Holland, as well as exhibition catalogues and art periodicals from the UK, US and the Continent. The shop regards art in a wide sense, to include fashion, photography, architecture and landscape gardening. It does not cover theatre, dance or cinema. In addition to their extensive holdings, Ian Shipley pride themselves on being able to obtain books from any part of the world.

Services: mail order, search service, special order
Catalogue: new title lists two to three times anually, together with a wide range of publishers' catalogues; monthly newsletter detailing new art and photography books and also out-of-print titles

Silver Moon   *(Leicester Square)*
68 Charing Cross Road WC2
836-7906

M–Sat 10:30–6:30

ground floor:
biography / black women / fiction / history / lesbian / sexual politics / work

basement:
arts (including literary criticism, media, plays, poetry) / children's books / crime / education / health / philosophy / religion / science fiction / second-hand / young women's section

Silver Moon is a bookshop especially concerned with women and women's studies. The staff are helpful and knowledgeable, and there is access for the disabled on the ground floor.

Non-book material: jewellery, postcards, records of women's music, T-shirts
Services: search service, special order
Catalogue: quarterly newsletter with new titles and reviews

James Smith   *(Chancery Lane)*
94 Gray's Inn Road WC1
405-5697

M–F 8:30–6:00

antiques / art / atlases / cars / clocks / collecting / cookery /
dictionaries / gardening / London / poetry / railways

While there is not much space in which to browse, James Smith
has a good selection of remainders and end-of-run books in
'practical' areas (e.g., collecting antique watches or restoring
furniture). The staff are very diligent about looking for recently
out-of-print titles, or ordering the last of an end-of-run book.

Services: mail order, search service

Solosy   *(Leicester Square)*
50-55 Charing Cross Road WC2
836-6313   434-0759

M–Sun 7:00a.m.–8:00p.m.

Army and Navy history / aviation and Air Force history / military
history and uniforms, weapons, equipment

This general newsagents and specialized bookshop deals with
new titles in the subject areas listed above. Predictably enough it
stocks a wide range of magazines in the fields of aviation, military
and naval history.

Non-book material: see above
Services: special order

Sportspages   *(Tottenham Court Road/*
Cambridge Circus Shopping Centre   *Leicester Square)*
Charing Cross Road WC2
240-9604

M–Sat 10:00–7:00

all sports – participating and spectating / card and board games /
children's / exercise / fiction / health and fitness

Sportspages might at first seem difficult to find, as it is in a cul-de-sac off Charing Cross Road, but if you are interested in sport it is well worth the effort. It is bright and welcoming and contains not only books but a developing sports video sale and hire service. There is a television in the shop which unobtrusively plays sports videos and programmes and on Saturdays the First Division football results are chalked up on a blackboard. Proud of being this country's first specialist sports bookshop, it stocks books imported from all over the world and covers all levels of interest and experience within each subject. These are too numerous to itemize but include hang-gliding, polo, cross-country, body-building, jogging, chess, dressage, baseball, curling, Australian Rules football, coaching and bird-watching.

Non-book material: videos, cards, calendars
Services: mail order, special order
Catalogue: specialist lists

Edward Stanford Ltd   *(Covent Garden)*
12-14 Long Acre WC2
836-1321

M–F 9:00–6:00   Sat 10:00–5:00

atlases / camping manuals and maps / cartography / geology / guide and travel books worldwide / historical reprints of maps / mountaineering / nautical books and charts / topography / walking guides

Acknowledged as the world's largest retail mapseller since 1852, Stanford's book stock reflects the kinds of title their traditional clientele wants, i.e., guides, outdoor activities, nautical and maritime subjects. Most of the shop is taken up by maps and charts. Downstairs you will find all the Ordnance Survey maps, geology and sea charts; upstairs on the ground floor are titles on Europe and foreign travel, as well as a good section on Britain.

Non-book material: compasses, esoteric maps of overseas countries, the best selection of globes in London, map measures, thematic maps, world area maps
Services: mail order, map mounting, special order
Publications: Stanford's is part of the George Philip group which publishes marine and country maps and charts

Rudolf Steiner Bookshop   *(Tottenham Court Road)*
38 Museum Street WC1
242-4249

M–F 10:00–5:30

This shop stocks a complete range of Rudolf Steiner's works, and other new books which are related to Steiner's interests (e.g. religion, philosophy and social commentary). A small selection of children's books is also available.

Non-book material: postcards, toiletries, toys
Services: mail order
Catalogue: annual selected listing
Publications: Rudolf Steiner Press imprint on works by and about Rudolf Steiner

Bernard Stone/Turret Bookshop   *(Russell Square)*
42 Lamb's Conduit Street WC1
405-6058

M–Sat 10:00–6:00

Bernard Stone's remains London's leading modern poetry bookshop. Many writers and illustrators congregate here and Ralph Steadman's books, illustrations and some original work are prominently featured.

Hours can easily be spent browsing through new and second-hand books (as well as a few remainders) of poetry and selected literature, looking at their candid photos of notable literary figures or chatting with the staff about the latest work and gossip in the world of modern poetry. Children's poetry and literature, books on music, biography and the performing arts are also stocked, and they carry a wide range of UK and US theatre, literary and poetry journals (back issues are also available).

Non-book material: cards, contemporary book illustrators' works, prints of local scenes
Services: mail order, special order
Catalogue: specialized lists, e.g., poetry, children's books
Publications: Turret Books publishes modern poetry

The Swedenborg Society Bookshop   *(Holborn)*
20-21 Bloomsbury Way WC1
405-7986

M–F 9:30–5:00

As the name suggests, this bookshop is quite literally devoted to the works of Emanuel Swedenborg. Most of the titles here are published by the Society and they include Swedenborg's works not only in Latin and English, but translated into a wide variety of European and African languages. Biographies, critical studies and books on the New Church, founded on the basis of Swedenborg's theology, make up the bulk of the stock. There is a small second-hand section covering the same ground. There is a large reference library and a smaller lending library on the premises.

Services: international mail order, library supply
Catalogue: catalogue covers the Swedenborg Society's own publications
Publications: books and a magazine published by the Society

The Theosophical Bookshop   *(Holborn)*
& Publishing House
12 Bury Place WC1
405-2309

M–Sat 9:30–5:00

astrology / Buddhism / diet / meditation / mythology / occult / philosophy / psychology / reincarnation / Sufism / Taoism / theosophy / Western mysticism

This firm has been established since 1881 and the shop has been in operation since 1926. In the relatively small shop space is a selective, high-quality stock of primarily scholarly books on theosophy and philosophy. Most of the titles are by Western writers, from UK publishers, and all of the books are new.

Services: mail order, special order in field
Catalogue: Theosophical Publishing House Ltd publications catalogue
Publications: Theosophical Publishing House Ltd publishes books in the fields of theosophy and philosophy

Triangle Bookshop   *(Tottenham Court Road)*
36 Bedford Square WC1
631-1381

M–F 10:00–6:00

aesthetics / architectural biography / architectural history / art
history / contemporary essays / crafts / landscape / photography /
theatre and stage

Triangle is a lovely shop tucked away downstairs in the
Architectural Association building (though run independently of
it), selling primarily new books on architecture and those subjects
that 'stimulate architects' (e.g., other visual arts and aesthetics).
Quality remaindered books can often be found here, as well as a
range of the leading architectural journals.

Services: mail order, special order, wants lists accepted
Catalogue: annual selected list

Travis & Emery   *(Leicester Square)*
17 Cecil Court WC2
240-2129

M–F 10:00–6:00   Sat 10:00–1:00

Antiquarian, second-hand and new books and musical scores
grouped according to country, composer and instrument are the
speciality of Travis & Emery.

Non-book material: musical ephemera, prints
Services: mail order, special order, search service
Catalogue: selected lists three times yearly

Tutor Tape Co. Ltd   *(Tottenham Court Road)*
100 Great Russell Street WC1
580-7552

M–F 10:00–6:00   Sat 10:00–1:00

This company specializes in language teaching courses and aids
for English as a foreign language, and all other languages for
which there is a demand. The course subjects range from

73

technical, sciences, maths and business shorthand dictation to drama, poetry and music. The books are sold in conjunction with cassettes, study tapes and video-tapes as part of ELT courses.

Non-book material: cassettes, records, slides, videos
Services: mail order, special order, demonstration room for audio-visual materials, language lab.
Catalogue: English/foreign languages annually
Publications: Tutor Tape Co. Ltd publishes books on foreign language teaching and English as a foreign language

University Press Books   *(Russell Square)*
13 Brunswick Centre
Brunswick Square WC1
278-6381

M–F 10:00–6:00

All the British university presses and the major American university presses are in stock here and the emphasis is firmly on the humanities, with very few science publications in sight. There is a large section on literary criticism and theory and a history section dominated by American, British and European history. The philosophy department is currently being enlarged, but any book that is not in stock can be ordered and the shop orders huge numbers of books from other American university presses on a regular basis. They also stock the Scolar Press publications and are willing to order titles from other publishers.

Services: international mail order
Catalogue: the shop is currently planning to compile individual subject lists

The Virago Bookshop   *(Covent Garden/Charing Cross)*
34 Southampton Street WC2
240-6638

M–Sat 10:00–6:00   W 11:00–6:00

ground floor: new books
biography / children's / cookery / criticism / drama / fiction / health / poetry / politics / psychology / reference / travel / Virago books / women's studies

basement: second-hand books by and about women

This is an attractive and well run bookshop just off Covent Garden specializing in titles published by Virago. Women's issues are important here, but a wide range of other subjects are also carried (these are very often by women writers).

Non-book materials: cards, stationery
Services: mail order, special order

Watkins Books Ltd   *(Leicester Square)*
19/21 Cecil Court WC2
836-2182

M–Sat 10:00–6:00

alchemy / astrology / Buddhism / Christian mysticism / consciousness / dreams / Egypt / healing / hermeticism / Indian philosophy / Judaism / Jungian psychology / Kabalah / meditation / new age / new sciences / occultism / para-psychology / psychical research / psychology / radiesthesia / reincarnation / spiritualism / Sufism / symbolism / Taoism / tarot / theosophy / Tibet / yoga / Zen

For books on esoteric subjects Watkins's large, elegant and friendly shop is one of the oldest and best-known in London. There are sections on new developments in holistic sciences and inner development and a number of related magazines and journals. Towards the back of the shop there is a substantial second-hand section.

Non-book material: astrological charts, pendulums, magazines, tapes, posters
Services: mail order, special order
Catalogue: annual catalogue of new and current titles

West End Books   *(Russell Square)*
82 Lamb's Conduit Street WC1
405-3029

M–F 9:30–6:00

anaesthesia / anatomy / biochemistry / cancer / cardiology / community medicine / dentistry / dermatology / diagnosis / dictionaries / embryology / endocrinology / gastroenterology / immunology / infectious diseases / medicine / microbiology / neurology / nursing / obstetrics, gynaecology / ophthalmology / orthopaedics / otolaryngology / paediatrics / pharmacology / physiology / psychology and psychiatry / radiology / surgery / tropical diseases / urology

West End Books is a new medical bookshop hoping to serve the doctors and nurses of the area's hospitals with a full range of books on medical and nursing subjects and specialities.

Non-book material: stethoscopes
Services: mail order, special order
Catalogue: in preparation – annual

Wildy & Sons Ltd   *(Holborn)*
Lincoln's Inn Archway
Carey Street WC2
242-5778

M–F 8:45–5:15

This is the oldest and grandest of London's law bookshops, tucked away behind the Law Courts in the archway into Lincoln's Inn. With possibly the widest selection of new, second-hand and antiquarian law books in the world, Wildy can cater to the student, practitioner, theoretician, legal philosopher, book collector and even the computer law specialist. Their stock is international in subject and language, and though Wildy does not provide a search service for out-of-print titles, they do keep requests on file indefinitely. Very few law journals are kept in the shop, but they do specialize in supplying sets of law periodicals (and individual back issues can be ordered).

Non-book material: modern and antiquarian engravings and prints, from serious to silly
Services: mail order, special order, wants lists accepted, book binding
Publications: Wildy & Sons Ltd publishes new law titles, while facsimile reproductions and reprints are published under the imprint of Carey

YHA Bookshop   *(Covent Garden)*
14 Southampton Street WC2
836-8541

M–Sat 9:30–6:00   Tue 10:00–6:00   Th 9:30–7:00

budget travel guides (international) / canoeing / caving / London guides / mountaineering, climbing guides / outdoor activities / phrase books / Sierra Club publications / ski guides (international) / treasure hunting / UK guides, illustrated / US sectional guides (Dollarwise) / Wainwright guides and picture books

YHA (Youth Hostels Association) is a complete outdoor sports shop, with a terrific travel and outdoor sport bookshop catering to both the low-budget traveller and the serious sportsperson. YHA pride themselves on their range of international mountaineering and climbing guides from all the major mountaineering clubs. They have excellent worldwide travel guides, including European guides and some general interest/hobby titles. Journals include *YHA Magazine* and *Descent*.

Non-book material: Ordnance Survey maps; UK, US and European maps; occasional posters; calendars
Services: mail order, special order
Publications: YHA publishes a *Guide to Europe* and the *YHA European Guide* to individual countries

Zeno   *(Tottenham Court Road)*
6 Denmark Street WC2
836-2522

M–F 9:30–6:00   Sat 9:30–5:00

archaeology / architecture / art / biography / Byzantium / children's books / classics / Cyprus / drama / Egypt / fiction / history / language teaching / literature / music / natural history / poetry / politics / religion / travel guides and maps / Turkey

Zeno is a long-established Greek bookshop selling new, second-hand and antiquarian books, in a variety of languages, on ancient and modern Greece. The shop carries popular Greek magazines and newspapers and, as well as being an active bookshop, Zeno prides itself on being a meeting place for Greek scholars, students and writers.

Non-book material: cards, engravings, maps, prints
Services: mail order, special order, search service
Catalogue: general catalogue annually; individual specialized lists throughout the year
Publications: Zeno publishes reprints of Greek history and travel

A. Zwemmer Ltd   *(Leicester Square)*
24 Litchfield Street WC2
836-4710

M–F 9:30–6:00   Sat 9:30–5:30

architecture / art history / costume / furniture / metalwork / modern art / monographs of artists / pottery and porcelain / prints and drawings / sculpture / textiles

This art bookshop is internationally renowned for the depth and range of its stock and the expertise of those administering it. Fine arts subjects are on the ground floor, which includes the widest selection of books on sculpture in London; architecture, applied art and remainders are in the basement; and antiquarian books are on the first floor (it is advisable to make an appointment to see this department). The shop carries a selection of major art and design periodicals, as well as local arts reviews and exhibition catalogues. They have a second shop at 80 Charing Cross Road, directly opposite this branch, which specializes in cinema, graphic design and photography. There is also another branch at the Whitechapel Gallery. See separate entries for both of these.

Services: mail order, special order
Catalogue: selected and special subject lists

A. Zwemmer Ltd   *(Leicester Square)*
80 Charing Cross Road WC2
434-4291

M–F 9:30–6:00   Sat 9:30–5:30

advertising / film / graphics / photography / typography

This branch of the excellent Zwemmer's has a wide range of stock in the above subjects. Fine and applied arts are in the shop directly opposite in Litchfield Street.

Services: mail order, special order
Catalogue: selected and special subject lists

Zwemmer's Oxford University Press Bookshop
(Leicester Square)

72 Charing Cross Road WC2
240-1559

M–F 9:30–6:00   Sat 9:30–5:30

architecture / art / bibles / biology / carol books / children's educational books / classics / economics / education / English as a foreign language / fiction / folk tales / geography / historical monographs / history / law / legends / linguistics / mathematics / medicine / Oxford companions / philosophy / physics / political science / prayer books / sciences

Zwemmer's OUP Bookshop stocks only OUP titles and has computerized inventory and stock ordering systems for quick delivery of whatever is not on the shelves. The OUP specializes in world classics, but the shop also has an excellent selection of books on English language teaching.

Non-book material: Oxford diaries, ELT cassettes and videos, some foreign language cassettes
Services: mail order, special order
Catalogue: OUP publisher's catalogue is available for a fee, selected specialized lists produced frequently

Zwemmer's Oxford University Press Music & Books
(Leicester Square)

26 Litchfield Street WC2
379-7886

M–F 9:30–6:00   Sat 9:30–5:30

This bookshop has been jointly set up by Zwemmer and OUP to specialize in music. This includes sheet music, scores, music manuscript paper and books on classical music and jazz – not just those published by OUP. The staff know their subject well and are always happy to help customers, whether they are interested in a first piano book or the biography of a great composer.

Non-book material: see above
Services: mail order, special order

Antiquarian and Second-hand Bookshops

John Adrian at A.W. Travel *(Leicester Square)*
12 Cecil Court WC2
836-2987

M–Sat 11:00–6:00

Baedekers / children's / Churchill / cricket / golf / Rider Haggard / history / Jennings / T. E. Lawrence / literature / Ward Locks / railways / Rupert annuals / William / Wodehouse

This is a second-hand and antiquarian bookshop with titles in the above subjects and many more. A pleasant background is provided by Radio 3 which is often playing.

Non-book material: old magazines
Services: search service

Any Amount of Books *(Leicester Square)*
62 Charing Cross Road WC2
240-8140

M–Sun 10:30–7:30

ground floor:
architecture / art / classics / cookery / education / fiction / film / gardening / history / illustrated books / language teaching / law / legends / literature / memoirs / music / myths / Penguin / philosophy / photography / plays / poetry (first editions) / politics / psychology / religion / science fiction / sociology / sports / theatre / travel

basement:
arts / bargains / children's / foreign language / literature / history / medicine / thrillers / travel

This bookshop is the sister shop to the original in Hammersmith and is conceived on exactly similar lines. It is a good, reasonably priced second-hand and bargain bookshop.

Services: mail order
Catalogue: first editions and art, twice yearly

M. Ayres Rare Books   *(Tottenham Court Road)*
31 Museum Street WC1
636-2844

M–Sat 10:00–6:00

art / children's Victorian books / illustrated books / individual illustrators / literature / philosophy / private presses

This antiquarian shop specializes in art and illustrated books from the 15th century onward, though most of their visible stock appears to fall into the eighteenth, nineteenth and twentieth centuries.

Non-book material: antiques, engravings, English and Continental prints
Services: mail order, wants lists accepted for collections of individual illustrators

Bell, Book & Radmall Ltd   *(Leicester Square)*
4 Cecil Court WC2
240-2161/836-5888

M–F 10:00–5:30

anthologies / autographs and manuscripts / fantasy and detective fiction / literary criticism / literature / modern first editions

For any student of modern literature (with a few quid to spare) the two floors of this shop are heaven. Bell, Book & Radmall have an impressive stock of modern first editions (1880 to the present) of English and American literature. The shelves are lined with first editions, alphabetical by author, but the most valuable titles are kept in cases. In addition to the subjects listed above, the shop carries classics in translation, back issues of literary magazines such as *Horizon* and *Criterion* and a few illustrated books. The shop's prices, though, are often as exclusive as their stock. (They have a distinct edge over their competitors in that many of their books have the original dust-jackets.)

Non-book material: literary prints and paintings
Services: mail order, search service in field of modern first editions
Catalogue: selected lists produced four to five times yearly

Andrew Block   *(Holborn)*
20 Barter Street WC1
405-9660

M–F 10:00–4:00 (opening hours can vary, ring for appointment)

architecture / art / botany / children's books / conjuring / drama / film / incunabula / literature / medicine / modern first editions / private press publications / reference / theatre / topography / typography

This antiquarian bookshop is one of the oldest bookshops in London. In its four jumbled rooms are a great many good books, but don't stop by expecting to browse as the quarters are tight with titles. If you are looking for a particular title there is a comprehensive index system originally designed by the late Mr Block himself. In it you will also find reference to prints, ephemera and general reference material for designers, interior decorators, etc.

Non-book material: prints, theatre posters, postcards

Bloomsbury Rare Books   *(Tottenham Court Road)*
29 Museum Street WC1
636-8206

M–Sat 10:30–6:00   Sun 12:00–6:30

antiquarian / English literature / history of science

Arthur Page stocks antiquarian books, especially medicine, history of science and English literature. These, remarkably, are available to browsers on the open shelves; the prices are as reasonable as the stock is varied and interesting. A recent speciality is that of medieval manuscript leaves – this is one of only a handful of bookshops that sell them.

The general second-hand section has not been neglected, ranging from academic texts to a good supply of early Penguins and Pelicans (and some original King Penguins). Runs of magazines, such as *The Strand*, can often be found here; so, too, can good sets of novelists and poets, such as Meredith, Conrad and the *Waverley* novels.

In addition to books, there is a small department specializing in prints and watercolours, mostly from the nineteenth century.

Services: mail order
Catalogue: specialized lists bi-annually, antiquarian list, general list

Horace C. Blossom, Booksellers   *(Covent Garden)*
36 Great Queen Street WC2
831-0381

M–Sat 11:00–5:00 (times are approximate)

art / cinema / history / London / Rupert / theatre / topography / P.G. Wodehouse

The stock here is largely second-hand but there are a few remainders.

Services: special order

Louis W. Bondy   *(Holborn)*
16 Little Russell Street WC1
405-2733

M–F 10:30–6:30   Sat 10:30–5:15

architectural history / ballet / bibliography / British history / British topography / caricature / children's books / English literature / fine art / French literature and history / miniature books / music / poetry / theatre

The owner of this antiquarian and second-hand bookshop is one of the few people in the world who specializes in miniature books, and he has published widely on the subject. In addition to miniatures, the shop's stock ranges from very rare, early printed books to 20th-century second-hand titles. Of particular interest in the shop are illustrated children's books, and books on art, architecture and caricature.

Non-book material: caricatures, ephemera, prints
Services: mail order, valuations
Catalogue: an irregular one of recent purchases; miniature and early printed books, four or five times a year

Alan Brett   *(Leicester Square)*
24 Cecil Court WC2
836-8222

M–Sat 9:00–5:30

Alan Brett specializes in antiquarian and second-hand books, maps and topographical prints. Also available are antiquarian fiction, gothic novels, antiquarian magazines and some theatre ephemera including a good collection of *Vanity Fair* prints.

Non-book material: boxes of prints grouped according to country, county and topic, e.g., fruits, caricatures, military, etc.
Catalogue: occasional catalogue of *Vanity Fair* subjects

Check Books   *(Tottenham Court Road)*
29 Museum Street WC1
637-5862

M–Sun 11:00–6:00

If you are gripped by the ancient mysteries of the British Museum you can find further inspiration in this basement shop in Museum Street, specializing in Middle Eastern and foreign travel. The stock is second-hand and antiquarian, with some general books as well as the specialist sections.

Services: mailing list
Catalogue: quarterly lists

The Economists' Second-hand   *(Holborn)*
Portugal Street/Clare Market WC2
405-8643

M–F 9:30–6:00   W 10:30–6:00

accounting / anthropology / applied economics / banking / development studies / economic history / economic theory / foreign policy / history / international economics / international politics / labour law / management / philosophy / politics / sexual politics / social history / social policy / sociology

This shop is the second-hand branch of The Economists' Bookshop and is an especially good source of affordable books for students from the LSE. Remaindered, out-of-print and an occasional antiquarian title on economics and the other social sciences are stocked in the shop, whose entrance is directly through the main Economists' Bookshop.

Services: mail order, out-of-print search service
Catalogue: annual list of sought after and out-of-print titles mainly in economics and banking

H.M. Fletcher   *(Leicester Square)*
27 Cecil Court WC2
836-2865

M–F 10:00–5:30

Despite the rather disorderly and slightly grubby appearance of this general antiquarian and second-hand bookshop, there is said to be a wealth of interesting stock out of sight. Second-hand paperbacks at 50p, modern private press and 16th century offerings are all available and give an idea of the range of books, and prices, to be found.

Services: mail order

Frognal Rare Books   *(Leicester Square)*
18 Cecil Court WC2
240-2815

M–F 10:30–6:00   Sat – by appointment

Early law, economics (especially banking) and history are the specialities of this elegant-looking shop. Two floors house books dating back to the 16th century, from all over the world and in a variety of languages.

Services: mail order
Catalogue: antiquarian law books, economics, special lists – four times annually

Holborn Books   *(Leicester Square/Charing Cross)*
14 Charing Cross Road WC2
240-2337

M–Sun: 9:00–7:00

'No Book Over £2' proclaims a poster in the window of this second-hand shop. Such a policy, while meaning that rare books are unlikely to be found here (and if they are one could make a quick profit by nipping round to Bertram Rota with them), is welcome in central London. The stock is of a general nature – from crime fiction to history and especially notable for its literature and art books – which makes a visit when passing likely to prove worthwhile. An interesting range of new and old Penguins is kept in several places around the shop.

Non-book material: old magazines, chiefly about the theatre and cinema

Images   *(Leicester Square)*
(Peter Stockham Ltd)
16 Cecil Court WC2
836-8661

T–F 11:00–6:00   First Sat of each month 11:00–2:00

Images specializes in children's, illustrated and art books, as well as children's and decorative ephemera. The stock consists of new, out-of-print and antiquarian titles. The shop also carries facsimile reprints of rare books, reference books and scholarly monographs on collecting, art and illustration.

Non-book material: ephemera new and antiquarian, games and toys

Services: mail order, special order, search service
Catalogue: many lists, e.g. children's literature, toys and games, antiquarian books
Publications: Peter Stockham publishes chap-books and facsimile reprints of children's illustrated books

Frew Mackenzie   *(Tottenham Court Road)*
106 Great Russell Street WC1
580-2311

M–F 10:00–6:00   Sat 10:00–2:00

Situated in the heart of Bloomsbury and the publishing world, and directly beneath the publishers André Deutsch, this is a delightful antiquarian bookshop. Its walls are lined with rare books, mostly in the humanities (18th- 19th- and 20th-century literature and travel accounts) and with its dark wood fittings, plush carpet and antique desk, it generates a restful air most conducive to browsing. Its directors also own the Primrose Hill Bookshop.

Catalogue: several issued per year

The Marchmont Bookshop   *(Euston)*
39 Burton Street WC1
387-7989

M–F 11:00–6:30 (hours may vary)

architecture / art / children's books / drama / history / literature / modern first editions / natural history / philosophy / poetry / topography

The Marchmont shop though rather jumbled has a fairly wide range of lower priced second-hand books, as well as a few remaindered titles and review copies. There is also a more specialized and more expensive range of better quality second-hand and antiquarian titles. Twentieth-century literature is one of their specialities.

Services: mail order, search service
Catalogue: modern first edition and private presses list

Pleasures of Past Times   *(Leicester Square)*
11 Cecil Court WC2
836-1142

M–F 11:00–2:30, 3:30–5:45   first Sat of each month 11:00–2:30
(other Sats by appointment)

This is a wonderfully colourful bookshop featuring second-hand children's literature along one wall, and books on entertainment and the performing arts on another. Books are brought into the shop according to the owner's taste, resulting in rows of bright bindings and familiar titles from the Edwardian and late Victorian eras. Collections of individual authors are stocked, and there are unusual sections on conjuring and the circus. Remainders, when relevant, are sold as well. The owner is always willing to help serious researchers.

Non-book material: another feature of the shop is the large collection of theatre ephemera (playbills, programmes, original designs, etc.). Also stocked are Valentines and similar Victorian ephemera in addition to many classified Edwardian postcards
Services: picture research and supply in children's literature and entertainment

Henry Pordes   *(Leicester Square)*
58-60 Charing Cross Road WC2
836-9031

M–Sat 10:00–7:00

art / Israel and Judaica / literature / modern first editions / philosophy / poetry / theology / topography / travel

Henry Pordes stocks second-hand, remaindered and a few antiquarian books of a general nature, with a particularly good selection of Judaica.

Provincial Booksellers Fairs Association   *(Russell Square)*
Royal National Hotel
Woburn Place WC1

Sun 5:00–8:00   M 10:00–8:00

also:
Imperial Hotel
Russell Square WC1

M 12:00–8:00   T 10:00–3:30

For three days each month, always beginning on the second
Sunday, the Provincial Booksellers Fairs Association (PBFA)
holds book fairs at the hotels listed above. Antiquarian and
second-hand booksellers from all over England come to London
to trade and buy books, and the general public is just as welcome
as those in the book business. This is one of Londoners' unique
opportunities to browse through a country bookseller's stock
without having to leave the city.

Quevedo   *(Leicester Square)*
25 Cecil Court WC2
836-9132

M–F 10:00–1:00 2:00–5:30

Quevedo is a general antiquarian bookshop specializing in travel
and English literature, mostly of the 16th-18th centuries, together
with a large number of foreign languages and some illustrated
books.

Services: mail order
Catalogue: irregular lists

Quinto of Charing Cross Road   *(Leicester Square)*
48a Charing Cross Road WC2
379-7669/7692

M–Sat 9:00a.m.–10:00p.m.   Sun 12:00–8:00

ground:
architecture / art / biography / cinema / dance / history / literary
criticism / literature / theatre

basement:
cookery / hobbies / medicine / military / natural history /
philosophy / politics / psychology / religion / science / sociology /
sports / topography / transport / travel / women's studies

This is a fairly large second-hand bookshop fronting the corner of Charing Cross Road and Great Newport Street. At the back of the ground floor are better quality books on all subjects including some antiquarian titles, while most of the paperbacks are to be found downstairs.

Catalogue: regular general catalogue of better quality second-hand and antiquarian books

Remington   *(Leicester Square)*
14 Cecil Court WC2
836-9771

M–F 10:00–5:00

Remington specializes in books dealing with voyages and travel, generally antiquarian and second-hand, from Hakluyt and earlier to the Kon-Tiki expedition and beyond. Such discursive writing, rather than guides, is the shop's interest; and it is the more adventurous who fill the reasonably-priced shelves – Africa, China and the Americas rather than Europe. There is a useful stock of more general, miscellaneous titles as well as natural history.

Non-book material: maps, prints
Services: mail order

Bertram Rota Ltd   *(Covent Garden)*
30-31 Long Acre WC2
836-0723

M–F 9:30–5:30   Sat by appointment

American literature / autographs / English literature / history / poetry / private presses / sciences / topography / travel accounts

With an international reputation to recommend it, this elegant shop is well worth a visit if you are looking for modern first editions (many of which have the original dust-jackets) and antiquarian books. Many of the choicest books are not on the shelves upstairs but may be lurking in the storage area below, so ask if you don't find what you want. There are some new titles as well, on topics which relate directly to modern literature. An added attraction are the glass cabinets in the centre of the shop which contain changing displays of particularly beautiful or unusually bound or printed volumes.

Services: mail order, search service in certain areas
Catalogue: numerous – produced six to eight times annually (e.g., poetry, rare books, fine printing)
Publications: the shop publishes limited editions of poetry and a few bibliographies

Skoob Books Ltd   *(Holborn)*
15 Sicilian Avenue
Southampton Row WC1
404-3063

M–Sat 10:30–6:30

antiques / architecture / art / chemistry / cookery / crafts / education / engineering / esoterica / Everyman Library / Folio Society / language / linguistics / literary criticism / literature / local history / medicine / modern prose / Oxford World Classics / Penguins / philosophy / physics / poetry / reference / theatre / theology / topography

The elegant Sicilian Avenue shop Skoob has established itself as the largest and best second-hand shop in central London where its interesting stock, with some emphasis on English and American literature, is frequently augmented. Its other sections, such as foreign literature and the sciences, are large, and all the prices are reasonable. Sets of authors, such as the *Waverley* novels, can occasionally be found here, together with some runs of magazines. The Penguin section is extensive; there is a good chance of finding any title that has been published there. More recently the shop has developed a section of modern first editions and antiquarian titles. Any visitor to London or inhabitant who does not visit Skoob will miss one of the capital's best assets.

Non-book material: a few second-hand records
Services: mail order, search service, 10% discount for NUS members
Catalogue: selected list

Stage Door Prints   *(Leicester Square)*
1 Cecil Court WC2
240-1683

M–F 11:00–6:00   Sat 11:30–6:00

The small stock of second-hand books here complements the antique theatrical prints which are the real specialization. Opera biographies, ballet, theatre and music generally make up the book section of this attractive shop.

Non-book material: antique prints, signed photographs of performers, Victorian greetings cards and Valentine cards

Harold Storey   *(Leicester Square)*
3 Cecil Court WC2
836-3777

M–F 10:00–6:00

This is a general antiquarian shop with a bias toward travel, exploration, voyages and illustrated books. It also carries a few second-hand books on aviation and naval history and has a good stock of sets of English literature (Dickens, *Waverley* novels, etc.) in fine bindings.

Non-book material: antique prints and engravings
Services: mail order

The Woburn Bookshop   *(Russell Square/Euston)*
10 Woburn Walk WC1
387-7340

M–F 10:00–6:00

Africa / biography / children's books / China / development studies / economics / history / India / Japan / Jewish history / Latin and Greek classics / Latin America / literary criticism / literature / medicine / Middle East / natural history / philosophy / poetry / politics / population / Russia / science / sociology / theology / travel / US

An antiquarian and second-hand bookshop with primary holdings in the humanities, The Woburn Bookshop was started by a man who has gone on to become a publisher but still keeps the shop as an active business concern.

Services: mail order, search service
Catalogue: by subject, bi-yearly
Publications: Frank Cass Publishers publish reprints and monographs

London EC

General Bookshops

The Bookcase *(St Paul's)*
26 Ludgate Hill EC4
236-5982

M–F 9:00–6:00   Sun 11:30–4:00

academic texts / art / biography / business / classics / collecting / cookery / crafts / economics / fiction / gardening / history / literary criticism / literature / natural history / Penguin / performing arts / poetry / politics / reference / royal family / science fiction / sociology / sports / technical / travel guides

The Bookcase sells new, but mainly remaindered books (prices start at 50p) in general subject areas, as well as the fields of business, academic texts and technical books. An odd second-hand title may turn up occasionally, as well as review copies, and the general subject areas vary weekly.

Services: mail order, special order (with publishers in stock)

Books Etc. *(Fenchurch Street/Bank)*
60 Fenchurch Street EC3
481-4425

M–F 8:30–6:00

antiques / art / biography / business / children's / classics / computers / crafts / crime / DIY / fiction / film / gardening / health / history / humour / literary criticism / literature / music / natural history / philosophy / photography / plays / poetry / politics / psychology / reference / religion / sports / thrillers / travel guides

This is the fifth of the Books Etc. shops to open. It is very large and its position is unusual in that it fronts onto three roads, one of which is directly opposite Fenchurch Street station. You can also actually see through into the basement from the street – not perhaps an original idea in itself, but one that succeeds in enticing passers by into the shop. It caters to the City trade – from Lloyd's underwriters to secretaries and clerks. Hence a wide choice of popular paperbacks rubbing shoulders with more exclusive items such as leather-bound dictionaries. There is naturally a large selection of business and computer books.

Non-book material: cards, wrapping paper, calendars, diaries
Services: special order

Chain Libraries Ltd   *(Moorgate)*
151 Moorgate EC2
606-5061

M–F 9:30–5:30

adventure / classics / cookery / crime / history / horror / non-fiction / Penguins / romance / science fiction

A general bookshop selling primarily paperback fiction.

Non-book material: cards, wrapping-paper, postcards
Services: special order

Dennys Booksellers Ltd   *(Barbican)*
2/4 Carthusian Street EC1
253-5421

M–F 9:00–6:00

general:
art / car manuals / children's books / cookery / crafts / economics / fiction / food / gardening / literature / management / natural history / Penguin / reference / travel guides

medical:
anaesthetics / anatomy / biochemistry / diagnosis / genetics / haemotology / histology / immunology / lecture notes / nursing / obstetrics, gynaecology / ophthalmology / surgery

Half of Dennys is a general retail bookshop with hardcover and paperback fiction and non-fiction. The other half of the shop features medical, technical and scientific books in a variety of specialized subject areas.

Non-book material: cards, posters, wrapping-paper, own greetings cards
Services: mail order, special order
Publications: Dennys Publications publishes medical, technical and scientific books

Note: There are two neighbouring branches of Dennys at 4 and 5 Carthusian Street (Telephone 253-1311). There is also a branch at Weston Street (see separate entry).

John Menzies   *(Liverpool Street)*
56 Old Broad Street EC2
588-1632

M–F 8:30–5:30

accountancy / biography / business / children's / computer / cookery / fiction / health / humour / reference / sport / travel

Situated two hundred yards from the Stock Exchange, this is quite a large shop on two floors (paperbacks upstairs) and is absolutely hectic at lunchtime. They have a much bigger area of books than any other branch of Menzies in London and the staff are helpful.

Non-book material: computer software, Ordnance Survey maps
Services: special order

John Menzies   *(St Paul's)*
50 Cheapside EC2
248-5315

M–F 7:30–6:00

autobiography / biography / business / children's books / commerce / cookery / fiction / sports / travel / wildlife

This is a small branch of Menzies with a large selection of books. There is a wide range of reference books, maps and guides as well as a section for paperback fiction.

Non-book material: stationery

New City Bookshop   *(Tower Hill)*
7 Byward Street EC3
626-3346

M–F 9:00–5:30

ground floor:
antiques and collecting / art / biography / classics / cookery / fiction / gardening / history / language teaching / literature / music / natural history / poetry / reference / sport

downstairs:
astronomy / business / children's books / crime / fiction / health / Open University / philosophy / photography / psychology / romance / science fiction / technology / travel

This bookshop, owned by The Booksmith, carries bargain hardbacks and full-price current hardcover and paperback books, all in a variety of subjects, with a special section on business and accountancy. The friendly, personable group of booksellers working at the shop are a pleasure to deal with.

Services: mail order through Bibliophile, special order
Catalogue: Bibliophile is the mail order arm of The Booksmith shops and produces frequent lists of bargain books available by post

Sherratt & Hughes   *(Bank)*
80 Cheapside EC2
248-2768

M–F 8:30–6:30

children's books / classics / cookery / cosmology / crime and adventure / dictionaries / fiction / games / gardening / history / horror / humour / literature / natural history / reference / romance / science fiction / sports / travel guides / war / westerns

This is a general bookshop primarily catering to the business people of the City with particularly strong sections of cookery and gardening books, dictionaries and paperback fiction.

Non-book material: cards, wrapping-paper
Services: special order

Sherratt & Hughes   *(Monument)*
64-72 Leadenhall Market EC3
626-5811

M–F 8:30–5:30

ground floor:
biography / children's / cookery / fiction / gardening / humour /
sport / sci-fi

mezzanine:
cards / stationery

basement:
art / bargain / business / history / plays / poetry / reference /
transport / travel

This is a spacious general bookshop in bustling Leadenhall
Market. Like other Sherratt & Hughes branches, it is owned by
W.H. Smith. There is a particularly large professional books
department in the basement catering for the regular City trade.
Subjects covered in depth include accounts, banking business,
economics, finance, insurance, investment, law, management,
shipping and taxation. The standard of service is high and it is
quite easy to find one's way around the shelves.

Non-book material: cards, gift-wrapping, stationery
Services: special orders

L. Simmonds   *(Temple/Chancery Lane)*
16 Fleet Street EC4
353-3907

M–F 9:00–5:30

The small front of L. Simmonds shop conceals an excellent general
bookshop with an academic section which has a good range of
new titles, both in paperback and hardback, as well as established
works. There is also a section of recent books at knock-down
prices which often contains interesting titles, and a
comprehensive range of books on journalism.

Services: mail order, special order, library supply
Catalogue: annual journalism list

W.H. Smith   *(Holborn)*
124 Holborn EC1
242-0535

M–F 8:30–5:30

Through the general news and stationery departments is a good book department. It has a particular interest in titles concerning the media and politics as it is in an area of newspaper publishing – in fact it is directly opposite the *Daily Mirror* building.

Non-book material: stationery, records, newspapers, etc.
Services: special order, post-a-book, tokens
Catalogue: *Bookcase* review of books twice yearly

W.H. Smith   *(St Paul's)*
145-147 Cheapside EC2
606-2301

M–F 8:30–5:30

The book department here occupies one half of the ground floor and has a comprehensive range including new hardback fiction.

Non-book material: stationery, cards, paper, news, magazines, etc.
Services: special order, post-a-book, tokens

W.H. Smith   *(Liverpool Street)*
Liverpool Street Station EC2
283-3825

M–Sat 7:00a.m.–7:30p.m.

The main shop in this station is by platform 9 and there is a smaller stall on platform 12 to supplement the bigger branch and make life easier for book-hungry commuters. The stock on platform 12 is largely paperback fiction, including crime, horror and westerns, while the main shop has a larger range of hardback titles. The usual subjects are covered, including biographies, cookery, gardening, entertainment and student books.

Non-book material: stationery, cards, paper, news, magazines, etc.

Speciality Bookshops

Barbican Business Book Centre *(Moorgate)*
9 Moorfields EC2
628-7479

M–F 9:00–5:00

accounting / banking and investment / business studies / commercial / computing practice / economics / finance / industrial relations / law / M & E handbooks / management / marketing / shipping / statistics / taxation / technology

Specializing in business, management and finance books for students and professionals, this shop is well organized, clearly labelled and has a good range of UK and US publishers in each subject area. They also stock many directories and yearbooks.

Services: mail order, special order
Catalogue: bimonthly catalogue – 'Barbican Business Book News'

The Barbican Centre *(Barbican/Moorgate)*
Silk Street EC2
638-4141

The Barbican remains a controversial building housing and hosting a cross-section of the arts. To some it is an impersonal, concrete labyrinth – windswept yet stifling, so that in its early day it became known as the 'barbecue' by those working there. To others it is a happy combination of exhibition hall, art gallery, concert hall and theatre, complete with playing fountains and panoramic restaurants. For our purposes it has three sales points for books which are listed below. Two are owned by the Barbican itself, the other is solely the concern of the Royal Shakespeare Company.

Barbican Bookshop
Level 4

M–Sat 11:00–9:30   Sun 12:00–7:30

This is the smallest of the bookshops in the Barbican, stocking a few play-texts, fiction and biography titles among the records, sweets, Alka Seltzer and key-rings.

Barbican Bookshop
Level 7

M 11:00–7:30   Tue–Sat 10:30–7:30   Sun 12:00–9:00

This is an expanded version of the Level 4 shop and has a much greater proportion of books. These cover fiction, theatre, music, performing arts in general and some hardback bestsellers. Also stocked are cards, art posters, classical tapes, souvenirs, glass, jewellery, etc. Although there is no mail order at present this may come in the future.

Royal Shakespeare Company Bookstall
Level 3, Stalls Left
628-3351 ext. 490

M–W/F 6:00–7:30p.m.   9:00–9:15p.m.   Th/Sat 1:00–2:00
3:30–3:45   5:00–5:15   6:00–7:30   9:00–9:15

This stall is run by the Royal Shakespeare Company who are now permanently installed at the Barbican. It sells a selection of theatre books amongst the clothing, souvenirs, cards, videos, records, tapes and posters. It naturally concentrates on Shakespeare. It also stocks theatre magazines, yearbooks and programmes.

Services: mail order
Catalogue: annual list

Barbican Music Shop   *(Barbican/Moorgate)*
Cromwell Tower
Silk Street EC2
588-9242

M–F 9:00–5:45   Sat (term time only) 8:30–4:00

This shop sells books on music, sheet music, scores, song books, educational music for schools and all examination music. It also sells chamber music, musical accessories and cassettes. It is a sister shop to Chimes Music Shop on Marylebone High Street.

Non-book material: see above
Services: mail order, special order

Books Nippon   *(St Paul's)*
(Nippon Shuppan Hanbai UK Ltd)
64-66 St Paul's Churchyard EC4
248-4956

M–F 10:30–7:00   Sat 10:00–6:00

Nippon have a large range of Japanese books and magazines, including Japanese fiction, reference and children's books. They also stock books in English about Japan, textbooks, language books and a selection on Japanese culture.

Non-book material: cards, dolls, postcards of Japanese prints, music cassettes, Japanese screens and stationery
Services: distribution of books on Japanese advertising, architecture, design, graphics and photography

Brown & Perring Ltd   *(Old Street/Moorgate)*
Redwing House
36-44 Tabernacle Street EC2
253-4517

M–F 9:00–5:15   Sat 9:00–12:00

Brown & Perring sell musical charts, but a portion of their business is in the field of nautical books as well. The shipping industry (vs. the pleasure boating public) is their principal clientele, with the result that Brown & Perring's stock is comprised of commercial and technical marine publications.

Nautical almanacs, Admiralty, IMCO, OCIMF, ICS and HMSO publications are constantly stocked. The shop claims to be able to get virtually all technical nautical publications in print, including restricted nautical publications when possible and appropriate, such as Admiralty charts.

An interesting service which Brown & Perring offers is the compilation of 'case histories' for old or antique nautical instruments.

Non-book material: nautical charts, ships' stationery, lights (indeed anything needed for a ship)
Services: mail order, special order

Christian Literature Crusade   *(St Paul's)*
St Paul's Shopping Centre
Cathedral Place EC4
248-5528/6274

Tue–F 9:30–5:30   Sat 9:30–5:00

ground floor:
archaeology and atlases / Bible study / bibles / biography / Christian home / Christian living / church growth / church history / commentaries / concordances / courtship and marriage / daily readings / evangelism / Greek and Hebrew / healing / missionary / Old and New Testaments / prayer / prophecy / renewal / sermon aids / theology / tracts

basement:
bible stories / biography / children's books / children's talks / hymn and chorus books / missionary / object lessons and games / teaching aids

Appropriately located next to St Paul's Cathedral, the Christian Literature Crusade bookshop is a large shop selling new books on all aspects of Christianity, from religion in daily life to academic texts on theology and comparative religion. The downstairs of the shop is devoted largely to children's books and teaching aids. Also available is a wide range of journals on Christianity and evangelism.

Non-book material: cards, cassettes, posters, records
Services: mail order, special order (in field of Christian books)

The City University Bookshop   *(Angel)*
Northampton Square EC1
608-0706

M–F 9:00–5:00   W 9:00–2:30

actuarial science / business and management / computer science / engineering / optometry / speech therapy

This bookshop caters mainly for the courses run at the university. Within the section on engineering are books on all branches of the subject including electrical, electronic control, mechanical, civil and aeronautical.

Non-book material: stationery

The Daily Telegraph Bookshop   *(Blackfriars)*
130 Fleet Street EC4
353-4242

M–F 9:00–5:00   Sat 9:00–12:00

business / cookery / gardening / sports / travel

Within the newspaper's own building is a shop stocking all the publications under the auspices of the *Daily Telegraph*, including its Sunday and Magazine off-shoots. The interests and preoccupations of the papers are reflected in the range of subjects available.

Non-book material: crosswords, diaries, maps and guides, wall charts
Services: mail order; back copies of the newspapers; 25%+ discount for NUJ members, trade and publishers

Genesis Books   *(Old Street)*
East West Centre
188 Old Street EC1
250-1868

M–F 11:30–7:00   Sat 11:00–3:00

acupuncture / astrology / child care and pregnancy / cookery / diet / Eastern classics / Eastern religions and philosophies / healing / health / herbs / history / macrobiotic nutrition / magic / massage and shiatsu / medicine / mysticism / psychology / society / women and sexual politics / yoga

Although run independently from the East West Centre in which it is located, this shop is, none the less, closely associated with the purpose of the centre. The shop specializes in new books on alternatives in health, medicine and spirituality, and carries titles on a range of subjects from diet to iridology to acupuncture to sexual politics. Also available are journals and magazines in these fields, especially in the areas of herbal and holistic medicine, psychology and nutrition. The owner is an acupuncturist and can give advice on literature in the field.

Non-book material: gifts, herb teas, badges, charts, aromatherapy oils, bach flower remedies, acupuncture needles, moxibustion rolls, incense, back and foot massage rollers, New Age music cassettes, meditation tapes and stools and relaxation stools
Services: mail order, special order
Catalogue: selected list
Publications: The centre publishes booklets on health and nutrition

Geographia   *(Blackfriars)*
63 Fleet Street EC4
353-2701

M–F 9:00–5:15

Travel guides for travel budgets of all sizes together with maps for practically every area of the world are Geographia's speciality.

Non-book material: maps, globes
Services: mail order
Catalogue: Geographia publications
Publications: Geographia publish maps and travel guides

Jewish Chronicle Bookshop   *(Chancery Lane)*
25 Furnival Street EC4
405-9252

M–Th 9:30–5:00   F 9:30–3:00

books for the younger reader / culture / ethics / history / holidays / Israel / Jewish legends / lifestyle / music / mysticism / reference / Talmudic studies / Torah

This bookroom, off the foyer of the *Jewish Chronicle* building, carries a well-chosen range of new books (mostly in English) on Judaism and Israel.

Services: mail order for books they distribute or publish
Catalogue: monthly book lists
Publications: Jewish Chronicle Publications publishes books about Jewish faith, culture, lifestyle, etc. They are distributors for: Behrman House (US); Jewish Publication Society of America; Jonathan David (US); Keter Publishing House (Israel); Ktav (US); SBS Publishing (US); Schocken Books (US)

Hammick, Sweet & Maxwell   *(Chancery Lane)*
Corner of Chancery Lane
191/192 Fleet Street EC4
405-5711

M–F 9:00–5:30

ground floor: general books
basement: law books

The floor space in this bookshop is evenly divided between general books and law books, but it is best known for the excellent range and depth of the latter. Titles stocked cover everything from common law to commercial law and all other matters touching the legal profession in the UK. Foreign legal texts can also be ordered and the major legal journals are carried. The general books department has a good selection of classics, fiction, drama, poetry, cookery and travel.

Non-book material: cards, 'legal' prints of personalities, wrapping-paper
Services: mail order, special order
Catalogue: annual catalogue and six special subject lists yearly
Publications: Sweet & Maxwell are publishers of law books

Jones & Evans Bookshop Ltd   *(Mansion House)*
70 Queen Victoria Street EC4
248-6516

M–F 9:30–5:15

art / biography / business / economics / finance / history / law / literature / management / natural history / politics / Royal Family

With a speciality in current business and finance titles, Jones & Evans reflects the interests of the working population in the City, although they also stock recent fiction and non-fiction.

Services: mail order, special order

MENCAP Bookshop   *(Barbican)*
Royal Society for Mentally Handicapped Children and Adults
123 Golden Lane EC1
253-9433

M–F 9:30–5:30

This bookshop provides a source of specialist literature on all aspects of mental handicap to parents and professional workers such as teachers, nurses and therapists. The shop is the sole UK distributor of SEFA (Social Education First Aid) Assessment and Teaching Materials and of Nicholls and Mott Individual Learning Programmes.
    An RSMHC Library Reference Set, which has been developed by the shop, is a useful foundation on which to build a library in this field and the staff are very willing to advise in this area.
    Also welcome are comments and suggestions from parents and teachers about books they have read which might be added to the RSMHC lists.

Non-book material: individual learning programmes
Services: mail order (cheques payable to RSMHC Ltd), special order
Catalogue: complete list of titles in stock, SEFA catalogue, Individual Learning Programmes Information Sheet
Publications: books on mental handicap are published by the NSMHC

The Museum of London Bookshop   *(Barbican)*
150 London Wall EC2
600-3699

T–Sat 10:00–5:40   Sun 2:00–5:40

This is a gift shop with a small selection of books on London history, architecture and monuments. They also carry some stock of general history books with urban connotations.

Non-book material: cards, gifts, posters
Services: mail order
Catalogue: list of museum publications and products
Publications: The Museum of London publishes books on particular periods of London's history, aspects of the museum's collection and special exhibitions

J. D. Potter   *(Aldgate)*
145 Minories EC3
709-9076

M–F 9:00–5:30

atlases / automation / biography / construction / electronics / encyclopedias / fiction / history / knots and splices / mathematics / miscellaneous business and law / model boats / naval architecture / navigation / oil / physics / pilotage / racing / radar / radio signals / sailing / sea stories / seamanship / signalling / voyages / yacht construction and design

J. D. Potter specializes in new books on sailing, yachting and boat racing. The shop is an agent for Admiralty publications and, though most of the shop space is devoted to books, marine instruments and equipment are available as well. Marine law, engineering and insurance are especially well represented.

Services: mail order, special order, marine equipment repair service
Catalogue: complete catalogue annually, specialized lists, ISSA catalogues

Protestant Truth Society   *(Blackfriars)*
184 Fleet Street EC4
405-4960

M–F 9:00–5:15

Banner of Truth / bibles / biography / children's books / church history / commentaries / contemporary church / daily readings /

death and life / Evangelical Press / Holy Spirit / Lakeland Series / Old and New Testaments / PTS publications / Pickering and Inglis / preaching / religion and society / sects and other religions / US publications

PTS is a bookshop selling new books on all aspects of the Christian faith.

Non-book material: cards, stationery
Services: mail order, special order

Stobart & Son   *(Liverpool Street/Moorgate)*
Technical Booksellers
67/73 Worship Street EC2
247-0501

M–F 9:30–5:30

building trades / crafts / forestry / timber technology and wood science / woodworking

This bookshop can supply you with almost anything to do with wood in all its aspects including turning, sculpture, toy-making, and furniture-making. It also sells technical books on plumbing, bricklaying, etc.

Non-book material: forest tools
Services: mail order, special exhibitions
Catalogue: specialist catalogues
Publications: publishers of woodwork and timber books

Third World Library and Bookshop   *(Old Street)*
173 Old Street EC1
608-0447/8

M–F 9:30–5:30   Sat 10:00–2:00

This bookshop specializes in Third World issues. A wide range of books includes politics, history and religion in the Third World and there is also a section for fiction and children's books from the Third World published here and abroad. There is a café and reading room attached to the bookshop so you can take your time choosing books and even break for a cup of coffee.

Services: mail order
Catalogue: the bookshop stocks all the books reviewed in its own journals
Publications: two journals: *Third World Book Review* and *Third World Women's News*

Tower Bookshop   *(Tower Hill)*
10 Tower Place EC3
623-1081

M–Sun 9:30–5:00

This shop caters largely to the tourist trade, selling full-price paperbacks, second-hand hardbacks, guides and illustrated histories of London together with gifts, records, cards, maps, etc.

Non-book material: see above

Witherby & Co. Ltd   *(Monument)*
147 Cannon Street EC4
626-1912

M–F 7:00–5:00

art / banking / business management / children's books / cookery / economics / export / fiction / insurance / language texts / law / M & E handbooks / marine and shipping / marketing / reference / travel guides

Witherby & Co. specializes in new books on insurance, shipping and business. A few general fiction and non-fiction titles are stocked alongside the business titles. This Cannon Street shop is also a newsagent and stationer which opens at 4.30a.m. and if such books are needed at that time they can be sold.

Non-book material: see above
Services: mail order, special order
Catalogue: Witherby Publications catalogue, book list on insurance and related subjects
Publications: Witherby Publications publishes books on insurance, marine business and insurance
Note: Books from Witherby & Co. can also be obtained from their mail order department: 32 Aylesbury St, EC1, 251-5341

Antiquarian and Second-hand Bookshops

Ash Rare Books   *(Bank)*
25 Royal Exchange
Threadneedle Street EC3
626-2665

M–F 10:00–5:30

general / first edition literature / natural history / sport / travel and topography

Located opposite the Bank of England, the shop's stock reflects the interests of the professional-class, 'local' population of bankers, stockbrokers and lawyers. The rather small premises hold a good amount of literature, mainly from 1800 to modern first editions, world history and London topography, among other subjects.

Non-book material: engravings, maps, prints
Services: mail order, search service, framing service, valuations
Catalogue: modern first editions listed annually, other lists by subject or author always available

The Clarke-Hall Bookshop   *(St Paul's)*
7 Bride Court EC4
353-4116

M–F 10:30–6:30

anthropology / architecture / astronomy / biography / Lewis Carroll / crafts / economics / fiction / fine printing / health / history / illustrated books / Samuel Johnson / literature and letters / local history / military history / modern first editions / poetry / politics / psychology / religion / sciences / sociology / transport / travel

This is a general second-hand and antiquarian shop which is usually bustling at lunch-time, the attraction being shelves of review copies of new titles and second-hand books. The specialities of the shop, however, are late 19th-century illustrated books – children's, art, natural history, etc. – the work of Samuel Johnson, his contemporary writers and his circle of friends, Lewis Carroll and his world and modern works. A few doors down the court is the Clarke-Hall Print Shop specializing in 19th-century topographical prints, cartoons and Victorian ephemera.

Non-book material: see above
Services: mail order
Catalogue: Johnson illustrated books, Lewis Carroll, modern first editions

East London

General Bookshops

Centerprise   *(Dalston Kingsland – British Rail)*
136 Kingsland High Street E8
254-9632

Tue–W 10:30–7:00   Th 10:30–2:00   F 10:30–5:30   Sat 10:30–5:30

biography / black history and culture / British politics / children's books / community publications / cookery / crafts / crime / DIY / feminism / fiction / film / gardening / gay health and sex / history / hobbies / Ireland / literacy / literature / local interest (biography, fiction, history, photography, pottery, politics) / numeracy / poetry / politics / reference / social sciences / sports / travel guides / Turkish books

The Centerprise bookshop is one of London's best examples of how books can form the nucleus of a community centre. Local shoppers, school kids and workers usually fill the shop, showing genuine interest in the books, journals and activities of the centre – so Centerprise is doing something right. Many of the Centerprise titles are politically oriented toward local politics, black, feminist and minority rights, and labour issues. The selection of children's books incorporates multiracial perspectives alongside classic fairy tales and fiction. Sections on Ireland, black America and the West Indies reflect the community's interest in political and social questions beyond the perimeters of London. Local history, fiction and poetry by authors from East London, and illustrated books about the area, comprise the section of 'local interest' titles – many of which are published by Centerprise.

Meeting rooms available for use by the community, a writers' workshop, a youth centre and the Hackney Reading Centre are also based at Centerprise, and a snack and coffee bar next to the bookshop, which also acts as an advice centre.

Non-book material: badges, cards, posters, book tokens
Services: mail order (Centerprise publications only), special order, supplies schools, colleges, etc.
Catalogue: Centerprise publications
Publications: books of local writers' works, history, adult literacy schemes and issues of local interest are published by Centerprise

Fanfare Bookcentre   *(Walthamstow Central)*
2 Chingford Road E17
527-4296

M–F 9:30–5:30   Sat 10:00–5:00

accounting / automotive engineering / bibles / biology / building / business / chemistry / children's books / classics / computing / cookery / crafts / current affairs / economics / electronics / fiction / gardening / geography / health and child care / history / humour / law / mathematics / music / natural history / nursing / Pelican, Penguin / physics / plays / poetry / politics / psychiatry / psychology / reference / science fiction / sociology / sports / technical / travel guides

General fiction and non-fiction, children's books and student text books are the three general areas in which Fanfare stocks books. This retail shop exists because of the success of their college bookstalls supplying students at Waltham Forest College, Redbridge and Havering Technical Colleges, and the North East London Polytechnic.

Services: special order

Paperbacks Centre   *(Upton Park)*
389 Green Street E13
470-1388

M–Sat 9:00–6:00

art / biography / children's books / classics / cookery / crime and thrillers / economics / fiction / health / history / labour and unions / Lenin / literature / Marx / music / Pelican, Penguin / philosophy / politics / reference / science fiction / sexual politics / sports and games / travel guides

This is one of three Paperback Centres carrying a general range of new books, but with particular emphasis on books about politics, the labour movement, unions and individual rights. It has the most extensive collection of Trotskyist books in London. Located in a working-class area the shop stocks titles which are relevant to the lives of those in the neighbourhood, and it also caters to the interests of football supporters who flock to nearby Upton Park during the season. Football programmes are sold in the shop.

Non-book material: calendars, cards, political periodicals
Services: mail order, special order, photocopying, special service for local schools and colleges
Publications: New Park Publications publishes books on political issues, and produces a series of Newsline Reports which focus on current political 'hot spots' throughout the world

W.H. Smith   *(East Ham)*
125 High Street North E6
552-4875/6

M–Sat 9:00–6:00 (8:30a.m. for news)

There is a well-stocked book department in this branch of W.H. Smith, including a large range of fiction, children's books and the usual selection of general interest titles.

Non-book material: stationery, cards, paper, news, magazines, etc.
Services: special order, post-a-book, tokens
Catalogue: *Bookcase* review of books twice yearly

W.H. Smith   *(Stratford East)*
The Stratford Centre
41-42 The Mall E15
534-5955

M–Th 8:30–5:30   Tue 9:30–5:30   F 8:30–6:00

The book section here stocks new hardback titles and the standard range of fiction, children's books and books of both general and special interest.

Non-book material: stationery, cards, paper, news, magazines, etc.
Services: special order, post-a-book, tokens
Catalogue: *Bookcase* review of books twice yearly

THAP Community Bookshop   *(Whitechapel)*
178 Whitechapel Road E1
247-0216

T–F 10:00–5:30   Sat 10:00–5:00

alternative technology / anarchy / anthropology / bicycling / biography / children's books / cookery / economics / education / fantasy / fiction / gardening / health and medicine / history / housing / humour / Ireland / language teaching / local interest (biography, fiction, history, photography, plays, poetry) / Marx, Russian history / nuclear power / poetry / politics / popular music / prison and crime / reference / rural Britain / science fiction / sexual politics / sociology / travel guides

THAP (Tower Hamlets Arts Project) Community Bookshop is one of two of the most exciting bookshops and community centres in London (the other is Centerprise). Each title in the shop is obviously chosen for its relevance to the East London community (with an emphasis on the arts and writing) from multiracial children's readers to books on realistic alternative technologies to urban gardening and contemporary literature from the Third World as well as the West. The books in the section 'local interest' feature photographic histories of East London, the poetry of local writers, fiction about East London (often by local authors) and books on race relations and local politics. All in all, THAP books are not just a mishmash of alternative literature and radical politics, but well chosen titles for a diverse audience.

The THAP has another dimension which includes aid for local authors and artists, helping them to work and be published, exhibited and staged. Workshops at the centre include writing, theatre, poetry and photography, as well as the children's workshop which has now split into teams of four, each making a super-8mm film. Printing facilities are open at the THAP Bookshop, consisting of a litho machine and professional advice on artwork, layout and paste-up. 'Controlled Attack' is another THAP group of writer/performers involved with street theatre – in short, the THAP's activities are wide-ranging, creative and distinctly community-oriented.

Non-book material: prints and original work by local artists and illustrators
Services: mail order, special order
Publications: THAP Publishing publishes poetry by local writers, as well as an anthology of those in the TH Worker Writers Group

Richard Tudor   *(Chingford – British Rail)*
135 Station Road E4
524-5518

M–F 9:30–5:00   Th 9:30–1:00   Sat 10:00–5:00

adventure fiction / biography / children's books / cookery / fiction / games / gardening / health / history / humour / language teaching / literature / natural history / pets / reference

This is a small friendly bookshop which also doubles as a picture gallery. Most of the books are paperbacks, although hard-cover illustrated books are available.

Non-book material: paintings, wrapping-paper, picture-framing
Services: special order, photocopying and litho printing

The Whole Thing   *(Stratford)*
53 West Ham Lane E15
534-6539

M–F 9:30–5:30   Th closed   Sat 9:30–4:00

African fiction / alternative technology / Caribbean fiction / children's books / cookery / crafts / diet and nutrition / education / environment / fiction / gardening / health / history / Indian fiction / Ireland / labour and unions / literature / local interest / Marxism / nuclear energy / philosophy / poetry / politics / psychology / social issues / South American politics / women's issues

The Whole Thing is a community-oriented co-operative which specializes in new books about political and social issues, but also has a good selection of black and Third World fiction. There are a variety of pamphlets and magazines on a range of subjects, from women to education to Ireland, and the tone of the stock as a whole is politically left-of-centre. They also have textbooks for the North East London Polytechnic which is nearby.

Non-book material: badges, cards, posters
Services: mail order (Page One Publications only)

Speciality Bookshops

Dillon's at Queen Mary College   *(Mile End)*
Mile End Road E1
980-2554

M–F 9:00–5:00   W 9:00–4:30

astronomy / biochemistry / biology / chemistry / classics /
computers / economics / engineering / fiction / genetics /
geography / history / law / mathematics / microbiology / Pelican,
Penguin / physics / plays / politics / sociology / zoology

This branch of Dillon's Bookshop is located in the main building of
Queen Mary College and stocks student textbooks.

Non-book material: cards, posters, stationery
Services: special order

Freedom Bookshop   *(Aldgate East)*
Angel Alley
84b Whitechapel High Street E1
247-9249

M–Sat 10:30–6:00

anarchy / communism / decentralization / ecology / feminism /
individual rights / libertarianism / pacifism / syndicalism / utopias

The Freedom Bookshop specializes in books and pamphlets on
anarchism and related literature. The small stock does include
some other subjects, though, such as feminism and ecology. The
sister company, Freedom Press, have been publishers of anarchist
literature since 1886 and publish the magazine *Freedom*. All three
are staffed by volunteers. The bookshop is situated between
Blooms and Whitechapel Art Gallery in Angel Alley. Once you
have found your way down this rather doubtful alley and up some

rickety old stairs you are quite likely to be rewarded with a cup of freshly ground Colombian coffee.

Non-book material: badges, posters
Services: mail order, special order
Catalogue: complete list of new titles annually
Publications: see above

R. Golub & Son Ltd   *(Aldgate East)*
27 Osborn Street E1
247-7430

M–Th 10:00–5:00   F 10:00–1:00   Sun 10:00–1:30

art / biography / culture and civilization / economics / fiction / Hebraica / Hebrew language teaching / Hebrew texts / history / holidays / Israel / Judaica / legends / literature / memoirs / music / philosophy / politics / prayer / religion / Talmudic studies / Torah – tradition and commentaries / travel guides / war and Holocaust

R. Golub is one of London's largest bookshops specializing in Judaica and Hebraica. With new books on a variety of subjects. R. Golub has a refreshingly enlightened view of those which are relevant to their field of speciality. Traditional and classical Hebrew texts are available, as well as books on subjects relevant to orthodox and reformed Judaism.

Non-book material: religious requisites
Services: mail order, special order
Catalogue: catalogue available

Kelvin Hughes Charts   *(Aldgate)*
and Maritime Supplies
31 Mansell Street E1
481-8741

M–F 9:00–5:30

ground floor:
astro charts / insurance / marine engineering / meteorology / nautical books (including fiction, history, humour) / navigation / pilotage / RYA publications / yacht racing

basement:
charts (Admiralty, Stanfords, etc.) / naval publications

Kelvin Hughes has a stock of new books on sailing and boating, some of which are geared to the pleasure-boating public or amateur boat-racing enthusiast, while other titles are in fields of interest to those in the shipping industry. The shop has a large range of Admiralty publications and charts (it is the world's largest chart agency), as well as nautical and marine supplies, including those necessary for yachting.

Non-book material: chandlery
Services: chart correction, mail order, special order
Catalogue: nautical book list and price list

The London Buddhist Centre Bookshop *(Bethnal Green)*
51 Roman Road E2
481-8741

M–F 10:00–5:00

Most of the books here are texts recommended by the founder of the Western Buddhist movement, Sangharakshita. Other sections include literature, art, comparative religion and body care techniques like yoga and the Alexander technique.

Non-book material: the shop has its own department of cassettes which includes lectures by Sangharakshita and instruction cassettes for yoga and massage, devotional objects, magazines, postcards
Services: mail order
Catalogue: available on receipt of a large s.a.e., covering the entire stock

London Yacht Centre Ltd   *(Liverpool Street)*
13 Artillery Lane E1
247-0521

M–F 9:00–5:30   Th (March–Sept.) 9:00–7:00

beginning yachting / cruising / design and construction / dinghies / fiction / meteorology / navigation / off-shore safety / power racing / reference / ropework / sails / singlehanded sailing / voyages

On the ground floor of the London Yacht Centre are new books on yachting and sailing. Admiralty charts for the channel are available, and the shop can order charts for waterways in the rest of the world. The rest of the shop is taken up with boating equipment and clothing.

Non-book material: charts, logs and maps for the British Isles and Continent
Services: mail order, special order

Newham Parents' Centre   *(Upton Park)*
747 Barking Road E13
552-9993

M–F 9:30–5:30   W closes 1:00   Th closes 6:00   Sat 9:30–5:30

This is a small shop on the ground floor of the Newham Parents' Centre, specializing in educational books and play materials for children. Indeed, improving the quality of education for adults and children in the borough is the function of the centre. Five general subject areas characterize the shop's stock: developmental books for pre- and early readers; pleasure books for children; titles for adults including science fiction, thrillers, art books and philosophy; classic works of drama, poetry, literature and non-fiction; reference books from dictionaries to cookbooks.

The staff of the centre are involved in a variety of education activities, including community publishing, outreach schemes, play groups, career advising, and literacy programmes and the centre has a worker for young families.

Non-book material: games, play material
Services: mail order, special order
Publications: Parents' Centre Publications publishes information about community education and literacy issues and programmes

Page One Books   *(Stratford East)*
53 West Ham Lane
Stratford E15
534-6539

M–Sat 9:30–5:30   closed Thursdays

This is a community bookshop run by a workers' collective unusual for its multi-cultural interests – no separatism here. The wide range of alternative subjects includes anti-sexist and anti-racist literature, political writings from socialism to Communism and everything in between, and a section for Virago and the Women's Press. They specialize in gay and African literature, and there is also a large media section and a very up-to-date selection of literary criticism. A wide and unusual variety of fringe magazines from all over the world emphasizes the broad range of interests catered for by Page One Books.

Non-book material: badges, mugs, records, T-shirts
Services: special order, evening talks in the bookshop covering a range of community issues
Publications: a large selection of alternative cards printed by Page One Ltd

Raymond Port   *(Wood Street – British Rail)*
4 Antique City Market
98 Wood Street E17
520-4032

M–Sat 9:30–5:00   closed Thursdays

Raymond Port specializes in local history and this covers the East End, Essex, Epping, Chingford and Walthamstow. William Morris was born in Walthamstow, so there is also a special collection of books on and by William Morris and the Pre-Raphaelites. There is a smaller selection of children's books, literature and some gay and feminist titles. The books are new and second-hand.

Non-book material: reproductions of old maps of Essex, reproductions of old postcards
Services: mail order
Catalogue: there is an occasional catalogue on special subjects, e.g. William Morris

Psychic Sense Bookshop   *(Wood Street – British Rail)*
1 Antique City Market
98 Wood Street E17
520-4032

M–W 9:15–5:15   F–Sat 9:15–5:30

Eastern religions / esoteric / occult / psychic / spiritualism

The owner of this shop is a spiritualist and a good authority on out-of-print books in this area of study. The stock covers new, second-hand and out-of-print books and helpful advice is on hand.

Services: mail order
Catalogue: catalogue covers the new and out-of-print books

St Andrew's Bookshop   *(Leytonstone)*
St Andrew's Road
Plaistow E11
474-0743

M–Fri 9:00–5:00

This bookshop specializes in bibles, Christian books, children's and Asian-language titles. It also covers other faiths, particularly Islam.

Catalogue: Christianity and world religions, Urban Mission

Society for the Protection of   *(Liverpool Street)*
Ancient Buildings
37 Spital Square E1
377-1644

M–F 9:30–5:00

There is a small sales area in the reception of this society's offices in Spital Square. Most of their book trade is in fact conducted by post and they supply a current list upon request. They specialize in books relating to vernacular architectural styles and technical leaflets on traditional building repair methods.

Catalogue: see above
Publications: technical pamphlets and information leaflets

Willen Ltd   *(Leytonstone)*
Howard House, Howard Road E11
556-7776

M–F 9:30–5:00

beauty therapy / dermatology / diseases of hair and nail / hairdressing / edged weapons / firearms antique and modern

Specializing in the rather odd combination of guns and hairdressing, Willen is actually a showroom and distributor for titles in these fields, although individuals are welcome to drop in to look at and purchase books.

Services: mail order, special order
Catalogue: guns, hairdressing annual lists

Zwemmer at the Whitechapel Gallery   *(Aldgate East/*
Whitechapel Hight Street E1   *Whitechapel)*
377-6225

Tue–Sun 11:00–5:00   W 11:00–8:00

This bookshop in the gallery sells titles on all aspects of the visual arts and books relating to current exhibitions. Most of the stock covers modern art.

Non-book material: artists' materials, magazines, postcards, posters

Antiquarian and Second-hand Bookshops

C. & J. Foster   *(East Ham)*
79 Shopping Hall
Myrtle Road E6
552-2263

M–Sat 9:00–5:00   Th 9:00–1:00

This is a small shop stocking second-hand books, including
children's books and annuals. They are quite happy to exchange
but will not longer accept Mills and Boon – the days of rose-tinted
romance are over and the tales of fluttering hearts and damsels in
distress just don't sell any more!

Non-book material: games, stationery

Norman Lord   *(Wood Street – British Rail)*
Antique City Market
98 Wood Street E17
520-8300

M–Sat 10:00–5:00   Th closed

This shop, which is close to a large, free car-park, has a general
stock from the eighteenth century onwards, with prices ranging
from 50 pence to £150 and more, and its antiquarian side is
continuing to grow. As well as having a large selection of
literature, travel and topography, natural history and gardening
are covered and there is a large section of biography,
autobiography and the performing arts. A number of association
copies can usually be found here.

Non-book material: antiquarian maps and prints
Services: mail order

North London

General Bookshops

The Angel Bookshop
(Angel)
102 Islington High Street N1
226-2904

M–Sat 9:30–6:00

antiques / art / biography / children's books / classics / collecting / cookery / drama / fiction / hardback fiction / literature / music / natural history / paperbacks / photography / poetry / travel guides

Because the Camden Passage Antique Market is only a few steps from the door of this general bookshop, Angel carries a large stock of books about antiques and collecting. The shop has a nice children's section as well as cookery and wine. It also boasts very good coverage of new hardback fiction and non-fiction titles.

Non-book material: calendars, children's friezes, cards, postcards
Services: mail order, special order
Publications: books on travel are published by Granville Publishing

Austen-Parish Ltd
(Archway)
162 Archway Road N6
340-2575

M–F 9:00–5:30

This is a full service, academic text bookshop supplying libraries, schools and other shops with books in all subject areas, but Austen-Parish is also happy to help individual customers. While most of the shop's stock is geared to the United Kingdom's university-level education system, the staff are very good about tracking texts from all over the world (although they do not handle any out-of-print material).

Non-book material: audio-visual teaching aids, cards, cassettes, posters
Services: mail order, special order, on request the shop will complete subject lists of the available stock

Bargain Bookshop *(Lower Edmonton – British Rail)*
2 The Concourse
Edmonton Green N9
807-7972

M 9:30–2:00   Tue–Th 9:30–5:00   F–Sat 9:30–5:30

Remainders make up the bulk of the stock here, but there is a small range of paperbacks and hardbacks on general topics.

Bookmarks *(Finsbury Park)*
265 Seven Sisters Road N4
802-6145/8773

M–Sat 10:00–6:00   W 10:00–7:00

ground floor:
African fiction / anarchism / anthropology / anti-nuclear / art / black struggle / British history / children's / cookery / diet and health / economics / education / family / feminism / feminist biography / feminist fiction / fiction / film / imperialism / Ireland / lesbian and gay / literary criticism / media / music / philosophy / poetry / political theory / politics / psychology / reference / rights / science / science fiction / sexual politics / social science / social work and welfare / state control / the state / theatre / travel

first floor:
Engels / Gramsci / labour history / Lenin / Rosa Luxemburg / Marx / remainders and second-hand books / SWP publications / trade unions / Trotsky

Bookmarks is one of the few alternative bookshops to make aggressive use of means other than a shop premises to sell books and disseminate information. The shop runs a quarterly book club – Bookmarx – which offers the best of new socialist books at low prices delivered to your door. Also affiliated with the shop is the Trade Union Bookservice, whose aim is to make new books, booklets and pamphlets on trade-union issues and history available to trade unionists and others interested in the movement, outside the major cities.

Bookmarks is affiliated to the Socialist Workers Party and has set up (at Seven Sisters Road) a publications and agitprop section of the party, which organizes distribution of pamphlets, books, posters and recordings. These items are listed with Bookmarks publications and SWP publications in a regular catalogue.

The shop itself is a specialist bookshop with two floors of varied stock and obvious strengths in their areas of labour relations and trade children's section with a wide range of picture books and story books divided by age group. In this part you will also find their international sections: Southern Africa, Africa, Caribbean, Latin America, North America, Far East, Middle East, USSR and Eastern and Western Europe. They also carry a large number of journals, magazines and newspapers.

Non-book material: badges, cards, posters
Services: mail order, special order
Catalogue: Bookmarks publications list, Agitprop list, Books for Socialists, Trade Union booklist
Publications: see above

Boots the Chemists   *(Wood Green)*
137-139 High Road
Wood Green Shopping City N22
888-0101

M–W 9:00–5:30   Th 9:00–7:30   F–Sat 9:00–6:00

On the first floor, a part of the computer department, the book section concentrates on paperback fiction, with a few reduced-price hardbacks. Its location in the shop seems to reflect the status awarded to it.

Non-book material: department store

Canonbury Bookshop   *(Highbury and Islington)*
(Islington Books Ltd)
268 Upper Street N1
226-3475

M–Sat 9:00–6:00

ground floor: general
antiques / art / classics / cookery / dance / fiction / film / gardening /
health / history / humour / language teaching / literature / local
history music / natural history / photography / poetry / pregnancy
and child care / psychology / reference / theatre / thrillers /
transport / travel guides

basement: children's books and toys
classics / fairy tales / fiction / Ladybird / non-fiction / novels /
nursery rhymes / poetry / Puffin / transport

The Canonbury Bookshop is a general bookseller with a
wonderful range of children's books. You will find these
downstairs in the main shop, passing on the stairs a marvellous
mural. The shop offers facilities to keep children occupied while
parents are browsing. It also specializes in local history (Islington,
Highbury and Highgate) and carries a large selection of general
fiction and non-fiction.

Non-book material: cards of local scenes, stationery, party gifts,
agents for Galt toys
Services: special order
Publications: Islington Books Ltd has published one title about
Islington and greeting cards of local scenes

Comyns Books   *(Silver Street – British Rail)*
61 Sterling Way N18
807-3427

M–Sat 9:30–6:00   closed Thursdays

A general range of both new and second-hand books, some maps
and what the owner describes as 'girlie magazines'. Exchange is
welcomed.

Crouch End Bookshop   *(Highgate/Finsbury Park)*
60 Crouch End Hill N8
348-8966

M–F 9:00–6:00   Sat 9:30–6:00

second-hand:
arts / biography / children's books / fiction / literary criticism /
literature / military history / natural history / poetry / theatre /
travel / UK guides

new:
anthropology / archaeology / art / astronomy / bibles / child care /
children's books / classics / cookery / Corgi, Pan, Penguin / crafts /
crime / drama / fiction / film / history / literature / mathematics /
music / philosophy / poetry / politics / psychology / reference /
science fiction / sexual politics / travel guides

With a general selection of new and second-hand books, the
Crouch End Bookshop has quite a good section on sexual politics
and alternative political literature, and also carries a range of
feminist, gay and leftist political magazines and newspapers.

Non-book material: postcards, magazines
Services: mail order, special order, wants lists accepted

Faculty Books   *(Finchley Central)*
98 Ballards Lane N3
346-0145

M–Sat 9:30–5:30

antiques / art / astrology / biography / children's books / classics /
cookery / drawing and painting / economics / feminism / fiction /
games and crafts / gardening / health and child care / history /
humour / literary criticism / literature / mathematics / military
history / music / mysticism / natural history / occult / Penguin /
philosophy / plays / poetry / psychology / reference / sociology /
sports / theatre / travel guides / young adults

This general bookshop is one large, airy room with particularly
good sections of poetry, literary criticism and children's books.
For the first few weeks after publication, newly released titles are
displayed separately.

Services: mail order, special order, library supply

Note: There is another branch of Faculty Books at:
Middlesex Polytechnic
The Burroughs NW4
202-3593
M–W 10:00–4:00

Fagin's Bookshop   *(Angel)*
76 Upper Street
Islington Green N1
359-4699

M–Sat 10:00a.m.–10:00p.m.

This is a medium-sized general bookshop, the seventh branch of the Fagin's Bookshops to open. A range of fiction and non-fiction is stocked, including academic titles.

Non-book material: cards, wrapping-paper
Services: post-a-book, special order

Fagin's Bookshop   *(Southgate)*
62 Chase Side N14
882-5690

M–F 9:30–5:30   Sat 9:00–5:30

art / biography / children's books / classics / cookery / crafts / drama / economics / education / fiction / film / gardening / health / history / literary criticism / literature / music / natural history / Penguin / philosophy / photography / plays / poetry / politics / psychology / reference / religion / revision aids for students / science fiction / sociology / transport / travel guides

Fagin's is a medium-sized general bookshop with current hardcover and paperback titles. Contemporary fiction and children's books form the largest sections of the stock, and the shop carries a few A-level student textbooks among the selection of non-fiction.

Non-book material: cards
Services: special order

Hamilton Books and Art Ltd   *(Finsbury Park/Highgate)*
3 Park Road N8
340-8084

M/Th 10:00–6:00   Tue/W 9:30–6:30   F 9:30–6:00   Sat 9:15–6:15

Hamilton's is a general bookshop, stocking mainly paperbacks with specialities in art, children's books, feminism and science fiction.

Non-book material: cards, giftwrap
Services: book tokens, book of the month delivered free locally, post-a-book, special order

Highgate Bookshop   *(Highgate)*
9 Highgate High Street N6
340-5625

M–Sat 9:30–5:30

art / biography / children's books / classics / cookery / economics / education / fiction / history / illustrated books / literature / music / mysteries / natural history / Penguin / philosophy / poetry / politics / psychology / reference / sexual politics / sociology / travel guides / women

As one might expect in well-heeled Highgate, this general, bookshop though small, is very complete and well-stocked, with good sections of literature, fiction and children's books, and coverage of the social sciences.

Services: mail order, special order, library supply

The Library Bookshop   *(Old Street)*
Shoreditch Library
Pitfield Street N1
729-4723

M–F 11:30–2:00   M 3:00–8:00   Tue–Th 3:00–7:00   F 3:00–6:00

The owner describes this shop as a 'general bookshop in miniature'. It specializes in local publications, in other words the East End. One of its functions is to serve the local college and so it stocks all the O and A level set books in addition to the general stock. The owner is Lithuanian and he has developed a fascinating side-line, specializing in books from, in or about Lithuania. These books are stored in a warehouse but clearly the specialists have no need to search on open shelves for Lithuanian rarities. The shop also supplies approval lists for libraries and as a result there are always interesting alternative titles passing

141

through the shop and a particularly comprehensive range of paperback fiction.

Services: special order, approval lists, library supply

Martin the Newsagent   *(Finchley Central)*
29-31 Ballards Lane N3
346-9303

M–W 8:30–6:00   Th–F 8:30–7:00   Sat 8:00–6:00   Sun 10:00–4:00

cookery / dictionaries / fiction / gardening / health / language / maps / reference / TV and entertainment

This newsagent has a general range of paperback fiction and reference books, including the usual selection of entertainment and comedy.

Non-book material: newsagents

Morgans & Co. Ltd   *(Totteridge)*
1287 High Road N20
445-2692

M–Sat 9:00–5:00   Th 9:00–1:00

This is a small bookshop with a range of paperback fiction.

Non-book material: cards and toys

Muswell Hill Bookshop   *(East Finchley/Highgate)*
72 Fortis Green Road N10
444-7588

M–F 9:30–6:00   Sat 9:30–5:30

alternative health / antiques / art / astrology / biography / child care / cosmology / classics / cookery / crafts / crime / drama / education / fantasy / fiction / films / games and sports / gardening / Gay Men's Press / health / history / literature / Marxism / medicine / music / natural history / non-fiction / Open University / Penguin, Picador, Pelican / philosophy / poetry / politics / psychology / reference / religion / science fiction / socialism / theatre / travel guides / women / young adult fiction

Muswell Hill is fortunate to have such a well stocked general bookshop, with an especially large Penguin section, while having a tendency throughout the shop towards the leftist and alternative approaches to issues and literature.

Non-book material: cards, postcards, wrapping paper, maps, specialist left-wing magazines
Services: mail order, post-a-book, special order

W.H. Smith   *(King's Cross)*
King's Cross Station N1
837-5580

M–Sat 7:00a.m.–8:45p.m.   Sun 8:00a.m.–8:00p.m.

The bookshop in the station concourse has a large range of both fiction and reference. The new hardback titles are clearly displayed and very popular here. Fiction is set out in alphabetical order by author and there is also a special section for the classics. Other areas covered include cookery, gardening, wildlife, railways and management.

Non-book material: stationery, cards, paper, news, magazines, etc.
Services: special order, tokens
Catalogue: *Bookcase* review of books twice yearly

W.H. Smith   *(Highgate)*
117 Muswell Hill Broadway N10
883-1706

M–Sat 8:30–5:30

The books run along one side of this branch of W.H. Smith and in the fairly limited space they stock a selection from the usual range, including the new hardback fiction, children's books and a variety of general titles. Fiction is divided both by author and by category, with the standard selection of science fiction, horror, crime and autobiography.

Non-book material: stationery, cards, paper, news, magazines, etc.
Services: special order, post-a-book, tokens
Catalogue: *Bookcase* review of books twice yearly

143

W.H. Smith   *(Woodside Park)*
766 High Road N12
445-2785

M–Sat 9:00–5:30

This is a fair-sized book department with the usual range of fiction, reference and children's books. There is an A-Z of general fiction in addition to the subject categories, a stock of new titles in hardback, and the general sections include humour, education and cookery.

Non-book material: stationery, cards, paper, news, magazines, etc.
Services: special order, post-a-book, tokens
Catalogue: *Bookcase* review of books twice yearly

W.H. Smith   *(Palmers Green – British Rail)*
5 Alderman's Hill N13
886-4743

M–Sat 8:30–5:30

The book section here occupies one-third of the shop and covers the general range of fiction and general interest with a particular emphasis on children's books.

Non-book material: stationery, cards, paper, news, magazines
Services: special order, tokens
Catalogue: *Bookcase* review of books twice yearly

W.H. Smith   *(Silver Street – British Rail)*
104-110 Upper Fore Street N18
807-7637

M–Sat 9:45–5:45

The book department here covers the standard range of subjects, from fiction to children's books and general interest titles including history, health and school books.

Non-book material: stationery, cards, paper, news, magazines
Services: special order, post-a-book, tokens

144

W.H. Smith   *(Wood Green)*
110 High Road
Wood Green Shopping City N22
889-0221

M–Sat 9:00–6:00   Tue 9:30–6:00   Th 9:00–8:00

This is one of the larger book departments in W.H. Smith branches and it has a comprehensive range, including a good section of new hardback fiction.

Non-book material: stationery, cards, paper, news, magazines, etc.
Services: special order, post-a-book, tokens
Catalogue: *Bookcase* review of books twice yearly

Speciality Bookshops

Arms and Militaria Bookshop
(Southgate)
34 High Street N14
886-0334

M/W/Sat 9:30–5:00   F 9:30–4:00 (spring and summer only)

arms of all periods / military history up to the Second World War / military uniforms of all periods / regimental histories

This is truly a specialist shop and, while the military and regimental history have a part to play, the owner is now concentrating largely on the arms and military uniforms.

Non-book material: badges, medals, toy soldiers

The Aviation Bookshop
(Archway)
656 Holloway Road N19
272-3630

M–Sat 9:30–5:30

aerodynamics / aeronautics / air battles / aircraft markings / construction / flight / history and development of aircraft / Iron Curtain / maritime aircraft / military / model aircraft / reference / rockets / space / technical

The shop's name is a dead giveaway, as new (about 80% of the stock) and second-hand books about aviation and aircraft are the only books here. I was told that if there's a book published on aviation the shop has it and if this claim won't actually fly, they do carry the majority of English and American aviation titles as well as titles in German, French, Italian and Japanese (in which the photographs are said to be most popular).

A wide range of aviation magazines and journals are sold and back issues are often available.

Non-book material: photographs, posters, slides, aeromodellers' plans
Services: mail order, special order, search service in field
Catalogue: complete annual catalogue

Basharan Turkish Bookshop *(Canonbury – British Rail)*
123 Green Lanes N16
226-3330

M–Sat 10:00–5:00 (by appointment)

children's books / cookery / dictionaries / fiction / linguistics / literature / poetry / reference / religion

The books in Turkish cover a wide variety of subjects, including a small selection of Turkish literature and poetry. There are English translations of Turkish novels and a section on the English language for Turks. The reference books are aimed both at the Turkish community and anyone else with an interest in Turkey.

Non-book material: cassettes of traditional Turkish music, story cassettes, framed pictures, postcards, posters
Services: mail order supply for bookshops, libraries and schools
Catalogue: catalogue available on request

Children's Bookshop *(East Finchley/Highgate)*
29 Fortis Green Road N10
444-5500

M–F 9:15–5:45   Sat 9:15–5:30

astronomy / Bible stories / biography / classics / dictionaries / encyclopedias / fairy tales / fiction / football / hobbies / horses / Ladybird / music / nursery rhymes / poetry and verse / Puffin / puzzle books / reading schemes / science fiction / songbooks / sports / transport / young readers

Walking into this colourful shop is, in itself, enough to make one want to have kids. The shop is devoted to new books for children from infancy up to twelve, and their goal is to make reading enjoyable. There is also a special teenage books section. The staff are happy to give advice on reading schemes, new books and books in specialized interest areas and must be among the most knowledgeable in this field.

Non-book material: cassettes, cards, birthday cards, birthday books, wrapping-paper
Services: mail order, special order

The Cholmeley Bookshop   *(Highgate)*
(W.E. Hersant Ltd)
228 Archway Road N6
340-3869

M–Sat 9:30–1:00 2:00–5:00   Th closed

aviation / military / naval

The Cholmeley Bookshop's stock consists of new and second-hand books on all historical aspects of aviation, the military and the world's navies. These books come from publishers throughout the world. In addition, the shop has magazines and journals specializing in these areas and some remaindered books.

Services: mail order, special order
Catalogue: aviation, military, naval

CND Bookshop   *(Old Street)*
22-24 Underwood Street N1
250-4010

Tue–F 10:00–5:30   Th 10:00–7:00   Sat 10:00–4:00

This bookshop, set up by CND to cater for the increasing interest in nuclear disarmament, also helps to fund the campaign by selling a wide range of books on all aspects of the subject.

Non-book material: badges, jewellery, mugs, postcards, posters, records, stickers, T-shirts
Services: mail order, special order
Catalogue: complete list of all anti-nuclear titles, with quarterly supplements; bookclub
Publications: CND publishes various books and pamphlets as well as cards and posters

Corner Stone   *(Woodside Park)*
The Finchley Christian Bookshop
638 High Road N12
446-3056

M–Sat 9:30–5:30   F 9:30–6:30

This evangelical Christian bookshop has the usual range of popular fiction, children's books and biblical studies.

Non-book material: video library
Services: educational supply, special order
Catalogue: lists for the video library

Earth Exchange Bookshop   *(Highgate)*
213 Archway Road N6
340-6407

F–Tue 11:00–7:00 (W/Th closed)

alternative medicine / astrology / children's books / feminist literature / occult / politics / psychology / sexual politics / vegetarian and vegan cookery

The Earth Exchange Collective is a workers' co-operative and the bookshop is on the second floor of a large Victorian house which also encompasses a food shop and a café. There is a wide range of alternative literature and some fiction – in particular the Virago Press and the Women's Press. All you need for a healthy and well-informed alternative life-style under one roof.

Non-book material: biochemic tissue salts, candles, cards, crafts, essential oils, medicinal and culinary herbs, homeopathic remedies
Services: food shop and café

Fantasy Centre   *(Highbury and Islington)*
157 Holloway Road N7
607-9433

M–F 10:00–6:00   Sat 10:00–5:00

149

For collectors of post-war science fiction, fantasy and horror books, Fantasy Centre is a treasure house of (unbelievably) moderately priced hardbacks, paperbacks and magazines. In one large room are second-hand books and magazines and a small, but up-to-date selection of new titles. Sci-fi fanatics will drool over the collectors' section at the back of the shop which holds rare first editions (some of which are signed) and vintage magazines.

Standard 19th-century sci-fi writers are kept, but the majority of the stock is post-1945.

Services: mail order, wants lists accepted
Catalogue: selected list every month

G.W. Foote & Co.   *(Archway)*
702 Holloway Road N19
272-1266

M–F 9:15–5:15

This bookshop is linked to the National Secular Society and the stock includes a range of books on free thought, humanism, rationalism, and philosophy. There is also a selection of pamphlets covering the same ground.

Services: mail order
Catalogue: the catalogue covers most of the stock
Publications: *The Freethinker* and a book commemorating the centenary of *The Freethinker*

Headstart Books & Crafts   *(Seven Sisters)*
25 West Green Road N15
802-2838

M–F 9:30–6:30   Sat 9:30–7:00

art / fiction / history / politics

The books here are concerned with all aspects of the African world. As well as a large reference section, there are novels in the original languages and in translation.

Non-book material: craft shop

Hebrew Book & Gift Centre *(Stoke Newington – British Rail)*
18 Cazenove Road N16
254-3963

M–Th 10:00–6:30   F 10:00–2:00   Sun 10:00–2:30

biography / cookery / culture / faith / folklore / Hebraica / history / holidays / Judaica / law / religion / Talmudic studies / Torah

The Hebrew Book & Gift Centre specializes in new books on Judaism, especially on religious heritage and the orthodox Jewish faith. Many of the religious books – Talmudic and Torah studies and commentaries – are in Hebrew, while the English-language books are concerned with Jewish culture, history and religious life. Fiction by Jewish authors, or about Israel and Judaism, is not, however, a strong element in the shop's stock.

Non-book material: gifts, religious requisites
Services: special order

Housmans Bookshop   *(King's Cross)*
5 Caledonian Road N1
837-4473

M–F 10:00–6:00   Sat 10:00–1:00 1:30–5:00

ground floor:
child-birth and child rearing / children's books / cookery (vegetarian) / drama / feminism / film and media / gay and lesbian / general fiction / health / Marxism / philosophy / poetry / psychology / radical politics / reference books / sub-culture music

downstairs:
anarchism / anti-militarism / ecology / education / Gandhi / Ireland / nuclear issues / pacifism / peace education / peace studies / reduced books / South Africa / Third World

Housmans, a pacifist bookshop owned by *Peace News* Trustees, opened in 1945 and has continued to specialize in books related to non-violence, anti-militarism and the peace movement. To support this core of politically-oriented titles, the shop sells a limited range of general titles. The staff, however, are very much involved with the main stock of alternative literature, and are generous with their time and knowledge. (The shop, collectively run, is a member of the Federation of Radical Booksellers.)

Non-book material: a wide range of magazines, newspapers and pamphlets on radical subjects and concerns; stationery; postcards; posters; badges; stickers; records
Services: mail order, special order
Catalogue: regular lists are issued on such subjects as peace education, feminism, anti-militarism
Publications: Housmans publishes pamphlets on such topics as pacificism as well as the annual *Peace Diary*. It also acts as UK distributor for Black Rose Books, Bradford School of Peace Studies, Bewick, Exitstencil Press, Navijavan, Porter Sargent, Ralph Myles and Telos

Manor House Books   *(Finchley Central)*
80 East End Road N3
349-9484   445-4293

M–Th 10:00–4:00   Sun 9:30–1:30

Specializing in Jewish theology, this bookshop caters for the Rabinical college in the Sternberg Centre. Middle Eastern studies, Old Testament theology and all aspects of Judaism are covered by their stock. The books are in English and Hebrew with a small selection in Yiddish. The bulk of the range is new with a few second-hand books. Children's books and literature also have their place in this shop.

Non-book material: cards, Judaica
Services: mail order
Catalogue: the catalogue covers most of the general stock

Model Railway (Manufacturing) Co. Ltd   *(King's Cross)*
12–14 York Way N1
837-5551

M–Sat 9:30–5:30

This shop primarily sells model railway equipment but has a section of new books about railway history, stations, steam wagons, liveries and road transport.

The Muslim Bookshop   *(Finsbury Park)*
233 Seven Sisters Road N4
272-5170

M–Sat 10:00–6:00

children's books / Christians / economics / faith / government /
health and welfare / history / human rights / Islam / Middle East /
politics / prayer / prophets / Quran / reference / religion / social
responsibility / society / sociology / understanding Islam / women /
worship

The Muslim Bookshop is part of Muslim Information Services, an
organization which is very active in the Muslim community
promoting the perpetuation of Islamic faith and culture. The
bookshop is for Muslim and non-Muslim alike, with new books in
English, Arabic and Urdu on all aspects of Islam, including
interesting titles on current political issues and the culture of the
Islamic world. There is a large section on the Quran, the text of
which is also available on cassettes.

Muslim Information Services also operates from the premises
and keeps a wide variety of literature on the Middle East and
Islam.

Non-book material: cards, cassettes, educational aids, posters,
video-cassettes and films
Services: mail order, special order
Catalogue: selected list
Publications: MWH publishes books on Islam and educational
material

New Beacon Bookshop   *(Finsbury Park)*
76 Stroud Green Road N4
272-4889

Tu–Sat 10:30–6:00

African fiction and non-fiction / Afro-American fiction and
non-fiction / anthropology / Caribbean fiction and non-fiction /
children's books / colonization / cookery / economics / education /
history / individual rights / literary criticism / literature / music /
philosophy / poetry / politics / science / social issues / sociology /
Third World / women

New Beacon Bookshop specializes in current titles about and from Africa, the Caribbean, Afro-America and Black Britain. Journals, magazines and newspapers on politics, social issues, women and education are available, and they have a large general stock of books as well. School texts for use by children of Caribbean and African origin are a peculiar speciality, and they carry a wide range of general children's books, including some Asian titles.

Non-book material: cards, posters
Services: mail order, special order (any book in print)
Catalogue: selected lists (e.g., children's books, African literature)
Publications: New Beacon Books Ltd publishes books on African politics, history, etc.

New Era Books   *(Finsbury Park)*
203 Seven Sisters Road N4
272-5894

M–F 10:00–5:30   Sat 11:30–4:30

Africa / anti-imperialism / Asia / children's books / China / class struggle / classics of revolutionary writing / communism / Engels / Ireland / labour / Lenin / literature / Mao Tse-Tung / Marx / Middle East / political philosophy / revolution / socialism / Stalin / Third World / women / worker's rights

New Era Books is independently operated, but stocks new books in line with the politics and philosophy of the Revolutionary Communist League of Britain. The shop specializes in progressive literature from the Third World, and as they are the wholesalers for the Foreign Language Press in Peking, the shop has unique access to anything published in China. The bookshop also stocks an extensive selection of material of Irish interest. Also on sale is a range of booklets on politics and community issues, magazines and newspapers, many from Third World countries. Yet despite the overt political identity of New Era, the shop also serves the needs of the neighbourhood as a general bookseller.

Non-book material: cards, T-shirts, gifts from China, crafts, paints and brushes, posters, paper cuts, fans
Services: mail order, special order
Catalogue: mail order and trade list for wholesalers

Oak Hill College Bookroom   *(Southgate)*
Oak Hill College
Chase Side N14
499-0467/0041

M–F 9:00–1:00

This is the bookshop for an Anglican theological college and the stock caters for the specific course demands. The range includes bibles, bible commentaries and prayer books.

Non-book material: cards
Services: special order

Operation Headstart Books and Crafts   *(Seven Sisters)*
25 West Green Road N15
800-2389

M–F 9:30–6:00   Sat 9:30–7:00

Africa / Afro-America / art / black studies / children's books / civil rights / cookery / history / law / literature / music / plays / poetry / politics / religion / sociology

Operation Headstart specializes in new books on black studies in the UK and abroad. Titles on political and social issues are especially prominent, but the shop also has African, Caribbean and black American fiction.

Non-book material: cards, crafts, gifts
Services: mail order, special order

Reading Matters Bookshop   *(Turnpike Lane)*
(Reading Matters Ltd)
10 Lymington Avenue N22
881-3187

M–Sat 10:00–5:30   Th–F 10:30–6:00

This is a community bookshop with an emphasis on multiracial children's books. There is a good section of women's fiction and women's issues and the other subjects covered by the shop include radical politics, community rights and cookery. Most of the stock is new but there is a small second-hand section.

Non-book material: calendars, diaries, postcards, posters, recycled stationery
Services: library and school supplies, book stalls for schools and community groups
Catalogue: issue occasional lists
Publications: the most recent publication from Reading Matters Ltd is a selection of writing by young women in Haringey

SCM Bookroom   *(Dalston Kingsland–British Rail)*
26-30 Tottenham Road N1
249-7262

M–F 9:00–5:00

The SCM Bookroom stocks an excellent range of books on Christianity, philosophy and theology, among other topics. There are some bargain books, either slightly damaged or remaindered, and a few recently out-of-print titles. Most of the shop's business is done by mail order and the staff says that it can get any theological title currently in print.

Services: mail order, special order
Catalogue: annual comprehensive list
Publications: SCM Press publishes standard works on religion and political theology, as well as prayer and educational titles

Sisterwrite Bookshop & Gallery   *(Highbury and Islington)*
190 Upper Street N1
226-9782

M–Sat 10:00–6:00   Th 10:00–7:00

birth and child care / black women / children's / death and dying / education / feminism / fiction / health / history / Irish women / Jewish women / language and literary criticism / lesbianism / matriarchy / media / myths / older women / peace and anti-technology / poetry / psychology / religion / science fiction and fantasy / sexuality / violence against women and children / women's liberation / women's rights / young women

Sisterwrite is a bookshop selling books by and about women. Their literature section is excellent as is the coverage of black women and women of colour. What feminist history that has been written is available and I was pleased by the inclusion of a section on myths, matriarchy and religion (those often insidious oppressors). An excellent range of UK and US feminist magazines, papers, booklets and pamphlets is also available. On the first floor is a craft shop and gallery. A variety of handmade items produced by women are sold here, including pottery, jewellery, clothing, sculpture and many prints and paintings. There is a small sitting area with a coffee machine if you want to relax or you can wander into the garden area through the back of the shop. There is no wheelchair access to the first floor.

Non-book material: see above
Services: bookstalls at conferences, library orders, mail order, monthly readings of their work by women writers, special order
Catalogue: monthly book list (write for subscription details)

Stoke Newington and North Hackney Labour Party Bookshop Service East Ltd

(King's Cross and then 73 bus)

96a Stoke Newington High Street N16
249-5624

M–Sat 10:30–4:30

economics / history / Labour movement / politics / sociology

A selection of Labour Party publications is just one section of this shop and there is quite a broad range of new and second-hand books in addition to those related specifically to the Labour movement and the political party. Some of the books are donated so the prices are generally very reasonable.

Non-book material: magazines and journals

Sunpower Food & Book Co-operative

(Finsbury Park)

83 Blackstock Road N4
226-1799

M–F 10:00–6:00   Tue 1:00–6:00   Sat 10:00–5:00

alternative medicine / astrology / black fiction / children's books / cookery / diet and health / feminism / fiction / mysticism / occult

Sunpower is a small community bookshop whose floor space is evenly divided between crafts, books and food. It specializes in titles concerning women, women's fiction, the environment and related subjects. It has a good selection of non-sexist, anti-racist children's books.

Non-book material: crafts, wholefood, magazines
Services: mail order, special order

Victor's (Model Railways)   *(King's Cross)*
166 Pentonville Road N1
278-1019

M–Sat 10:00–5:30

This shop is a specialist in model railways and the books cover all aspects of railways and model railways around the world. Most of the books are published in America and Europe; a few are second-hand.

Non-book material: model railways
Services: mail order

Women's International Resource Centre   *(Archway)*
173 Archway Road N6
341-4403

M–Sat 10:00–6:00

The centre has a library specializing in women's international issues and educational resource material. There are occasional sales of books from the library and the above opening hours refer only to the library. The centre organizes discussion groups on women's issues, sponsors courses at the Mary Ward Centre and has links with women's organizations and the trade-union movement all over the country.

Services: mailing list, newsletter, including book reviews

Antiquarian and Second-hand Bookshops

Bonaventure   *(Highgate)*
259 Archway Road N6
341-2345

W–Sat 10:30–6:00

This general second-hand shop, which also keeps a number of antiquarian titles, covers such subjects as English literature, history and fiction but has an emphasis on travel around the world, particularly Latin America.

Non-book material: maps and prints
Services: mail order, wants lists accepted

Camden Passage Antique Market   *(Angel)*
Camden Place N1

Market days: W and Sat

Scattered around the arcades at Camden Passage are a number of booksellers whose stands and stocks may change location from week to week. Of particular note, though, is Martin Stone (usually found early Saturday mornings along the Camden Passage pavement near Carrier's restaurant) who specializes in collectors' science fiction and detective fiction. Nearby is Ian Sinclair whose special interest is second-hand contemporary poetry and the beat poets of the 1950s and 60s.

Fisher & Sperr   *(Highgate)*
46 Highgate High Street N6
340-7244

M–Sat 10:00–5:30 (hours may vary)

basement:
economics / politics / sociology / sports

ground floor:
art / chess / children's books / classics / economics / fiction / film / gardening / geography / history / humour / illustrated books / law / literary biography / criticism / history / literature / London / mountaineering / music / natural history / occult / ornithology / Penguin and Pelican / philosophy / poetry / psychology / topography / travel guides

first floor:
art / topography / travel accounts

second floor:
Judaica / medicine / military history / modern first editions

Fisher & Sperr is a large general second-hand and antiquarian shop, neatly laid out on four floors, in a charming 17th-century listed building – one of the oldest in Highgate. The shop's stock is particularly strong in the areas of literature and topography. It is a fine shop to browse in and prices range from £1.00 upwards.

Non-book material: engravings and prints (some local scenes)
Services: mail order, search service, framing service
Catalogue: occasional special list
Publications: Fisher & Sperr have published a pamphlet about the history of Highgate Village

Helgato Books   *(Arnos Grove)*
2 The Broadway
Friern Barnet Road N11
361-8326

W–Sat 9:30–5:30

archaeology / art / history / London and the counties / military / natural history / philosophy / topography

Helgato Books have a very comprehensive range of books in the above subjects. Their collection is antiquarian and second-hand and they also stock a selection on nineteenth-century maps and prints.

Non-book material: antique shop in the building, maps and prints
Services: special order

The History Bookshop   *(Arnos Grove)*
2 The Broadway
Friern Barnet Road N11
368-8568

W–Sat 9:30–5:30

ground floor:
architecture / art / cinema / English local history / gardening / history (general, military, UK) / illustrated books / London / mountaineering / music / natural history / Scotland / sport / theatre / theology / topography / transport / travel

basement:
anthropology / archaeology and ancient history / aviation / British and foreign history (all nations) / detective fiction / economics / fiction / historical periodicals / law / literary criticism / literature / music / natural history / naval history / philosophy / plays / poetry / politics / psychology / science and history of science / social history / social sciences

One could do worse than spend a morning or afternoon getting to this bookselling outpost in North London where the speciality is second-hand (and some antiquarian) history books. Military, local history and travel are the largest subject categories in the stock, but books on economic, political and social history are also on the shelves. Titles on transport, guides to the English counties and London can be found on the ground floor as well.

There are also books on a range of general subjects, and these shelves no doubt hold one or two collectors' items in each category. Of special interest is the collection of illustrated books, many of which are interesting examples of printing, engraving and book-making techniques. As a group, the illustrated books provide a telling history of the evolution of printing and book-making from the mid-nineteenth century.

The staff at The History Bookshop is as unusual as their stock. They seem less concerned with the money you spend than with your interest in and pleasure from the books on hand.

Non-book material: antique china, glass *objets d'art*, maps, prints (antiquarian and later)
Services: mail order, search service, special order: any book in print from UK or US and Germany
Catalogue: a separate list for military history

K.L. Books   *(Archway)*
614 Holloway Road N19
272-1754

M–Sat 12:00–6:00

Sharing premises with the A1 Records shop, this bookshop has a collection of second-hand and antiquarian books covering a general range of subjects with a particular emphasis on art and literature. They have paperbacks and hardbacks and a permanent sale on selected stock.

Non-book material: record shop

Open Way Books   *(Stoke Newington – British Rail)*
7 Cazenove Road N16
806-0638

M–Sat 10:00–6:00   closed Wednesdays

A variety of second-hand books, with a particular interest in mysticism and Sufism. Other sections include sociology, psychology and philosophy. There is a small academic stock.

Non-book material: bric-a-brac, jewellery, old furniture, ornaments
Services: special order

Upper Street Bookshop   *(Highbury and Islington)*
182 Upper Street N1
359-3785

Tue–Sat 9:30–6:00

A general second-hand bookshop with a special interest in art, architecture, design and books on Islington.

Services: book search

Vortex Galleries   *(King's Cross and then 73 bus)*
139-141 Stoke Newington Church Street N16
254-6516

M–Sat 9:30–6:00   Sun 1:00–6:00

The bookshop here has a general range of second-hand and antiquarian books, including a selection of paperback fiction. The bookshop is attached to an art gallery, art shop and a café, so you are not restricted to the written word alone.

Non-book material: artists materials, cards
Services: mail order
Catalogue: Vortex are currently compiling a catalogue to cover their entire stock

Wade Galleries   *(Angel)*
12b Camden Passage
Charlton Place N1
226-3803

W–Sat 9:00–5:00

Wade Galleries is an antique shop dealing with, among other things, books with fine bindings which are used for decorative purposes. If you need a fill a lovely, antique shelf, Wade Galleries can fix you up with the desired number of attractively spined volumes to create that studied air of erudition. The content of their books is less important to the dealers than the condition and colour of the spine. I did notice, though, that the books were predominantly literary or historical, English and French, and from the 18th and 19th centuries.

Non-book material: antiques
Services: mail order (reluctantly)

G.W. Walford   *(Highbury and Islington)*
186 Upper Street N1
226-5682

M–F 9:30–5:00 (appointment sometimes advisable)

A general stock of fine, rare and antiquarian, rather than routine second-hand, books is kept here with some emphasis on economics, illustrated books, natural history, sciences and travel, as well as a number of sets of standard literary authors.

Services: mail order
Catalogue: frequent, general

Whetstone Books   *(Totteridge/Arnos Grove)*
368 Oakleigh Road North N20
368-8338/445-8667

T–W F 10:00–3:00   Sat 10:00–5:00

This small, full corner-shop puts many larger ones in central London to shame. Certainly it makes a trip to this corner of London more than worth its while. The stock is general but of a high quality, the limited space meaning that the friendly, knowledgeable owner cannot keep rubbish. All in good condition, the stock ranges from cookery, history, topography and biography to fiction, foreign literature and hobbies. Especially good are the sections of poetry and of Penguins and Pelicans – many of these are the sought-after, out-of-print titles. There is an interesting section of Everyman and the original World's Classic series. All of the books are at prices considerably lower (indeed, often as much as two-thirds) than one would pay in more central London. Its lower rents mean that Totteridge could well become a focus for the second-hand book trade if Mr Carty's excellent shop is anything to go by.

Non-book material: a few prints and postcards
Services: mail order, occasional specialized lists, search service

Edna Whiteson   *(Arnos Grove)*
343 Bowes Road N11
361-1105

M–T Th Sat 10:00–5:00   F 10:00–6:00

art / biography / cookery / fiction / gardening / literary criticism / modern first editions / music / natural history / plays / politics / transport / travel

Edna Whiteson is a second-hand bookseller specializing in modern first editions and 20th-century literature. The selection of general fiction and non-fiction is strong as well, and the shop also carries a large selection of 19th-century prints and maps.

Non-back material: see above
Services: mail order, search service for modern first editions
Catalogue: modern first editions

North West London

General Bookshops

Belsize Bookshop   *(Belsize Park)*
193 Haverstock Hill NW3
794-4006

M–F 9:30–6:30   Sat 9:30–5:30

art / biography / children's / classics / cookery / crime / drama /
essays / fiction / guides / health / history / humour / medical /
Pelicans / poetry / Picador / reference / science fiction / social
sciences / sport / travel

In a relatively small space the Belsize Bookshop manages to
contain an excellent range of titles, a large proportion of which are
in paperback; the owner, however, is extremely keen to promote
new fiction and a good number of these are in recent hardback.

Non-book material: a range of literary magazines, maps
Services: rapid special order, mail order

Boots the Chemists   *(Hendon Central)*
Brent Cross Shopping Centre NW4
202-5256

M–F 10:00–8:00   Sat 9:00–6:00

There is a small general selection on the shelves here, including
popular fiction and some reference books.

Non-book material: department store

C. & L. Booksellers   *(Hendon Central)*
13 Sentinel Square
Brent Street NW4
202-5301/6288

M–Sat 9:30–5:30

art / BBC language teaching / business / children's books / classics / collecting / cookery / crafts / crime / dictionaries / economics / fiction / film / gardening / health / literature / military history / natural history / Pelican, Penguin / sciences / sculpture / sports / technical textbooks: O and A level / transport / travel guides

C & L is a general bookshop selling new and remaindered books (from 50p) with a section of academic textbooks and study aids.

Non-book material: cassettes, records, stationery
Services: mail order, special order

Compendium   *(Camden Town)*
234 Camden High Street NW1
485-8944

M–Sat 10:00–6:00   Sun 12:00–6:00

ground floor:
acupuncture / astrology / art / Black and Third-World fiction / blues, country, folk, jazz / civilizations (Egyptian, Mayan, North American) / diet and nutrition / family therapy / feminism: black women, fiction / Gestalt / health / Indian cookery / Indian philosophy and religion / magic / modern fiction / mysticism / mythology / numerology / occult / Oriental philosophy and religion / poetry / pregnancy and childbirth / psychic literature / psychology / rock 'n' roll history / religion / sexuality / social work / symbolism / tarot / transactional analysis / women's rights

basement:
architecture / building / communities / economics / gay literature / green politics / linguistics / nuclear issues / philosophy / politics / semiotics / travel

Compendium is at the top of the list of London's alternative bookshops, in terms of size, the depth of their stock and the range of the subject areas they cover. The books in the major sections are ordered by individual buyers who bring substantial knowledge to the areas in which they specialize. Poetry, literature, feminism, philosophy and politics are particularly strong sections, and a wide range of magazines, specialist journals, pamphlets, booklets, etc. are kept in all major subject areas. The shop specializes in American paperback books in all subject areas.
   With Compendium's growth in size and range has come a rise

in their public's expectations of what the shop is able to supply in addition to books. One buyer told me that the telephone rings all day with questions about workshops, meetings, marches and films which the public *thinks* Compendium will know about, not realizing that the shop doesn't function formally as an information centre.

Non-book material: postcards, political posters, tarot cards
Services: mail order, special order

Fenwick   *(Hendon Central)*
Brent Cross Shopping Centre NW4
202-8200

M–F 10:00–8:00   Sat 9:00–6:00

The books are a part of the toy department on the first floor in Fenwick's and the largest section is devoted to children's books. There is also a selection of popular fiction and general reference books.

Non-book material: department store

Gilberts Bookshop   *(St John's Wood)*
(H.M.P. Confectioners Ltd)
26 Circus Road NW8
722-8863

M–F 8:00–6:30   Sat 8:30–6:00   Sun 9:00–2:00

children's books / cookery / fiction / guides to London / medical books / reference / travel

The book section here has a large range of general reference books and the usual stock of popular fiction.

Non-book material: confectionery, stationery

Hampstead Village Bookshop   *(Hampstead)*
17 Flask Walk NW3
435-4741

M–Sat 10:00–6:00   Sun 11:00–5:00

ground floor: hard and paperback fiction / other general hardbacks

basement: second-hand books

This is a very small bookshop on the corner of picturesque Flask Walk. It frequently displays and sells rather charming paintings by local artists. A good place to browse on a Sunday outing to Hampstead.

Non-book material: cards, watercolours
Services: special order, book tokens

High Hill Bookshops Ltd   *(Hampstead)*
6-7 Hampstead High Street NW3
435-2218

M–Sat 9:30–6:30

general:
antiques / archaeology / architecture / art / biography / bargain books / business management / cinema / classics / cookery / crafts / Eastern philosophies and religions / fiction / gardening / health / history / humour / literature / local history / music / natural history / nostalgia / occult / Open University / philosophy / photography / plays / poetry and verse / politics / reference / science fiction / Shakespeare / sport / TV and movie guides / transport / travel guides / women

children's books:
arts / Asterix / bible stories / board books / chess / classics / Dr Seuss / early learning / early readers / fiction / games / geography / history / hobbies / Ladybird / music / myths / natural history / poetry / pop-up books / pre-school readers / puzzles / reference / younger tales

The High Hill Bookshop is extraordinary in the depth and range of its stock. It comprises, in fact, three interlinked shops. The first has new hardbacks for adults and also many paperbacks in the field of cookery, history, etc. There is, in addition, a separate section at the rear devoted to travel books both in cloth and paper. The middle shop has colourful and informative children's books covering a wide range of ages and reading levels, together with bargain books for adults and children, Open University and educational titles; while the third shop stocks paperbacks for adults. The undeniably literary and artistic personality of Hampstead Village itself is reflected in constantly renewed window displays of the latest biographies, letters, memoirs, fiction, essays, art books and literary criticism.

Services: mail order, special order

The Kilburn Bookshop   *(Kilburn Park)*
8 Kilburn Bridge
Kilburn High Road NW6
328-7071

M–Sat 9:30–5:30

alternative religions / art / astrology / biography / black studies / business studies / children's books / classics / cookery / cosmology / crime / drama / economics / education / fantasy / feminism / fiction / gardening / health / history / humour / Ireland / literature / media / music / mysticism / natural history / occult / philosophy / poetry / politics / psychology / reference / religion / science fiction / sociology / sports, games / thrillers

The Kilburn Bookshop is a good literary and general bookshop. It is relatively small but bright and open, and it carries an interesting selection of titles, including a good section of sci-fi and fantasy books, and special sections on feminism, Ireland, black culture and leftist politics, reflecting the ethnic and political mix of the area. While most of the stock is in paperback, the new titles' table also features many of the latest hardbacks in fiction and non-fiction. A useful range of political, feminist and community magazines, journals and papers are sold as well.

Non-book material: cards, wrapping-paper
Services: library and school supply, mail order, special order

Martin the Newsagent   *(Golders Green)*
26 Market Place
Falloden Way NW11
455-9720

M–Sat 7:30–5:30   Sun 8:30–1:00

The book section in this newsagents shop includes bestselling fiction, general reference books and a selection of children's books including some Ladybirds.

Non-book material: newsagents

John Menzies Ltd   *(Euston)*
The Colonnade
Euston Station NW1
387-5354/4640

M–Sat 7:00a.m.–10:00p.m.   Sun 7:00a.m.–9:00p.m.

children's books / fiction / humour / reference / TV and entertainment

The book section here stocks a general range of reference books including guides, phrasebooks, dictionaries and encyclopaedias as well as bestselling fiction.

Non-book material: stationery

Owl Bookshop   *(Kentish Town)*
211 Kentish Town Road NW5
485-7793

M–Sat 9:30–6:00

art / biography / British history / children's books / classics / cookery / current affairs / economics / education / feminism / fiction / gardening / health / literary criticism / literature / music / natural history / philosophy / photography / plays / poetry / politics / psychology / reference / science fiction / sociology / thrillers / travel guides / women's literature / world history

This is a spacious, general bookshop, whose stock reflects a special interest in literature and children's books, with a wide range of titles in the arts and social sciences. The Owl Bookshop is one of the better, medium-size general shops that I've found and is far stronger on academic books than most shops of this size.

Services: mail order, special order

Paraphernalia   *(Finchley Road)*
2 Midland Crescent
Finchley Road NW3
435-4634

M–Sat 9:30–6:30

This shop has a range of general paperbacks and second-hand books from 25p up. They specialize in studies of the occult and folklore and they have a selection of early children's annuals, film books and theatrical books.

Non-book material: film posters and stills
Publications: studies in mythology

The Penguin Bookshop   *(Camden Town)*
2 Plaza House
Camden High Street NW1
Telephone number not available at publication

M–Sat 9:30–5.30   Sun 11.30–5.30

art / biography / business and economics / children's / classics / cooking / crime / drama / education / feminism / fiction / film, TV / games, sports / history / humour / literary criticism / literature / music / natural history / philosophy / poetry / politics / psychology / reference / religion / science, mathematics / science fiction / sociology / travel guides

Penguin's newest and largest shop (4,000 square feet) offers more than the familiar stock – an interesting line in 'reduced price' books, which, it claims, does *not* mean the usual kind of uselessly glossy remainder, but rather hardback biographies, say, or literary fiction whose saleability has been hard hit by paperback editions.

Non-book material: literary magazines, postcards, greeting cards, wrapping-paper, children's book-related merchandise
Services: mail order, Penguin monthly stocklist

Primrose Hill Books   *(Chalk Farm)*
134 Regents Park Road NW1
586-2022

M–Sat 10:00–6:00   Sun 12:00–4:00

art / automobiles / children's books / classics / cookery / fiction / gardening / literature / natural history / photography / plays / poetry / psychology / reference / social sciences / travel accounts

This general shop has an unusual combination of new and second-hand titles. The books are divided according to price and type: new books ('up-market' paperbacks and hardcover titles, children's books, art cookery, etc.) are on the ground floor of the shop and general second-hand books are located downstairs. The sister bookshop, Frew Mackenzie (see separate entry), now deals with the antiquarian books which used to be here. It also keeps a stall in the Portobello Road on Saturdays.

Services: special order, book binding and repair service, photocopying

Regent Bookshop   *(Camden Town)*
73 Parkway NW1
485-9822

M–Sat 9:00–6:30   Sun 12:00–5:00

adventure and crime / architecture / art / biography / Britain / children's books / classics / cookery / economics / education / fiction / film / health / history / literature / Penguin / philosophy / poetry / psychology / reference / science fiction / sciences / sociology / travel guides

The Regent Bookshop is a straightforward, friendly neighbourhood shop selling a good range of general paperback and hardcover titles.

Non-book material: cards, stationery, wrapping-paper
Services: mail order (infrequent), special order

St John's Wood Newsagents   *(St John's Wood)*
134 St John's Wood High Street NW8
722-8800

M–F 7:30–7:30   Sat 8:30–6:30   Sun 9:00–3:00

The book stock in this newsagents includes bestselling fiction, children's books, a range of general interest books and a few books in Arabic.

Non-book material: newsagents
Services: special order

W.H. Smith   *(St Pancras)*
St Pancras Station NW1
837-5703

M–F 7:00a.m.–8:00p.m.   Sat 8:00–7:00   Sun 8:00–6:00

The bookstall in this station concentrates on paperback fiction, including the new titles, bestsellers and a section for the classics. There is a very small reference section largely made up of maps and guides.

Non-book material: stationery, cards, paper, news, magazines
Services: special order

W.H. Smith   *(Willesden Green)*
82 Walm Lane NW2
459-0455

M–Sat 8:30–6:00

This book department stocks the standard range of fiction, children's books and general interest. They keep the new hardback titles, and the general subjects include cookery, transport, school books and sport. The children's books range from Ladybirds through to teenage titles.

Non-book material: stationery, cards, paper, news, magazines
Services: special order, post-a-book, tokens
Catalogue: *Bookcase* review of books twice yearly

W.H. Smith   *(Finchley Road)*
9-10 Harben Parade
Finchley Road NW3
722-4441

M–Sat 8:45–5:30

There is a reasonable variety of books here, including all the standard Smith's categories with a section for new hardback titles.

Non-book material: stationery, cards, paper, news, magazines
Services: special order, post-a-book, tokens
Catalogue: *Bookcase* review of books twice yearly

W.H. Smith   *(Hendon Central)*
Brent Cross Shopping Centre NW4
202-4226

M–F 10:00–8:00   Sat 9:00–6:00

The book department of this branch of W.H. Smith is really
excellent and is in fact the biggest book department of the chain in
the whole country. They are situated on the upper floor and
occupy most of the floor space there, having a special children's
books section at the back and a very good stock of paperbacks
towards the front of the shop. Escalators carry you down to the
stationery, cards, records, etc., on the lower floor.

Non-book material: see above
Services: mail order, special order
Catalogue: *Bookcase* review of books twice yearly

W.H. Smith   *(Kilburn Park)*
113 Kilburn High Road NW6
328-3111

M–Sat 8:30–5:30

The book department here has a sufficiently large range to make it
the main suppliers of reading matter in the immediate area. The
usual range of subjects are covered and they keep the new
hardback titles.

Non-book material: stationery, cards, paper, news, magazines
Services: special order, post-a-book, tokens
Catalogue: *Bookcase* review of books twice yearly

W.H. Smith   *(Mill Hill Broadway – British Rail)*
29 The Broadway NW7
959-1316

M–Sat 8:30–5:30

This is a small shop so the book department covers the standard
range of fiction, children's books and general interest as best it can
within the limited space available. To compensate for the lack of
space, the ordering service is very popular.

Non-book material: stationery, cards, paper, news, magazines
Services: special order, post-a-book, tokens
Catalogue: *Bookcase* review of books twice yearly

W.H. Smith   *(Golders Green)*
889 Finchley Road NW11
455-0036

M–Sat 8:30–5:30

The comprehensive range of books in this department occupies one half of the ground floor and the new hardback titles are on display by the front door. A wide range of general interest books includes a particularly strong section on sport.

Non-book material: stationery, cards, paper, news, magazines
Services: special order, tokens
Catalogue: *Bookcase* review of books twice yearly

W.H. Smith   *(Golders Green)*
22 Temple Fortune Parade NW11
455-2273

M–Sat 9:00–6:00

This is a fairly small book department but it does cover the usual range of subjects and keeps a selection of the new hardback titles.

Non-book material: stationery, cards, paper, news, magazines
Services: special order, post-a-book, tokens
Catalogue: *Bookcase* review of books twice yearly

Strathmore Book Shop   *(Chalk Farm/Kentish Town)*
22 Cheriton, Queen's Crescent NW5
482-4446

M–F 9:00–5:00

children's books / classics / cookery / fiction / gardening / literature / Pelican, Penguin / poetry / reference / travel guides

Strathmore carries a limited amount of stock in the above subjects, its chief business being with college and university library supply.

Services: mail order, special order

Swiss Cottage Books Ltd   *(Swiss Cottage)*
4 Canfield Gardens NW6
625-4632

M–Sat 9:30–7:00

ground floor:
art / children's / classics / cookery / fiction / gardening/ women's fiction

first floor:
biography / drama / health / performing arts / poetry / reference / revision aids / social sciences / sport / travel / women's studies

This bookshop, just off the Finchley Road, is of very modern design with bright red and green tubular fittings and a staircase leading from the centre up to a first-floor gallery. They specialize in fiction, women's fiction, classics both in English and other languages, travel, poetry, biography and drama.

Non-book material: cards
Services: special order

West End Green Bookshop   *(West Hampstead)*
339 West End Lane NW6
431-0881

M–Sat 10:00–6:00

art / child care / children's / classics / cooking / drama / fiction / gardening / health / history / languages / music / philosophy / poetry / reference / religion / second-hand / travel

This is a fairly small but very friendly local bookshop just opposite West End Green. It has a particularly good choice of up-market fiction and poetry, mostly in paperback, but also stocks current hardback bestsellers. The owners are Australian and have a strong background in the book trade 'down under' – this is not revealed in the stock so much as in the warm and open atmosphere in the shop.

Non-book material: art, cards, postcards, wrapping-paper
Services: special order, search service

Speciality Bookshops

J. Aisenthal *(Golders Green)*
11 Ashborn Parade
Finchley Road NW1
455-0501

M–F 9:00–6:00   Sun 9:30–1:00

art / biography / children's books / civilization / cookery / ethics / faith / Hebrew language-teaching / history / holidays / Israel / Jewish authors / literature / music / prayer books / religious philosophy / religious practice / Talmudic studies / Torah

Aisenthal is a bookshop selling new books on all aspects of Jewish culture, religion and politics. The shop's stock is generally pro-Zionist, but Aisenthal carries books for those interested in reformed as well as orthodox Judaism. About half of the books are in English, the rest in Hebrew.

Non-book material: religious requisites
Services: mail order, special order

Al-Noor Bookshop *(Baker Street)*
54 Park Road NW1
723-5414

M–Sat 10:00–5:00 (hours are flexible)

This bookshop stocks books on Islam in Arabic and Urdu, with a few in English. The range includes studies on Islamic culture and history as well as the specifically religious works.

Non-book material: cassettes, including recordings of the Quran; pictures; prayer mats; jewellery
Services: special order

179

Basilisk Press Ltd   *(Swiss Cottage)*
10 Adamson Rd NW3
722-2142

By appointment only

architecture / art / calligraphy / children's books / gardening /
Hawk Press / Hippopotamus Press / horticulture / literature /
maritime / natural history / Northern House / Permanent Press /
poetry and verse / printing / Taurus Press / Thornhill Press / Triton
Press

Basilisk carries books, booklets, leaflets and pamphlets, mostly of
poetry and verse, literature, natural history or art, all of which are
beautifully designed and printed. The above listing is only a
smattering of the presses which are represented, most of which
are from the USA.
   This is not a bookshop – all purchases are through mail order or
by special appointment.

Non-book material: original calligraphy, cards, hand-marbled
paper
Services: mail order, special order
Catalogue: selected listing (£2.50)
Publications: Basilisk Press publishes in the fields of natural
history, history of landscape and illustrated literature

Bellman Bookshop   *(Tufnell Park)*
155 Fortress Road NW5
485-6698

M–Sat 10:00–5:00 (closed W)

Africa: economics, politics, society / Americas: economics,
politics, society / anthropology / Asia: economics, politics, society /
British history / children's books / classics / cookery / drama /
Europe: economics, politics, society / fiction / folk traditions /
Ireland and IRA / language teaching / Marxism and Lenin / myths /
poetry / psychology / reference / social history / travel guides

This is the bookshop of the Communist Party of Britain (M-L),
selling new books which are curiously divided between general
subjects and communist literature. I was treated to an extended
ideological harangue from the woman who was staffing the shop.

In spite of the staff's enthusiasm, the stock is scanty, though Bellman is one of the few places which has literature from the Communist Party of Ireland.

Non-book material: badges, cards, games, posters
Services: mail order, special order
Catalogue: a listing of Party publications and related political titles
Publications: see above

The Business Bookshop   *(Baker Street)*
72 Park Road NW1
723-3902

M–F 9:00–5:30   Th 9:00–7:30

accounting / analytical techniques / banking / behavioural sciences / business strategy / economics / finance / information technology / law / management / organization theory / personnel / production / reference / small business / statistics

This is a well-organized bookshop specializing in new books on business. Stock comes from the UK, US and Europe and covers a wide range of practical and theoretical business subjects.

Non-book material: stationery, cards
Services: mail order, special order, express delivery
Catalogue: monthly bulletins in business, technical, EEC, directories and reference. Stock lists by subject available
Publications: Alan Armstrong Ltd produces reference material for libraries and also owns this bookshop

Changes Bookshop   *(Kilburn Park)*
242 Belsize Road NW6
328-5161

M–F 10:00–6:00   Sat 10:00–5:00

bodywork / counselling / groupwork / hypnosis / Jung / mythology / psychoanalysis / psychology / psychotherapy / spiritual issues

Changes specializes in books on psychology and psychotherapy, and prides itself on having probably the largest selection of hypnosis and neurolinguistic programming in the world. The shop stocks second-hand books within its subject areas and will look out for customers' out-of-print wants. It also specializes in imports from the USA. It offers a bookstall service to appropriate conventions and issues a three-monthly news-sheet and occasional subject catalogues. The friendly atmosphere doesn't change; there's free coffee and a box of toys for children.

Non-book material: magazines, meditation and psychological tapes
Services: mail order, special order, and see above
Catalogue: subject catalogues, three-monthly newssheet
Publications: distributors of Future Pace Press and Syntony Publishing

Chapter Travel   *(St John's Wood)*
102 St John's Wood Terrace NW8
586-9451

M–F 9:30–6:00   Sat 9:30–1:00

This is a bookshop run in tandem with a travel agency, so you can book your holiday and then find out all about it under the same roof. The books include travel, cookery and fiction related to foreign travel. The owners have a particular interest in Italy which is reflected both in the book selection and their own tour operations.

Non-book material: travel agency, motoring accessories, language tapes
Services: special order
Catalogue: four annual booklists are issued to cover Italy, France, Greece and combined list for Austria, Germany and Switzerland
Publications: brochure for villas in Tuscany with an accompanying booklist

East Asia Company   *(Mornington Crescent)*
101-103 Camden High Street NW1
388-5783

M–Sat 10:00–5:30

lower ground floor: oriental subjects
cookery / folk art / language and culture / martial arts / philosophy

upper ground floor:
acupuncture, general health for the layman / holistic medicine /
homeopathy

Now expanded into two shops, East Asia has an extensive range
of activities: selling new, out-of-print and antiquarian books on
East Asia and other oriental countries; publishing both the *East
Asia Bibliography*, which contains detailed notes on new books
about East Asia, and language teaching books; as well as selling
sophisticated acupuncture and homeopathy books and
equipment. Books in Chinese are at the back of the lower floor.

Non-book material: acupuncture charts and equipment, cards,
cassettes, crafts, gifts, homeopathic practitioners' aids, natural
health and beauty products, *objets d'art*, paintings, prints
Services: mail order, special order, wants lists accepted
Catalogue: East Asia Bulletin, specialized lists
Publications: see above, also *Acumedic Series*

Faculty Books   *(Hendon Central)*
Middlesex Polytechnic
The Burroughs NW4
202-3593

M/W/F 10:00–4:00   Tue/Th 10:00–6:30 (term time only)

business / catering / computing / law

This shop stocks books specifically ordered for courses at the
polytechnic and the main subjects are business and law. It is open
to the general public and the staff are very friendly.

Non-book material: stationery
Services: special order

The Folk Shop   *(Camden Town)*
Cecil Sharpe House
2 Regent's Park Road NW1
485-2206

M–F 9:30–1:00

festivals / folk crafts / folk customs / folk dancing / folk music / history / Ireland / Scotland / traditions / US folk traditions

Although this is only a small shop on the premises of the English Folk Dance and Song Society, there is a lot of information available about the history and practice of folklore, history, song and dancing in the UK and, to a lesser degree, in the USA. The books here are new; there are magazines about dancing and music, as well as song books and folk song records.

Non-book material: crafts, folk instruments, music, records
Services: mail order, special order in field
Catalogue: large annual list of 'folk' books and song records
Publications: The English Folk Dance and Song Society publishes books and records

Friends Book Centre   *(Euston)*
Friends House
Euston Road NW1
387-3601 ext. 23

M–F 9:30–5:30   Tue 10:00–5:30

alcoholism / children's books / Christianity / comparative religion / cookery / Eastern religions / elderly / faith / fiction / non-fiction / non-violence and peace / Pelican and Penguin / Quaker faith / social issues and responsibilities

The Friends Book Centre carries general literature on religion with a specific concentration on literature about the Quaker faith. Ninety per cent of the books are new, although the Book Centre does have second-hand and rare books on Quaker topics and religion.

Non-book material: cards, posters, maps, guides
Services: mail order, special order, search service for out-of-print and rare Quaker titles
Catalogue: annual new title list of books on Quaker faith; second-hand book list; list of Swarthmore lectures, including out-of-print; Quaker poster lists
Publications: The Religious Society of Friends publishes a variety of books in the field of religion and Quaker Faith

Hampstead Bible School of Faith   *(Finchley Road)*
339 Finchley Road NW3
794-7353

M–F 9:00–5:00

This bookshop has a wide range of Christian books concerned with faith and its relation to the body, soul and spirit. There is a large choice in children's books and a selection of American publications.

Non-book material: teaching and music cassettes, videos
Services: special order

Islamic Book Centre   *(Warren Street/Euston)*
120 Drummond Street NW1
388-0710

M–F 10:00–6:00   Sat 10:00–8:00 (closed 1:00–2:00 each day)

art / calligraphy / history / philosophy / politics

The Islamic Book Centre sells Islamic religious books primarily in the areas listed above, the first such shop in the centre of London.

Non-book material: Quranic cassettes, rugs, posters, cards, postcards
Services: mail order, special order

H. Karnac (Books) Ltd   *(Swiss Cottage/Finchley Road)*
118 Finchley Road NW3
431-1075

M–Sat 9:00–6:00

This is the sister shop to Karnac in Gloucester Road, also specializing in psychoanalysis, analytical psychology, psychotherapy and related subjects. They sell general books too and have a good selection on social work and counselling.

Services: mail order, specialist conference bookstalls
Catalogue: yes

Jerusalem The Golden   *(Golders Green)*
146a Golders Green Road NW11
458-7011   455-4960

M–Th 9:30–6:00   F 9:30–2:30 (summer 6:00) Sun 9:30–4:30

art / biography / children's books / civilization / cookery / ethics / Hebrew language teaching / history / holidays / Israel / Jewish authors / literature / politics / prayer books / religious philosophy / religion practice / Talmudic studies / Torah

The majority of titles at this Jewish bookshop are in English and focus on subjects of interest and importance to the movement of Reformed Judaism. There are some religious and secular titles in Hebrew, and books are imported from the US and Israel. They boast the largest stock of Jewish and Hebrew records in Europe.

Non-book material: cassettes, records, religious requisites
Services: mail order, special order

LCL Benedict Ltd   *(Camden Town)*
65 Camden Road NW1
267-3247/3673

M–F 9:00–6:00

Language teaching texts and courses are the specialities of LCL Benedict. Approximately 50% of their stock is devoted to books for teaching English as a foreign language, while the rest of the titles are on learning a wide variety of foreign languages including Serbo-Croatian, Vietnamese, Mandarin Chinese and Urdu. LCL Benedict's books are usually sold in conjunction with audio-visual learning aids and are most useful to the home student.

Non-book material: audio-visual language teaching aids
Services: mail order, special order in field
Catalogue: on request

MCC Bookshop   *(St John's Wood)*
Lord's Cricket Ground
St John's Wood NW8
289-1957

M–F 9:45–5:45 (winter)   open match days during the cricket season

This small bookshop is really only for sports and particularly cricket fans. It was initially created to serve spectators at Lord's and is consequently quite difficult to find, being inside the ground near the stands. It has a decent stock of cricket books, sports joke books, etc., as well as other cricketana.

Services: mail order

Menorah Print & Gift Centre/ Hebrew Booksellers   *(Brent Cross)*
227 Golders Green Road NW11
458-8289

M–F 10:00–6:00 (closed 1:00–2:00) Sun 9:00–1:00

biography / child raising / commentary and analysis / cookery / culture and civilization / ethics / faith / Hebrew language / history / holidays / Jewish life / literature / music / philosophy / religion / Torah

Many of the books here are in English, but there are also religious texts in Hebrew imported from the US and Israel. The emphasis in all subject areas is on orthodox Judaism and the preservation of the laws of the Torah.

Non-book material: religious requisites

Methodist Church Overseas Division Bookshop   *(Baker Street)*
25 Marylebone Road NW1
935-2541

M–F 9:00–5:00

bibles / children's books / China / commentaries / contemporary issues / dictionaries / ethics / evangelism / faith / family / Far East / Middle East / missions and missionaries / political and social change / prayer / religion and Third World

This is a small shop with new books covering Christian and religious subjects from evangelism and missionaries to the history of the high church. The staff are friendly, helpful and respond quickly to mail order requests.

Non-book material: cards, cassettes, jewellery, posters, records, song books
Services: mail order, special order
Publications: Cargate Press occasionally publishes books on religion

Mustard Seed   *(Camden Town)*
21 Kentish Town Road NW1
267-5646

M–Sat 10:00–7:00 (hours may vary; often open later)

bibles / children's books / C. S. Lewis / family / inspirational biography / religion

This small shop sells new books about Christian-based alternatives to the conventional church. A community fellowship is run in conjunction with the shop, for those who are looking for a locally based christian group. One of their most important and interesting sections deals with the creation/evolution debate.

Non-book material: cards
Services: mail order, special order
Publications: Mustard Seed produces leaflets on Christian issues

OCS Bookshop   *(Camden Town)*
67 Parkway NW1
485-4201

Tu–Sun 10:00–6:00

OCS carries new books in Japanese about Japan. Language teaching books are the only titles in English, but for those who can read Japanese the rest of the books cover every aspect of history, art, culture and politics in Japan. The shop imports all its books and is the distributor for the Japanese Government Printing Office.

Non-book material: cards, origami, stationery
Services: mail order, special order

Offstage Theatre Shop and Gallery
(Chalk Farm/Camden Town)

37 Chalk Farm Road NW1
485-4996

T–Sat 10:00–5:30 Sun 11:00–6:30

ballet and dance / biography / children's theatre / cinema / criticism / jazz / media studies / music hall / play texts / puppet theatre / reference / stagecraft / television / theatre history

The ground floor of this shop has new books covering all aspects of the performing arts, together with a second-hand department and a few antiquarian titles; upstairs is a gallery displaying a collection of theatre designs both by 19th- and early 20th-century designers. Outside exhibitions, talks and play-readings are also held and there is a studio theatre downstairs.

Non-book material: cards, magazines, stage designs and prints, theatre and cinema posters
Services: mail order, special order, wants lists accepted

Skola Books
(Camden Town)

27 Delancey Street NW1
388-0632   387-0656

M–F 9:30–5:00

Specialists in EFL material, Skola Books cater for foreign students and teachers and the bulk of their business is wholesale supply to schools and colleges. They have a large selection of language books and some stock for English speakers learning a foreign language.

Non-book material: language cassettes, stationery and equipment for schools and colleges
Services: international mail order; supplies for schools and colleges; organize student accommodation for foreign students on short courses; language courses and information on courses

SPCK Bookshop
(Great Portland Street)

Holy Trinity Church
Marylebone Road NW1
387-5282 (second-hand dept ext. 237)

M–Th 9:00–5:30   F 9:00–5:00

new books:
bibles / children's books / Christian education / church history /
commentaries / comparative religion / evangelism / Fontana,
Hodder & Stoughton, Lion, Penguin / monuments and cathedrals /
Old and New Testament / prayer / religious philosophy / theology /
Third World

antiquarian and second-hand books:
apocrypha / bible background / Byzantine / church history / church
unity / collections of authors / commentaries / comparative
religion / essays / French, German, Hebrew, Latin texts / hymns
and music / lectures / Middle Ages / missions / moral and pastoral
theology / patrology / philosophy / prayer, liturgy, worship /
psychology / reformation / religious biography / religious
denominations / religious poetry and literature / sermons / social
order and the church / spiritual life / theology

The long list of categories in SPCK's second-hand and antiquarian
department is evidence of their extraordinary stock – to my mind,
the finest religious holdings in London.

   In the new-book section of the shop the scope of Christian
education material is particularly broad, geared to young learners
as well as adults, but a fine range of all recent Christian and
religious titles is sold here.

Non-book material: cards, cassettes, creche figures, films,
posters, slides, tapes, records, compact discs
Services: mail order, special order, search service
Catalogue: new books listing only
Publications: Religious books are published under the imprints of
SPCK, Sheldon and Triangle; and the shop distributes Abingdon
and Seabury in the UK

Rudolf Steiner Bookshop   *(Baker Street)*
35 Park Road NW1
723-4400/8219

M–Sat 10:00–6:00   during school term 10:00–7:30

agriculture / art / children's books / education / health / meditation /
occult / Penguin / philosophy / religion / Rudolf Steiner

This small shop sells new books, primarily of and about Rudolf
Steiner's work, but with a selection of books on other general

subject areas as well. Although run independently from the Rudolf Steiner Bookshop in Museum Street, WC1, the two shops are affiliated through the Anthroposophical Association and share the speciality of Steiner's life and work. Journals sold here are connected to Steiner in some way.

Non-book material: cosmetics, elixirs, paints, postcards, prints, shampoos, wooden toys
Services: mail order, special order in any field
Publications: Rudolf Steiner Press

Westfield College Bookshop   *(Hampstead)*
Westfield College
Kidderpore Avenue NW3
794-7911

M–Th 10:00–4:00 during term time only (hours flexible – ring first)

classics / English literature / history / history of art / modern languages

This is a campus shop but it is open to the general public. The stock is geared towards the courses at Westfield College and includes a wide range of history textbooks and paperback literature.

Non-book material: greetings cards
Services: special order

Antiquarian and Second-hand Bookshops

Archive Bookstore

(Edgware Road)

83 Bell Street NW1
402-8212

M–Sat 10:00–6:00

art / dictionaries / history / literature / music / natural history / occult / travel

This antiquarian and second-hand shop is run by a man who seems to know good books and also knows how to restore them well. A lovely hour's browse can easily be had here and I found the prices reasonable, the shop well ordered and the books and business well cared for. Bargain books are to be found here especially on Saturdays when there is a street market for household goods in Bell Street.

Non-book material: maps, music
Services: mail order, search service, restoration of fine bindings, valuations

Bibliopola

(Edgware Road)

Alfie's Antique Market Room 603
13 Church Street NW8
724-7231

Tue–Sat 10:30–5:30

ancient history / classics / cookery / English literature / history / limited editions / modern first editions / natural history / private presses / travel accounts and guides

This nicely organized general antiquarian bookshop stocks books in the noted categories, including 16th- and 17th-century Italian and Latin texts and 19th-century illustrated books. The books are in good condition and prices reflect their fine quality.

Services: mail order, search service
Catalogue: selected lists

P.J. Cassidy   *(Edgware Road)*
95 Bell Street NW1
724-0876

M–Sat 10:30–5:45

Africa / art / biography / Christianity / economics / English classics /
fiction / French and German texts / gardening / history / hobbies /
literature / local guides / military history / poetry / politics /
reference / witchcraft

This bookshop is nicely ordered, with general, second-hand stock
and a few remainders and review copies. All the books are in good
condition and at reasonable prices. In the basement, open from
Thursday to Saturday, you will find antiquarian, illustrated books
and modern first editions

Non-book material: engravings, ephemera, maps, prints
Services: picture-framing and mount-cutting

The Corner Bookshop   *(Chalk Farm)*
Camden Lock
Chalk Farm Road NW1
no phone

Sat–Sun 10:00–6:00

Africa / art / astronomy / biography / cookery / fiction / gardening /
health / heraldry / history / letters / literature / London / Middle
East / music / natural history / topography / travel guides

This is a second-hand and antiquarian bookshop which is always
packed with market browsers on Saturdays and Sundays. The
stock is general, with illustrated books from this century and the
last, travel guides, a bit of literature and a reasonably large section
of books about London. Prints, book plates, engravings and
water-colours of theatre scenes, landscapes, animals and people,
are also plentiful and pleasant to leaf through.

Non-book material: see above
Services: mail order (through shop in Hertfordshire)

Fitzjohns Books   *(Swiss Cottage)*
27a Northways Parade
College Crescent NW3
722-9864

M–Sat 11:00–6:00

Fitzjohns stock a general selection of second-hand books, with a specialized antiquarian stock and some remainders. Medicine and psychiatry take first place in the pecking order here, but that should not discourage the less scientific browser from investigating the other areas of the shop.

Services: mail order
Catalogue: a catalogue for the more specialized stock is available

The Flask Bookshop   *(Hampstead)*
6 Flask Walk NW3
435-2693

Tue, W, F, Sat 10:00–6:00

antiques / architecture / art / drama / fiction / gardening / history / literary biography / literary criticism / literature modern first editions / music / natural history / poetry / porcelain

This is my favourite Hampstead bookshop because, though there is the feeling of a 19th-century bookseller's pride in his stock, the shop's contents are far from stuffy. The general collection of second-hand books and a large number of review copies is marked by an excellent section of reduced-price art books, a small but select section of modern first editions and a literary criticism section which is substantial and up-to-date, not full of jumble sale cast-offs.

Because of the regularity with which the shop gets review copies, newly published fiction, biography and art, for example, can often be found here at reduced prices. The owner is also an author (he has written on collecting modern first editions, P.G. Wodehouse and Jerome) and the shop keeps a small Wodehouse section. The bias of the shop is toward the humanities, with a twist here and there, and the stock changes regularly.

Non-book material: Hampstead prints

Gabriel's Bookshop   *(Willesden Green)*
47 Walm Lane NW2
451-2047

M–F 10:00–6:30   Sat 9:30–6:00

accountancy / biography / children's books / classics / cookery / crafts / crime / dance / economics / engineering / fiction: English, French, Spanish / film and TV / history / medicine / plays / romance / science fiction / sociology / westerns

There is a strange mix of books in this shop, including second-hand textbooks in the sciences, new and second-hand romance, fiction and sci-fi in English and Spanish, a collection of second-hand film, TV, detective and romance magazines and a section of children's books. The main speciality is in Spanish books, new, stocked for schools and colleges.

Services: mail order

Game Advice   *(Hampstead Heath – British Rail)*
1 Constantine Road NW3
482-5677

M–F 9:30–5:00

chess / cookery / games / psychology

This is primarily an antiquarian and second-hand bookshop specializing in the above areas, though some new chess books are also sold. They are one of the few shops to sell antiquarian psychology books.

Non-book material: games, tarot cards
Services: mail order, special order, search service in field
Catalogue: antiquarian and second-hand catalogue half-yearly

Lionel Halter   *(Mill Hill Broadway – British Rail)*
7 Hale Lane NW7
959-2936

M–Sat 9:30–5:30

annuals / art / biography / boxing / children's books / cinema / cookery / fiction / film / gardening / history / Judaica / literature / natural history / reference / religion / theatre / travel and topography

This shop, a little awkward to reach by London Transport, is close to a British Rail station. Its stock is general and its prices reasonable. As well as a useful specialist section on boxing, it has a number of sets of encyclopaedias and standard authors.

Non-book material: postcards
Services: photocopying and general printing

Charles Higham   *(Great Portland Street)*
Holy Trinity Church
Marylebone Road NW1
387-5282

M–Th 9:00–5:30   F 9:00–5:00

This is an extensive second-hand and antiquarian collection and a department of the SPCK Bookshop, housed in Holy Trinity Church. The emphasis is clearly on theology but the other sections include art, literature, history and a variety of books in foreign languages.

Services: mail order, special order
Catalogue: annual catalogue covering rare books, manuscripts and autographed material

A.A. Miles   *(Edgware Road)*
105 Bell Street NW1
723-8455

M–Sat 10:30–6:00 (days open may vary)

This jumbled, nay chaotic, general second-hand bookshop is run by an ailing gentleman with an interest in industrial history, art and architecture. Books can be found from 50p, at what is said to be Marylebone's second oldest bookshop. Some remainders and review copies are sold, particularly in the field of art.

Services: wants lists accepted

Phase One Books   (*Finchley Road*)
1 Midland Crescent
Finchley Road NW3
435-4634

M-Sat 11:00–7:00

This is a small general second-hand shop whose moderately price stock changes almost fortnightly. The owner buys one large collection of books, the contents of which may be fiction, natural history, science, travel or Czech cookery, to name only a few possible subject areas. He also stocks over 2,000 second-hand Penguins and has a good section on London.

Services: mail order, search service

Smith & Fawkes Bookshop   (*Hampstead*)
1-3 Flask Walk NW3
435-0614

M–Sat 10:00–5:30

anthropology / antiquities / architecture / art / ballet / biography / children's books / classics / cookery / crafts / crime / dictionaries and grammar / drama / essays / exploration and travel / fables / fiction / folklore / gardening / history / interior design / literature / local history / marine life / modern first editions / music: classical and contemporary / natural history / Penguin / philosophy / poetry and verse / science fiction / sociology / stage history / theology / thrillers / transport

Approximately 20% of the books here are antiquarian, the rest being second-hand in a wide range of subject areas. The shop is a good stop for browsers, it is relatively large, its shelves are well marked and the contents are nicely organized. Also, the flavour of old village Hampstead floats in from historic Flask Walk. Strong sections among the books are literature (French, German and Spanish in translation, as well as English) exploration and travel, art and biography.

Non-book material: occasionally engravings and prints
Services: mail order

Eric & Joan Stevens Booksellers   *(West Hampstead)*
74 Fortune Green Road NW6
435-7545

Sat 10:00–5:30 and by appointment

anthologies / art / bibliography / biography / cinema / cookery / economics / feminist history / fiction / history / Israel / law and crime / literary criticism / literature / Middle East / modern first editions / music / natural history / photography / plays / poetry / psychology / religion / sexual politics / theatre / thrillers / travelogues / women writers

What a shame that this shop is not open more hours during the week because in the relative desert north of central London this general bookshop is something of an oasis. There are three rooms filled with second-hand books, a few remainders and review copies, and some antiquarian titles.

The shop specializes in literature, art, poetry and feminism, the latter being a solid section of literature by women or about sexual politics and feminist history. The section of literary criticism is also good and there is a nice selection of modern first editions. They have a special section on Edward Thomas and the Powys family.

Non-book material: cards
Services: mail order, search service
Catalogue: five specialized catalogues yearly (e.g. feminism, literature, art, poetry)
Publications: Eric and Joan Stevens privately publish (indeed, they privately *print*) original poetry and contemporary writing

The Village Bookshop   *(Belsize Park)*
46 Belsize Lane NW3
794-3180

M–Sat 11:00–5:30

archaeology / architecture / art / astronomy / biography / children's books / crime / detective fiction / fiction / food / Germany / history / illustrated books / Judaica / literature: English, French, German / military history / modern first editions / mountaineering / music / natural history / philosophy / photography / poetry / psychology / sport / theatre / topography / travel / war / women

There is a large general stock with noteworthy sections of Victorian illustrated and children's books, literature and modern first editions. The owner has a special interest in books on all aspects of Germany, both in German and English, and has filled a good half of a wall with titles on the subject.

Services: mail order

Walden Books   *(Chalk Farm/Kentish Town West – British Rail)*
38 Harmood Street NW1
267-8146

Th–Sun 10:30–6:30

antiques / architecture / art / biography / children's books / cookery / dance / education / fiction / film / gardening / history / humour / literary criticism / literature / modern first editions / music / natural history / Penguin / philosophy / plays / poetry / psychology / romantic fiction / sciences / sports / theatre / travel

Located on the ground floor of the owner's home, this general second-hand bookshop takes on the comfortable air of its context, and customers can browse through a large stock of paperbacks in a variety of subject areas. The books are bought quite selectively by the owner and the stock changes from week to week, with 19th- and 20th-century literature as the main area of interest.

Services: mail order, search service (antiquarian books as well)

West London

General Bookshops

Athena   *(Piccadilly Circus)*

The Trocadero
Coventry Street W1
734-5061

M–Sun 10:00a.m.–11:00p.m.

ground floor: paperbacks
biography / cinema / fiction (hard and paperback) / humour /
popular music / travel

upper floor:
art / bargain books / cookery / health / history / militaria /
photography / reference / sport / transport

Situated in this ultra-modern complex in Piccadilly, Athena caters
largely to the tourist market, who will find their long opening
hours very convenient. It is owned together with its sister branch
on Oxford Street by the Pentos Group (who also owned Dillons).
It is a comfortable shop – large, spacious, brightly-lit and
air-conditioned.

Athena   *(Oxford Circus/Tottenham Court Road)*

119-121 Oxford Street W1
734-3383

M–F 9:30–8:00   Sat 10:00–8:00

astrology / bargains / cartoons / crime / fantasy / fiction / foreign
language fiction / horror / health / humour / occult / popular music /
reference / romance / sociology / science fiction / travel

There is a fairly large book department on the lower ground floor
of this branch of Athena. It caters in the main for the many tourists
flooding Oxford Street, also the generally young and trendy
popping in from neighbouring Soho. There is an extensive range

of Athena posters, prints, cards and stationery on the ground floor.

Non-book material: see above

Basketts Bookshops   *(Ealing Broadway)*
201 Uxbridge Road W13
567-5356

M–Sat 9:00–5:30

This is a general bookshop, including children's books and a section on religion.

Non-book material: cards and gifts
Services: special order

Bookcase Too   *(Baker Street/Bond Street)*
22 Baker Street W1
935-3483

M–F 9:00–6:00   Sat 10:30–5:00

This bookshop, owned by the remainder merchants Roy Bloom Ltd, sells general new and remaindered books. The ratio of remaindered to new books is about 3 to 1.

Services: special order

Book Cellar   *(Bond Street)*
(Fenwick of Bond Street)
63 New Bond Street W1
629-9161

M–Sat 9:30–6:00   Th 9:30–7:30

children's books / cookery / fiction / gardening / humour / reference / sport / travel

This basement book department in Fenwick's has a range of general reference books, hobbies and fiction, supplied by W.H. Smith.

Non-book material: department store
Services: special order

Bookends   *(Piccadilly Circus/Oxford Circus)*
172 Regent Street, W1
734-5886/7

M–Sat 9:30–6:30   Th 9:30–8:00   Sun 12:00–5:00

This colourful shop sells mainly bargain and remainder books. They also sell full-price books in the basement, together with stationery, wrapping paper, cassettes for children, cards and Beatrix Potter merchandise. An attractive marble and brass spiral staircase leads down from the centre of the ground floor into the basement. It is echoed by a round hole in the ceiling forming a gallery for those upstairs. A range of general subjects in hard and paper covers are stocked here. They open till 10:00p.m. during the Christmas period.

Non-book material: bookmarks, and see above

Bookcase Too   *(Warren Street)*
121-122 Tottenham Court Road W1
387-9212

M–F 9:00–6:30   Sat 10:00–6:00

This is a small general bookshop selling new and remaindered titles in both hard and paper. Some of their reduced stock is bought in from unwanted review copies and warehouse soiled stock. Prices vary from 50p to £50. Like its sister shops it is owned by Roy Bloom who himself specializes in remainders, and supplies the shops with exclusive stock from his own warehouse.

Services: special order, mail order

Books Etc.   *(Goodge Street)*
222 Tottenham Court Road W1
636-3270

M–Sat 9:00–6:30   Th 9:00–7:00

This is one of the smaller branches of the Books Etc. chain, stocking a general array of paperbacks and new hardbacks. Situated adjacent to the many video, computer and electronic hardware shops on Tottenham Court Road, it also naturally has a good selection of related titles.

Non-book material: calendars and diaries
Services: special order

Boots the Chemists   *(Oxford Circus)*
182 Regent Street W1
734-4934

M–Sat 9:00–5:30   Th 9:00–6:30

The book department here is on the first floor, near the stationery. It is a small section, with popular paperbacks and a few hardbacks.

Non-book material: department store

Bush Books   *(Shepherd's Bush)*
113 Shepherd's Bush Centre
Shepherd's Bush W12
749-7652

M–F 10:00–6:00   Sat 10:00–5:00

ground floor:
children's / fiction / humour / travel

basement:
antiques and collecting / architecture / art / bargain books / biography / business and law / computer books / cookery / crafts / drama / economics / education / feminism / film / gardening / health / history / Irish studies / media / militaria / motoring / music / mythology / natural history / occult / philosophy / photography / poetry / politics / psychology / reference / religion / science / sociology / sport / transport

Bush Books is in the centre of the shopping centre and is a bright, open shop. It stocks a general range of new books, including recent bestsellers. There is a separate record department in the basement. Take advantage of your visit and pop into the Italian coffee shop next door for the best home-made croissants in London.

Non-book material: book and gift tags, cards, magazines (literary and radical), records (classical and jazz), wrapping-paper
Services: special order

Elgin Books   *(Ladbroke Grove)*
6 Elgin Crescent W11
229-2186

Tue–Sat 10:00–6:00

ground floor:
art / biography / classics / fiction / history / literature / photography /
poetry / politics / reference / travel guides

basement:
children's books / cookery / feminism / history / natural history /
reference / science fiction / theatre / thrillers / travel guides

Elgin Books is a distinctive looking bookshop just off the
Portobello Road. On the ground floor, amid wall-to-wall
carpeting and dark wood, is a fine selection of current hardcover
and paperback fiction, literature and poetry with recent book
reviews and news conveniently pinned up on a bulletin board on
one wall. Downstairs is a spacious basement full of children's
books with a table and chairs in which adults and kids can sit to
read. This is one of the nicest small bookshops in London.

Services: mail order, special order

D.H. Evans   *(Bond Street)*
318 Oxford Street W1
629-8800

M–S 9:30–6:00   Th 9:30–8:00

On the fourth floor of D.H. Evans the books section includes
children's books, paperback fiction, popular reference books and
maps and guides.

Non-book material: department store

Christopher Foss   *(Baker Street)*
120 Baker Street W1
935-9364

M–F 9:00–6:00   Sat 10:00–5:00

art / astrology / biography / business / child care / children's books / classics / cookery / crime and adventure / economics / fiction / film / games / health and medicine / history / humour / languages / literature / music / natural history / philosophy / photography / plays / poetry / psychology / reference / religion / science fiction / sociology / travel guides

For a small shop Christopher Foss has a surprisingly good range of subjects packed onto the shelves, together with a wide variety of postcards and greetings cards.

Non-book material: stationery
Services: special order

Fountain Books   *(Turnham Green)*
229 Chiswick High Road W4
994-9500

M–F 9:30–6:00   Sat 9:30–5:30

ground floor:
biography / children's / classics / fiction / foreign literature / humour / science fiction / travel

basement:
art / computers / cookery / design / DIY / drama / feminism / film / gardening / health / history / leisure / music / natural history / philosophy / poetry / politics / psychology / reference / religion / sociology / study aids / travel guides

This is a bright and modern local bookshop selling a good range of titles in the above subject areas.

Non-book material: cards, wrapping paper, calendars, diaries
Services: special order, mail order
Catalogue: health/psychology list and other special subject lists

Claude Gill Books   *(Tottenham Court Road)*
19–23 Oxford Street W1
734-5340

M–Sat 9:30–8:00

antiques / art / biography / business and marketing / children's books / classics / computer / cookery / crime / fiction / film / gardening / health / history / humour / literature / music / natural history / Penguin / philosophy / photography / plays / poetry / reference / science fiction / social sciences / teach yourself / transport / travel guides / women's interests

Along with a wide range of current fiction and non-fiction, this Claude Gill shop has a particularly good selection of poetry titles (they have a poet working in the shop) and social sciences. About 12% of the stock is remaindered books, while the rest of the books are current general hardcover and paperback titles. This is the largest of the Claude Gill bookshops, which are all part of the Hatchard Group.

Non-book material: cards, stationery

Claude Gill Books   *(Bond Street)*
10-12 James Street W1
629-4773

M–F 9:30–8:00   Sat 9:30–8:00

antiques / art / astrology / beauty / biography / children's books / cinema / classics / cookery / crafts / crime / fiction / gardening / health / humour / music / natural history / non-fiction / Penguin / photography / poetry / reference / science fiction / sport / TV, film / transport / travel guides

This branch of Claude Gill carries a general range of new titles, particularly paperback fiction, but also has bargain tables of remaindered hardback books. Being just off Oxford Street and the only bookshop for quite a long way they do extremely well and are particularly busy at Christmas.

Non-book material: cards
Services: special order
Catalogue: Spring and Autumn selections

Claude Gill Books   *(Piccadilly Circus)*
213 Piccadilly W1
734-0681

M–Sun 10:00–7:00

ground floor:
biography / classics / crime / fiction / humour / literature /
non-fiction / occult / Pelican, Penguin / science fiction / teach
yourself / travel guides

basement:
antiques / art / children's books / cookery / crafts / DIY / film /
gardening / health / music / natural history / photography / plays /
poetry / sex / sports and games / transport

This Claude Gill branch has a broad range of new books, and in
the spacious basement is a good number of remaindered books at
bargain prices.

Non-book material: cards

Claude Gill   *(Ealing Broadway)*
64 Ealing Broadway Centre
The Broadway W5
840-5905

M–Sat 9:30–6:00

ground:
biography / children's / cinema / classics / DIY / fiction / humour /
music / plays / poetry / science fiction / travel

basement:
architecture / art / astronomy / cookery / crafts / gardening / health /
natural history / reference / religion / sport and games / study aids /
transport

This is the best bookshop in Ealing, being large, attractive,
well-stocked and well-staffed. It sells both hard and paperbacks,
some remainder books as well as new titles on both floors. There is
a good travel section and the children's department downstairs is
fun, with little tables and chairs for dedicated young readers.

Non-book material: cards, diaries, stationery, wrapping-paper
Services: mail order (through Hatchards at Piccadilly), special
order
Catalogue: Spring and Autumn selections

Green's Bookshop   *(Baker Street)*
17 Marylebone High Street W1
935-7227

M–F 9:00–6:00   Sat 9:00–1:30

children's books / current affairs / feminism / fiction / languages /
reference / travel

Downstairs from the newsagents is a bookshop covering a wide
range of subjects including the latest fiction publications and a
section for Virago books. Helpful advice is always on hand.

Non-book material: newsagents
Services: special order, photographic developing and printing

Hammick's Bookshop Ltd   *(Hammersmith)*
Unit 9 King's Mall
King Street W6
741-2467

M–Sat 9:00–5:30

architecture / art / biography / childcare and pregnancy / children's /
commerce / cookery / fiction / gardening / history / mysticism /
natural history / performing arts / social sciences / sports and
hobbies / travel

This is a well laid out family bookshop, with all general-interest
subjects covered.

Non-book material: cards, calendars, diaries, talking books,
wrapping-paper
Services: special order, post-a-book

Hatchards   *(Piccadilly Circus)*
187 Piccadilly W1
439-9921   437-3924 (24 hours)

M–F 9:00–5:30   Sat 9:00–5:00

basement: paperbacks
biography / business / classics / cookery / crime / drama / fiction /
history / humour / literature / music / nature and countryside /
poetry / politics / psychology / science fiction / social sciences

ground floor:
astrology / astronomy / biography / business / energy / fiction / history / humour / language / military / naval / occult / politics / reference / travel guides

first floor:
antiques / architecture / art / book-binding / calligraphy / cookery / costumes / crafts / gardening / natural history / pets / sports and games / textiles

second floor:
children's books / cinema / classics / fine bindings / literature / music plays / poetry / theatre

Hatchards on Piccadilly is one of London's largest and most respected booksellers. It is one of only a few bookshops to have the honour of the title 'by appointment to Her Majesty the Queen'. It is owned by the Collins group and now has several sister shops in London and throughout the UK. A few doors down from Fortnum & Mason, it preserves a similar air of grace and quality both in design and service. The expansion into the neighbouring premises has greatly increased the stock in some departments, especially the travel and paperback sections. The children's section is also worthy of note. The staff throughout are helpful and knowledgeable. The shop's position and reputation make it a favourite for signing sessions by famous authors.

Services: binding, mail order, picture-framing, second-hand search service, special order
Catalogue: Spring and Autumn catalogues, monthly review, gardening and art catalogues

G. Heywood Hill Ltd   *(Green Park)*
10 Curzon Street W1
629-0647

M–F 9:00–5:30   Sat 9:00–12:30

antiques / architecture / art / biography / children's books / classics / cookery / crafts / design / fiction / graphics / history / humanities / jewellery / literature / music / natural history / philosophy / porcelain / pottery / stage design / travel

Heywood Hill have a lovely combination of new, out-of-print and antiquarian books on the arts and humanities. The shop's holdings are particularly strong in fine art, 19th-century English literature, modern first editions and children's books (which take up most of the basement). The staff are knowledgeable, helpful and extremely industrious but the shop maintains an atmosphere from the era of the genteel 'gentlemanly booksellers'.

Services: mail order, special order, search service for out-of-print and antiquarian, valuations
Catalogue: new book lists

Liberty and Co. *(Oxford Circus)*
210 Regent Street W1
734-1234

M–Sat 9:30–6:00   Th 9:30–7:00

art / biography / children's books / classics / collecting / cookery / fiction / gardening / history / hobbies / literature / music / natural history / poetry / Reader's Digest books / travel guides

The small book department on the ground floor at Liberty has, a general selection of new best-selling fiction and literature, illustrated books about Great Britain and the arts, and a section of children's books.

Non-book material: department store
Services: mail order, special order

Mandarin Books *(Notting Hill Gate)*
22 Notting Hill Gate W11
229-0327

M–F 10:00–6:30   Sat 10:00–6:00

art / biography / childbirth / cookery / drama / education / energy / environment / family / fiction / games / history / literary criticism / literature / music / natural history / occult / philosophy / poetry / politics / psychology / reference / religion / science fiction

While you can find the newest, best-selling hardcover and paperback books at Mandarin, the shop tends to carry less 'popular', somewhat more obscure titles in the range of subjects outlined above. The section on education is strong, with a well-chosen range of both practical and theoretical titles. Books about energy and environmental issues, usually found only in large general bookshops, are available at Mandarin, despite the shop's small space. Indeed, all manner of good fiction and non-fiction are packed onto the shelves.

Services: mail order, special order

John Menzies Ltd   *(Paddington)*
Paddington Concourse
Paddington Station W2
723-3153

M–Sun 7:00a.m.–10:00p.m.

The book stock in Paddington Station is surprisingly large. There is a children's section including revision aids, a bargain basement selection with a tendency towards gardening books, and the usual selection of general reference books. The fiction is divided by publisher but also includes the statutory bestsellers. There is a particularly good section on the railway, appropriately enough for the home of Brunel's Great Western Railway.

Non-book material: stationery

The Modern Book Co.   *(Edgware Road)*
19–21 Praed Street W2
402-9176

M–F 9:00–5:30   Sat 9:00–1:00

accounting / art / building / communications / computers / cookery / economics / electronics / engineering / fiction / gardening / hi-fi and audio / hydraulics / management / mathematics / medical / microprocessors / natural history / non-fiction / nursing / Pelican, Penguin / photography / radio and TV / reference / sport / structures / technical / transport / travel guides

This spacious shop specializes in new technical and medical books, and also carries general fiction and non-fiction. The shop is particularly proud of its selection of books on radio and TV, computers, electronics, hi-fi and audio equipment and microprocessors. In these technical areas, The Modern Book Co.

stocks the latest US, as well as UK publications. I have found no other shop in London with as wide a range of technical books on modern electronic equipment.

Services: mail order, special order
Catalogue: numerous lists in specialized areas

Mowbray's Bookshop   *(Oxford Circus)*
28 Margaret Street W1
580-2812

M–F 9:00–5:30   Th 9:00–6:00 (November and December M–F 9:00–6:00   Th 9:00–7:00   Sat 11:00–4:00)

lower ground floor: paperbacks
crime / fiction / literature / music and performing arts / Penguin, Pelican / science fiction / sports and pastimes

ground floor:
antiques / archaeology / art / biography / business / classics / cookery / crafts / drawing and painting / fiction / film / gardening / health / history / humanities / literature / music / natural history / photography / plays / poetry / printing / publishing / reference / secretarial / sports and pastimes / theatre / travel guides / yoga

gallery:
bible / church requisites / fine bindings / hymn and song books / prayer books / records / second-hand books / theology

first floor:
biography / children's books / church history / commentaries / concordances / confirmation / dictionaries / lexicons / Mowbray paperbacks / prayer / religion / saints / sermons / spiritual reading / theology

Mowbray's is a two-part shop. Half is a general bookshop with good coverage of the arts, humanities and children's books, while the gallery and first floor house books on the shop's speciality, religion and theology.

Non-book material: cards, church stationery, records, religious requisites
Services: mail order, special order (antiquarian, religion and theology second-hand books by post only)
Catalogue: Mowbray's publications, Christmas books
Publications: Mowbray publishes religious and theological books

Paperbacks Centre   *(Goodge Street)*
28 Charlotte Street W1
636-3532

M–F 10:00–6:00   Sat 10:00–5:00

first room:
biography / children's books / classics / cookery / fiction / health / humour / literary criticism / literature / Penguin / plays / poetry / reference / science fiction

second room:
Africa and Caribbean / China / feminist fiction and non-fiction / labour history / Latin America / literary criticism / Marxism / philosophy / politics / psychology / sciences / sociology

This is one of three shops owned by the socialist New Park Publishers. General hardcover and paperback titles are at the front of the shop, while books in the shop's speciality, left-wing and socialist literature, can be found in the rear of the shop. They have a good selection of women's titles and a second-hand social history section. A good range of magazines and newspapers on the arts, literature and radical politics is also available.

Non-book material: cards
Services: mail order, special order

Penguin at Liberty's   *(Oxford Circus)*
210 Regent Street W1
734-1234

M–Sat 9:30–6:00   Th 9:30–7:00

This is the paperback bookshop at Liberty's, just round the corner from their own, chiefly hardback, book department. The small shop is brimming with titles on all subjects usual in a general bookshop and each section is clearly marked. Their stock is about 40% Penguin titles, 60% other publishers'.

Non-book material: postcards
Services: special order
Catalogue: Christmas

Quartet Bookshop   *(Oxford Circus)*
45/46 Poland Street W1
437-1019

M–F 10:00–6:00   Th 10:00–7:00 (open Sat at Christmas)

art / biography / Robin Clark Publications / classics / cookery /
fiction / film / jazz / literary / biography / literature / Middle East /
non-fiction / Penguin / photography / poetry / Quartet Books /
theatre / travel / USSR / Virago / Women's Press

Quartet is a general bookshop with a selection of new
middle-of-the-road fiction and non-fiction. They stock a full range
of Quartet, Robin Clark and The Women's Press publications, and
these provide interesting titles in literature, jazz and sexual
politics – to name a few of the diverse subject areas. There is also a
limited range of arts and literary magazines.

Non-book material: cards, wrapping-paper
Services: mail order, special order
Catalogue: Quartet Books, Robin Clark, Women's Press
Publications: The shop is owned by Quartet Books, which also
owns Robin Clark, The Women's Press and *Literary Review*.

Red and Green Books   *(Acton Town)*
144 Churchfield Road W3
992-6029

Tue–Sat 10:00–6:00

art / biography / children's books / classics / commerce / cookery /
economics / education / environment / feminism / fiction / history /
mathematics / Open University / peace/ plays / poetry / politics /
science and technology / social studies / statistics / Third World

This is a workers' co-operative bookshop. They have special
sections on, among other things, feminism, peace, environment
and politics, and their children's books are multi-cultural and
non-sexist. At weekends they also trade at the Waterman's Arts
Centre in Brentford, and if you want information about events
and services in the community there is a noticeboard in the shop.

Non-book material: greetings cards, postcards, stationery
Services: bookstalls at community events, special order

Riverside Studios Bookshop   *(Hammersmith)*
Crisp Road W6
741-2251

M–Sun 12:00–8:00

art / biography / children's books / classics / cookery / dance / drama / feminism / film / literary criticism / literature / music / Gay Men's Press, OUP, Panther, Penguin, Quartet, Virago, Women's Press / performing arts / philosophy / poetry / visual arts

Although the shop is small in size, and despite recent difficulties, Riverside Studios continues to keep an appealing and selective stock of mostly paperback titles. Contemporary fiction, titles on feminism and children's books comprise the primary sections in their stock, alongside a range of titles on the performing arts – titles which vary to complement the theatre or dance programmes on offer at the studio. A large range of literary, political and arts magazines are also available.

In addition to the bookshop, Riverside operates two studios where there are always film series or modern dance, theatre or ballet companies performing. The separate art gallery has frequent exhibitions and there is a restaurant and bar in which to relax.

Non-book material: cards, posters for events at Riverside Studios
Services: mail order, special order
Publications: a series of Riverside Interviews with people such as Allen Ginsberg have been published by the Studios

Selfridges   *(Bond Street/Marble Arch)*
400 Oxford Street W1
629-1234

Spring: M–Sat 9:00–5:30   Th 9:00–7:00
Summer: M–Sat 9:00–6:00   Th 9:00–7:30
Christmas: M–F 9:00–5:30   Th 9:00–8:00   Sat 9:00–6:00

antiques / art / BBC publications / biography / children's books / classics / cookery / crafts / crime and thrillers / drama / fiction / film / gardening / historical romance / history / humour / Ladybird / medicine and health / music / natural history / occult and horror / poetry / reference / religion / romance / science fiction / sport and pastimes / theatre / transport / TV / war

Selfridges book department on the first floor carries a general range of new books, with a large selection devoted to children's fiction, picture books, crafts, etc., and is especially useful in the almost bookless Oxford Street. In the same department all manner of religious artefacts are also sold.

Non-book material: department store
Services: mail order, special order

W.H. Smith   *(Chiswick Park)*
370 Chiswick High Road W4
995-9427

M–Sat 8:30–6:00   Tue 9:30–6:00 (8:30 for news)

A respectable book department in the branch of W.H. Smith stocks the predictable range of subjects, including children's books and a section of new hardback fiction.

Non-book material: stationery, cards, paper, news, magazines
Services: special order, post-a-book, tokens
Catalogue: *Bookcase* review of books twice yearly

W.H. Smith   *(Ealing Broadway)*
21-23 The Broadway W5
567-1471

M–Sat 9:00–6:00   Th 9:00–7:00

The entire top floor of this shop is devoted to the book department and they stock a very wide range in all the usual subjects. The paperbacks are on display at the entrance to the department and there is also a selection of new hardback fiction.

Non-book material: stationery, cards, paper, news, magazines
Services: special order, post-a-book, tokens
Catalogue: *Bookcase* review of books twice yearly

W.H. Smith   *(Hammersmith)*
Kings Mall
King Street W6
748-2218

M–Sat 9:00–6:00

This is one of the larger book departments and they cover a wide range of subjects, with a particularly good children's section. The new titles in hardback are displayed at the front of the shop and the paperback fiction is classified by both subject and author. The children's books are divided up according to age groups, just one section in this comprehensive department.

Non-book material: stationery, cards, paper, news, magazines
Services: special order, post-a-book (home and abroad), tokens
Catalogue: *Bookcase* review of books twice yearly

W.H. Smith   *(High Street Kensington)*
132-136 Kensington High Street W8
937-0326

M–Sat 9:00–6:30   Th 9:00–7:00

A substantial book department is to be found on the basement floor of this branch of WHS. The stationery, magazines, etc., are all on the first floor. The subjects covered are similar to all other bookholding branches, but the range within each subject is greater and the bookshop manager is extremely helpful and knowledgeable should you need guidance.

Non-book material: see above
Services: special order, post-a-book, tokens
Catalogue: *Bookcase* review of books twice a year

W.H. Smith   *(Notting Hill Gate)*
92 Notting Hill Gate W11
727-9261

M–F 9:00–6:30   Sat 9:00–6:00

This is one of the branches with quite a substantial book department. All the books are on the first floor and there is usually a good window display featuring current bestsellers. A range of general subjects is covered and they stock a fair number of new hardbacks.

Non-book material: records, stationery, news on ground floor
Services: special order, vouchers/tokens, post-a-book
Catalogue: *Bookcase* review of books twice a year

W.H. Smith   *(Ealing Broadway)*
64 The Broadway W13
579-3461

M–Sat 9:00–6:00

This modest branch of W.H. Smith gives over a third of its floor space to the book department and the usual range of subjects are in stock, with a limited reference section and more emphasis on fiction, including children's books.

Non-book material: stationery, cards, paper, news, magazines
Services: special order, post-a-book, tokens
Catalogue: *Bookcase* review of books twice yearly

Waterstone's   *(Piccadilly Circus)*
88 Regent Street W1
734-0713/4

M–F 9:30–9:00   Sat 10:00–7:00   Sun 12:30–7:00

ground floor:
antiques / art and architecture / biography and memoirs / classics / crafts / dictionaries / fiction / humour / languages / literary criticism / literature / photography / poetry / theatre / travel guides / travel literature

basement:
business and economics / children's / computers / cookery / gardening / health / history / music / natural history / occult / philosophy / political science / psychology / reference / religions / sports and games

At the Piccadilly Circus end of Regent Street, Waterstone's attracts a lot of business from lunchtime shoppers, browsing tourists, and EFL students. Its coverage of the humanities is comprehensive, with a particularly good paperback fiction section. Also good is the EFL department. The staff know their particular departments well and the shop is open long hours, including Sundays.

Non-book material: maps, postcards
Services: mail order, search service for account holders, Waterstone's credit card which can be used in all branches and by telephone

Catalogue: free annual catalogue
Publications: literary diary, postcards

Waterstone's   *(High Street Kensington)*
193 Kensington High Street W8
937-8432/3

M–F 9:30a.m.–10:30p.m.   Sat 9:30–7:30   Sun 12:00–7:00

basement:
business and economics / children's books / computer science /
drama / history / performing arts / poetry / politics / psychology /
reference / religion and philosophy / sport

ground floor:
biography and memoirs / fiction / literature / travel

first floor:
antiques / art and architecture (new and second-hand) / beauty /
collecting / cookery / crafts / DIY / gardening / health / natural
history

Waterstone's chain of bookstores is the most important
development of the London retail book trade in recent years. Tim
Waterstone has put range, imagination and good service back into
heavyweight bookselling. Each of his stores is an oasis of good
layout, informed help and abundant stock. The managers are
accessible, the staff are friendly and with an apparent sense of
identification with their work. A distinctive feature of the chain is
the range of services it offers, especially to account customers.
Those who hold a charge account credit card can order books by
telephone or post, have them gift-wrapped (as can the ordinary
customer) and packed off worldwide. They are invited to
book-signings and other special events, and can make use of the
firm's search facility for out-of-print books.
   Kensington is, in fact, the largest of the Waterstone's in
London, with particularly stong art and literature departments.
The shelves of this branch hold about 50,000 titles, and the
warehouse stock is moving towards half a million. They have an
enviable expanse of window on two sides of the shop to mount
some really good displays.

Non-book material: maps, literary magazines, postcards
Services: mail order, and see above
Catalogue: free annual catalogue
Publications: literary diary, postcards

Speciality Bookshops

Academy Bookclub   *(Oxford Circus)*
51 Beak Street W1
437-2131/2

M–F 9:30–6:00

This is a literary book club with a showroom in Soho. Membership, currently running at 700, is free on the understanding that one buys at least four books a year at a discount of 25% or more on the published price. There is a back list of 140 titles and this covers a wide range of literature, with a particular interest in literary biographies.

Services: quarterly mail-out with between ten and twelve new titles

Academy Bookshop   *(High Street Kensington)*
7 Holland Street W8
937-6996

M–Sat 9:30–6:00

antiques and collecting / art deco / art history and theory / art nouveau / artists' monographs / calligraphy and printing / carpets and rugs / ceramics / colour theory / country crafts and book binding / design manuals / design and pattern source books / early photography / ethnic crafts / furniture / gardens / glass / glassmaking / illustrations / illustrators and monographs / interior design / landscape design / metal work and jewellery / painting and drawing / paper / photography collections / photography criticisms and history / photography monographs / photography techniques / posters and postcards / pottery / prints and print-making / sculpture / silver / textiles / wood

The Academy Bookshop is run in tandem with the London Art Bookshop, but here the new books are on all aspects of fine and applied arts. A particularly rich harvest of books on photography can be found here, but even in the more specialized fields of carpets, furniture, patterns and textiles, they stock a good range of titles. As in the London Art Bookshop, the Academy Bookshop is distinguished by the extraordinary range and depth of its holdings.

Services: mail order, special order
Catalogue: Academy Editions list
Publications: Academy Editions publishes books in the fields of architecture and the arts

Al-Majid Bookshop
18-24 Westbourne Grove W2
727-6199

M–Sat 10:00–7:00

This small bookshop sells books concerning the current affairs of Middle Eastern countries, including coverage of the Iraq-Iran war, the Gulf, and matters of Islam.

Services: mail order, special order
Catalogue: booklist available

Al Saqi Books   *(Queensway)*
26 Westbourne Grove W2
229-8543

M–Sat 10:00–6:00

academic texts / art / biography / business / children's books / culture and civilization / economics / education / fiction / history / linguistics / literature / music / philosophy / poetry / politics / reference / religion / science / sociology / technical

The emergence and success of Al Saqi reflects the interest and growth of the Middle Eastern population in London. With the exception of language teaching and English language titles, relevant to the Middle East, all the books here are in Arabic languages. New, second-hand and antiquarian books are sold and the shop prides itself on a comprehensive coverage of subject areas for the interests of a diverse clientele. A Middle East centre is being constructed in the building in which Al Saqi is located, due to be completed in 1987.

Services: mail order, special order
Catalogue: one catalogue per year, with general supplements
Publications: Al Saqi books publishes books on the history, sociology, arts, literature and politics of the Arab world as well as books teaching the Arabic language

Atoz Book Centre   *(Piccadilly Circus)*
3 Macclesfield Street W1
734-4142

M–Sat 11:00–6:00

This is a relatively small shop which, none the less, carries a complete range of new books (in English and Chinese) on all aspects and forms of martial arts for beginner and black belt. The majority of these are imported from Japan, the US and Hong Kong.

Non-book material: martial arts equipment
Services: mail order, special order, wholesale and retail
Catalogue: bi-annual comprehensive list

Automobile Association Bookshop   *(Leicester Square)*
Fanum House
5 New Coventry Street W1
839-4355

M–F 9:00–5:00   Sat 9:00–12:30

The bookshop in the A.A. head office has a large selection of atlases, guides and maps as well as some general books on the English countryside and related subjects.

Publications: A.A. maps and guides

Automobile Association   *(Hammersmith)*
24 King Street W6
748-0444/0555

M–F 9:00–5:00   Sat 9:00–4:00

There is a small section within the A.A. insurance offices that stocks the standard maps and guides for motorists and tourists.

Publications: A.A. maps and guides, *Drive* publications

The BBC Bookshop   *(Baker Street)*
35 Marylebone High Street W1
580-5577

M–F 9:30–5:30   Sat 9:30–1:00

architecture / art / children's books / cookery and nutrition / crafts and hobbies / drama / education and literacy / engineering / gardening / health and welfare / languages / music / natural history and environment / politics and economics / religion / science

This is the main BBC Bookshop, selling general BBC merchandise and books. BBC publications cover a wide range of subjects, including educational material and books derived from television series. There are other shops at:

BBC Broadcasting House   *(Oxford Circus)*
Portland Place W1
580-5577

M–F 9:30–5:15

BBC World   *(Aldwych)*
Bush House
Strand WC2
240-3456

M–F 9:30–6:00

BBC Television Centre   *(White City)*
Wood Lane W12
743-8000

M–F 9:30–5:30

Books for Cooks   *(Ladbroke Grove)*
4 Blenheim Crescent W11
221-1992

M–Sat 9:30–6:00

This shop is unique in that it specializes solely in books on cooking. Just off the Portobello Road, it is a pleasant shop to browse in with its terracotta-tiled floor, sofa and brightly-lit shelves. There is also a kitchen area and breakfast bar at the rear of the shop which are ideal for the cooking demonstrations and book launches which often take place here. Every conceivable aspect of food and drink is covered and there is a fine collection of second-hand and unusual cookery books. You might even bump into your local chef searching for a particular title. There is also a room upstairs which is used to host press launches, dinners and conferences.

Services: mail order, special order, book binding

Books on Sport   *(Piccadilly Circus)*
3rd Floor Lillywhites Ltd
Piccadilly Circus W1
930-3181

M–Sat 9:30–6:00   Th 9:30–7:00

cricket / equestrian / fishing / fitness / football / golf / racket games / rugby / skiing

This bookshop is actually a concession of Pipeline wholesalers within the Lillywhites store. Their sports books cover a wide range beyond those mentioned above, including good selections on windsurfing, croquet, martial arts and weightlifting. In the appropriate season they have among the best choice of skiing books on offer in London – understandably good business considering that practically the whole of the third floor is devoted to skiing clothes and equipment during that period.

Non-book material: videos, calendars
Services: special order, mail order

The Boosey and Hawkes Music Shop   *(Oxford Circus)*
295 Regent Street W1
580-2060

M–F 9:00–5:00   Sat 9:00–1:00

biography / counterpoint / dictionaries / harmony / musical instruments and teaching / opera libretti / popular music / theory

This shop is devoted to sheet music, musical scores and songbooks (including educational songbooks for children), in both classical and popular music. There is a limited selection of mainly hardbook books about composers, conductors, theory and music analysis, and a few specialized music journals are available.

Services: mail order
Publications: Boosey and Hawkes publishes sheet music and allied music books

The Bournemouth English Book Centre   *(Green Park)*
(International House Bookshop)
106 Piccadilly W1
493-5226

M–F 10:00–6:00 (closed 1:30–2:30)

A large and specialized range of English language teaching books for students and teachers. There is a teacher in charge of the shop, qualified to give advice to the customers.

Non-book material: English language cassettes
Services: mail order conducted through the head office in Bournemouth
Catalogue: a complete book of English language teaching materials is available

Cambridge House   *(Oxford Circus)*
English Language Bookshop
28 Market Place W1
242-5577

M–F 10:00–6:00

This is a large language bookshop with textbooks and teaching guides for both students and teachers concerned with the study of English as a foreign language.

Non-book material: audio cassettes, computer software, videos
Services: mail order, educational supply

The Catholic Marriage Advisory Council Bookroom
(Holland Park)

15 Lansdowne Road W11
727-0141

M–F 9:30–5:00

The bookroom at the Catholic Marriage Advisory Council carries new books on the subjects of the family, marriage, family counselling, child raising, psychology, sociology, sex and sex education. Despite this being run by a Catholic organization, the titles in the bookroom have less to do with religion than with the psychology of human sexual and social behaviour.

Non-book material: book marks, posters
Services: mail order
Catalogue: complete book list
Publications: the CMAC publishes booklets and pamphlets on marriage and the family

Chappell
(Bond Street)

50 New Bond Street W1
491-2777

M–F 9:30–6:00   Sat 9:30–5:00

ballads / ballet / biography / dictionaries / history / hymns / instruments / jazz / opera / rock

Chappell have a selection of new books about music and dance covering the categories listed above. They are however best known for their huge selection of classical and popular sheet music – they pride themselves on having the largest selection in London. They also sell musical instruments and hi-fi and electronic equipment, with a particularly fine range of pianos.

229

Non-book material: see above
Services: mail order, special order, same day sheet music mail order
Publications: Chappell publishes books about music

The Chimes Music Shop   *(Baker Street)*
65 Marylebone High Street W1
935-1587

M–F 9:00–5:30   Sat 9:00–2:00

biography / composition / criticism and analysis / dance / dictionaries / harmony / history / instruments / music notation / music reading / opera / orchestration / sight reading and singing / song / teaching / theory

The Chimes Music Shop has one of the most diverse stocks of new music books in London. They cater to all levels of ability and interest in music and instruments, carrying everything from elementary teaching guides to specialized texts.

Non-book material: records, scores, sheet music, song books, violin and guitar accessories, cassettes, gifts related to music
Services: mail order, special order

Christian Books and Music   *(Notting Hill Gate)*
Kensington Temple
Kensington Park Road W11
727-8684

M–F 10:00–5:30   W 10:00–7:00   Sat 10:00–4:00

As its name suggests, this shop stocks Christian literature of all kinds – popular Christian fiction, bibles, commentaries and guides for students of Christianity.

Non-book material: cassettes and records

The Craftsmen Potters Shop   *(Oxford Circus)*
William Blake House
7 Marshall Street W1
437-7605

M–Sat 10:00–5:30

ceramic techniques / Chinese ceramics / clays / glazes / health and safety / history / kilns / porcelain / pottery / raku / stoneware

This spacious shop, in a corner of the modern building which houses The Craftsmen Potters Association, is primarily a display space for members' work. There is a selection of new books on all aspects of applied ceramics and pottery, as well as the history of ceramics, pottery, porcelain and stoneware around the world. There are also ceramics magazines and exhibition catalogues.

Non-book material: see above
Services: mail order (books and pottery tools), special order
Catalogue: book list regularly
Publications: The Craftsmen Potters Association publishes bi-monthly, *Ceramic Review*; an illustrated directory of members' work, *Potters*; and *The Ceramic Review Book of Glaze Recipes*

Dar Al Dawa Bookshop   *(Bayswater)*
32 Hereford Road W2
221-6256

M–Sat 9:00–7:00

children's books / education / history / linguistics / politics / religion

This shop specializes in issues concerning the Muslim world. The stock ranges from Middle Eastern politics to a section of children's books in Arabic. The language department has books in English and Arabic, for students of both languages. Currently it is works in Arabic that make up the majority of the stock, but the owner is planning to expand the English section.

Non-book material: educational cassettes, music cassettes of children's songs from Kuwait, Islamic gifts including a computer watch which alerts its owner to the hours of prayer, videos
Services: mail order; educational supply; distributors of magazines published in this country, Egypt and Kuwait.
Catalogue: comprehensive catalogue available

The David & Charles Bookshop   *(Baker Street)*
36 Chiltern Street W1
486-6959

M–F 9:30–5:30   Sat 10:00–1:00

ground floor: general

basement: railway transport

Owned by the Devon publisher of the same name, this is basically a general bookshop, but it is particularly well-known for its comprehensive section on railways and other methods of transport.

Non-book material: railway posters, prints, videos
Services: mail order, special order
Catalogue: complete railway catalogue

The Dawn Horse Bookshop   *(Oxford Circus)*
28a Poland Street W1
734-4219

M–Sat 10:00–6:00   Th 10:00–9:30

homeopathy / macrobiotics / mystical teachings / saints / spiritual teachers / yoga

The umbrella term for the wide variety of spiritual life covered in The Dawn Horse Bookshop is New Age Studies. The books are organized according to the seven stages of life. The first three foundation stages, from childhood through puberty to young adulthood, include studies on the physical, emotional, sexual and mental needs by thinkers like Steiner. The subjects covered in the remaining stages of human development include the mystics, yogis, Tibetans and Zen. This shop is part of an international chain and the only one of its kind in Europe.

Non-book material: candles, cards, incense, New Age music, oils, wrapping-paper
Services: mail order for European sales; lunch time video presentations; film series on the great teachers in the hall below the bookshop

Early Learning Centre   *(High Street Kensington)*
225 Kensington High Street W8
937-0419

M–Sat 9:00–6:00   Th 9:00–8:00

The centre specializes in books and toys for children from six months up to ten years. In the early years the emphasis is on manipulative skills, music and activity. The books are largely aimed at children from three to seven years when reading and writing, numbers, creative play, puzzles and games are all involved in the learning process.

Non-book material: toys
Services: mail order
Catalogue: comprehensive catalogue for the whole shop

Esperanto Centre   *(Holland Park)*
140 Holland Park Avenue W11
727-7821

M–F 9:30–6:00

Located in the administration offices of The British Esperanto Association, this is the only Esperanto bookshop in Britain. Three hundred current titles are in stock, including Esperanto language teaching books, and magazines and journals are available as well. Approximately 50% of the titles are in technical subject areas (e.g., construction and the sciences) while the other half of the stock is in the field of the humanities. Original literature in Esperanto is available as well as Esperanto works translated into English.

Non-book material: cassettes, records (language and entertainment), insignia, stationery
Services: mail order, special order, reference library
Catalogue: complete list of titles
Publications: *Labrita Esperantisto, Esperanto News* (fortnightly magazines)

European Bookshop   *(Piccadilly Circus)*
4 Regent Place W1
734-5259

M–F 9:30–6:00   Sat 9:30–1:00

art / children's books / classics / Classiques Larousse / commerce / cookery / dictionaries / drama / economics / fiction / history / language teaching and course books / literature / Livres de Poche / philosophy / politics / psychology / science / travel guides

This shop just behind Regent Street sells only books to do with Europe and its languages. There is a very large stock of French books and guides, an excellent range of German books and smaller sections of Italian and Spanish books. A smattering of other languages is carried too. Educational material, the latest paperback fiction from France and German current affairs magazines may all be found rubbing shoulders companionably. There are two floors.

Non-book material: language teaching materials
Services: mail order, special order
Publications: European Schoolbooks, the associated company, publish a few titles

Family Planning Association Book Centre

(Goodge Street)

27-35 Mortimer Street W1
636-7866

M–Th 9:30–5:00   F 9:30–4:30

abortion / birth control / breast feeding / children's information books / fertility / history / medical / nursing / population control / pregnancy and childbirth / psychology / sex and marriage / sex education / sex technique / sociology

As part of the Family Planning Association, the Book Centre stocks new books, leaflets, fact sheets, studies and reports on all aspects of family planning in the UK.

Services: mail order, special order
Catalogue: selected annual list

Foyles Educational Bookshop

(Marble Arch)

37 Upper Berkeley Street W1
262-4699/5310

M–F 9:00–5:30

ground floor:
art / biography / cookery / fiction / gardening / history / languages / miscellaneous / music / natural history / photography / plays / poetry / reference / religion / sport / travel guides / war

basement: children's books:
alphabet and counting / arts and crafts / Batsford books / classics /
encyclopaedias / fiction / geography / history / hymn books /
Ladybird / literature / Macdonald reference / mathematics / music /
readers / theology / transport

text books:
adult education / business / careers / drama / economics / English
grammar / geography / history / language teaching / law and
politics / mathematics / Open University / poetry / psychology /
sciences / sociology / teaching / technical

There is no connection between this shop and Foyles on Charing
Cross Road. The Educational Bookshop carries a stock of general
books on the ground floor, while downstairs is an extensive range
of children's educational material. Also in the basement is a
comprehensive display of books and cassettes in English for
foreign students and the textbooks stocked range from primary to
A-level studies in all subjects.

Non-book material: educational aids
Services: mail order, special order

R.D. Franks Ltd   *(Oxford Circus)*
Kent House
Market Place
Great Titchfield Street W1
636-1244/5/6

M–F 9:00–5:00

This is an appropriate setting for a fashion specialist and Franks
provide the perfect background material to the fashion designers
and textile retailers in this area of London. They have a large range
of fashion books and magazines, pattern books and a section on
fashion history.

Services: mail order, special order
Catalogue: comprehensive catalogue available

French's Theatre Bookshop   *(Warren Street)*
52-56 Fitzroy Street W1
387-4356/9373

M–F 9:30–5:30

audition material / biography / children's theatre / illustrated theatre history / libretti / musical plays / one-act plays / play texts / technical theatre history / vocal scores

French's, London's oldest theatre bookseller, now occupies larger premises where it continues to offer a comprehensive stock and service. Only new books are stocked and these do include titles in the more technical areas, such as stage management, design and lighting. The staff will help to find out whether a title is in print, and the shop carries a useful stock of theatre magazines, both current and back-issues, from the UK and US.

Non-book material: dialect recordings; musical scores; original cast recordings of Broadway and West End musicals and plays; postcards; sound-effects; spoken-word records
Services: mail order; special order; a variety of amateur rights for play productions are handled; musical scores and libretti are for hire
Catalogue: many on specialized subjects
Publications: play texts and audition material are published by Samuel French

Grant & Cutler Ltd   *(Oxford Circus)*
55-57 Great Marlborough Street W1
734-2012

M–F 9:00–5:30   Sat 9:00–1:00

Grant & Cutler is the largest foreign-language bookshop in the country, with one mile of shelving carrying over 100,000 books. They are strong in French, German, Spanish, Portugese, Italian, Dutch and Scandinavian languages. The range of subject areas is varied, including contemporary literature, classics, cinema, history, linguistics, politics, the social sciences and the sciences. They are also specialists in technical dictionaries. New and second-hand titles are sold, and because most of the shop's stock is on the premises mail orders are quickly filled.

Non-book material: cassettes
Services: mail order, special order
Catalogue: for each language, new titles lists are produced two to three times annually; school texts with relevant critical works; lists of technical dictionaries
Publications: Grant & Cutler publish literature, primarily in Spanish, French and German

Grass Roots Storefront   *(Westbourne Park)*
61 Goldborne Road W10
969-0687

M–Sat 9:30–6:30

Africa / Afro-America / architecture / art / black studies / Caribbean / children's books / China / cinema / cookery / economics / education / environment / fiction / history / language teaching / Latin America / literature / music / poetry / politics / race relations / rights / women

As a community-based black bookshop, Grass Roots carries current titles relevant to class and race relations in Britain, as well as fiction and non-fiction by, and about, blacks from around the world. Magazines, newspapers and journals about community politics, Third World issues, individual rights and women's issues are also available, as is a range of children's books and learning material.

Non-book material: African and Caribbean arts and crafts, posters, cards, batiks, maps
Services: mail order, special order
Catalogue: selected catalogue
Publications: Grass Roots publishes a newspaper

G.L. Green   *(Hanger Lane)*
104 Pitshanger Lane W5
997-6454

W–Sat 9:30–5:00

Three rooms of specialist naval and maritime books, largely second-hand and antiquarian with some recent publications. The highly specialized stock also includes magazines and journals.

Services: international mail order
Catalogue: issued every month

Nigel Greenwood Books   *(Green Park/Bond Street)*
4 New Burlington Street W1
434-3797

M–F 10:00–6:00   Sat 10:30–1:30

architecture and design / artists' books / contemporary art
magazines / photography / sculpture / video and performance

Approaching this unassuming residence one would hardly expect
the marvellous range of books on contemporary art to be found in
the basement. Nigel Greenwood encourages browsers but not all
the stock can be fitted on the shelves. It is primarily an art gallery,
and much of its book business is conducted by mail. They publish
lists of titles on all aspects of contemporary art – the particular
focus of the gallery – and recent lists have included titles on
futurism, art and psychoanalysis, experimental theatre and
performance texts, exhibition catalogues and reproductions of
artists' notebooks. A particular interest of Nigel Greenwood is
bookworks, or examples of artists using the book as an artistic
medium. Their books come not only from the UK, but also the
USA, France, Germany, Italy and the Netherlands. Their lists also
feature a wide range of art journals and magazines.

A regular perusal of Nigel Greenwood's book list is enough to
keep contemporary art enthusiasts up-to-date on the people and
movements which are shaping modern art around the word.

Non-book material: postcards by Glen Baxter
Services: mail order, special order
Catalogue: comprehensive lists three times yearly
Publications: Nigel Greenwood Inc. occasionally publishes
material about the artists whose work is shown in the gallery

Hamley's of Regent Street Ltd   *(Oxford Circus)*
188-196 Regent Street W1
734-3161

M–Sat 9:00–5:30   Th 9:00–8:00

art / children's books / crafts / fiction / nature / transport

As you would expect, the largest section in Hamley's book
department is devoted to children's books. They have a large
range aimed at children up to sixteen years and the adults' books
are a sub-division of the same department, with some fiction and a
variety of reference books.

Non-book material: toy shop
Services: mail order
Catalogue: catalogue available for the whole shop

Hudsons Bookshop   *(Ealing Broadway)*
Ealing College of Higher Education
St Mary's Road W5
579-4111 ext. 3255

M–F 9:00–5:00

business / catering / humanities / languages / law / literature

This is the college bookshop with a stock of books ordered by the lecturers for specific courses, but it is open to the general public.

Non-book material: stationery
Services: special order

Japan Centre   *(Piccadilly Circus)*
66-68 Brewer Street W1
439-8035

M–F 10:00–7:00   Sat–Sun 10:00–6:30

art / children's books / dictionaries / economics / hobbies / language / literature / martial arts / politics

The Japan Centre has a huge range of books in Japanese and books in English about all aspects of Japanese life and culture. They stock novels in Japanese and in translation along with a selection of Japanese magazines.

Non-book material: crafts, food store, restaurant, stationery, videos (including martial arts videos)

Japanese Publications Centre   *(Piccadilly Circus)*
5 Warwick Street W1
439-8035

M–F 10:00–7:00   Sat & Sun 10:00–6:30

The majority of books here are imported from Japan, in Japanese, covering all aspects of the country and its history. A few titles on art, history, healing arts, religion, language and the martial arts are in English. Magazines, comics and children's books are available too.

Non-book material: cards, fans, gift items, prints
Services: mail order, special order

Kanoune Ketab Ltd   *(High Street Kensington)*
2a Kensington Church Walk W8
937-5087

M–Sat 9:30–6:00 (closed 12:30–1:30)

art / current affairs / dictionaries / history / literature / philosophy / poetry / reference

This is a Persian language bookshop with some books about Iran in English and a selection of novels in translation.

Non-book material: Iranian prayer cards and Christmas cards
Services: mail order
Catalogue: the catalogue is in Persian

Keltic   *(Notting Hill Gate)*
25 Chepstow Corner
Chepstow Place W2
229-8560/8456

M–F 10:00–5:30   Th 10:00–8:00   Sat 10:00–1:00

adult language courses / commercial English / English as a foreign language / English for specific uses / practice books / primary language course / reading / reading comprehension / reference / secondary language courses / speaking / teachers' manuals / writing

Keltic is a shop specializing in teaching books for English as a foreign language. Students and teachers alike will find a complete range of current titles from the major language text publishers.

Non-book material: cassettes, video-tapes, journals
Services: mail order, special order
Catalogue: selected lists of titles
Publications: *ELT Update*, the complete guide to ELT materials is annually updated

Kimpton's Medical Bookshop   *(Great Portland Street)*
205 Great Portland Street W1
580-6381

M–F 9:00–5:30   Sat 9:30–5:00

acupuncture / anaesthesia / anatomy / biochemistry / cancer / cardiology / dentistry / dermatology / dictionaries / dietetics / ear, nose, throat / embryology / endocrinology / forensic medicine / gastroenterology / geriatrics / haematology / histology / hospitals / immunology / medical genetics / medicine / microbiology / neurology / nursing / nutrition / obstetrics / occupational medicine / ophthalmology / orthopaedics / pathology / paediatrics / pharmacology / physiology / physiotherapy / pregnancy and baby care / psychology and psychiatry / public health / radiology / respiratory medicine / rheumatology / sexology / speech therapy / statistics / surgery / toxicology / tropical medicine / urology and renal / veterinary sciences

As the list shows, a great deal can go wrong with the human and animal body. Kimpton's, one of the leading specialist booksellers and library suppliers, stocks works on almost all cures; most of its stock is directed towards the medical and paramedical professions, but there is an amount for the layman to experiment with as well. Kimpton's has two smaller branches, one opposite Guy's Hospital, the other opposite the Middlesex Hospital Medical School (see separate entries), this branch is close to the Royal College of Physicians.

Services: mail order; special order; visits to medical meetings and schools of nursing for the display and sale of books; the Teviot subscription agency is able to handle orders for all British and international periodicals and journals
Catalogue: Kimpton's monthly Book News; specialized subject lists
Publications: Kimpton's and Teviot Scientific publish books in the field of medicine

Kimpton's Medical Bookshop   *(Goodge Street)*
49 Newman Street W1
580-4250

M–F 9:30–5:30   Sat 9:30–1:00

This branch of Kimpton's stocks the same subjects as its larger sister branch in Great Portland Street, with the exceptions of dentistry, speech therapy and veterinary sciences

Services: mail order; special order, visits to medical meetings and schools of nursing for the display and sale of books; the Teviot

subscription agency is able to handle orders for all British and
international periodicals and journals
Catalogue: Kimpton's monthly Book News; specialized
subject-lists
Publications: Kimpton's and Teviot Scientific publish books in the
field of medicine

Ksiegarnia S.P.K.   *(Ravenscourt Park)*
P.C.A. Publications Ltd
238 King Street W6
748-5522

M–F 10:00–6:00   Sat 10:00–2:00

history / literature / politics / reference

This shop is a part of the Polish Social and Cultural Association
and it covers a wide range of subjects related to Poland in both
Polish and English. The literary, political and historical material in
Polish is all from publishers outside Poland while some of the
dictionaries, encyclopaedias and general reference books come
directly from Poland. They stock Polish magazines and a daily
paper, again published outside Poland.

Services: international mail order; educational supply,
particularly for language teaching

John Lewis & Co.   *(Oxford Circus)*
279-306 Oxford Street W1
629-7711

M–Sat 9:00–5:30   Th 9:30–8:00

John Lewis has a section devoted entirely to children's books near
the toy department on the fourth floor. It is aimed at children up to
thirteen years and set out according to age and reading needs.
Starting with 'bath books' (printed on plastic for floating in the
bath) and moving up to 'board books' (durable and brightly
coloured on stiff cardboard), the books range up to atlases,
dictionaries and general reference for older children. This range
includes a selection of Ladybird books, general fiction and a
knowledge section.

Non-book material: a wide range of cassettes including nursery rhymes, stories, music and musical education
Services: special order

Linguaphone   *(Oxford Street)*
207-209 Regent Street W1
734-7572

M–F 9:30–6:00   Sat 10:00–4:00

The Linguaphone Institute has developed, and sells, comprehensive language teaching courses for home use. Included in a course package are cassettes or records, textbook, course handbook, self-correcting written exercise book, and an oral exercise book. The Institute also offers an advisory service via the post for student questions and written work. Languages include German, French, Spanish, Italian, Persian, Arabic, Chinese, Norwegian – 32 in all.
   The shop will be moving in 1987, so it is best to phone the Linguaphone head office (741-1655) to check its whereabouts.

Non-book material: see above
Services: mail order
Publications: course material is published by The Linguaphone Institute

The Literary Guild Bookshop   *(Goodge Street)*
89 Newman Street W1
637-0341

M–F 10:00–6:00

arts / bestsellers / biography / children's books / classics / cookery / fiction / gift books / history / literature / natural history / new titles / reference

Only members of the W.H. Smith/Doubleday book clubs can purchase books here. All titles are hardback and available through the Guild's mail order service, and the shop does attempt to stock books from past book offerings. The Literary Guild can be joined here, and details of the other clubs are available.

Services: mail order, back order
Catalogue: separate catalogues for each club, produced quarterly

London Art Bookshop Ltd   *(High Street Kensington)*
8 Holland Street W8
937-6996

M–Sat 9:30–6:00

administration / Africa and South America / alternative technology / American architecture / Baroque and Renaissance / building construction / building regulations / castles and country homes / church architecture / classical architecture / counties / Eastern Europe and Russia / exhibition catalogues / France / Georgian and Victorian architecture / Greece and Southern Europe / housing / industrial archaeology / interior design / Islamic and Oriental architecture / London and suburbs / medieval architecture / offices and shops / perspective and drawing / Scandinavia and Northern Europe / tourism and restaurants / town planning / towns and cities / vernacular architecture

Though small, this well organized shop specializes in new books on all aspects of architecture. The wide range of subject areas within the specialized stock is remarkable in a shop where an exhaustive survey of Renaissance architecture can be found as well as a highly specialized text on industrial archaeology. Indeed, almost all possible divisions within the field of architecture are acknowledged. A few second-hand books are available, and a selection of magazines and journals on architecture and design is on hand.

Across the street is the Academy Bookshop, which is under the same ownership as the London Art Bookshop, and carries books on fine and applied arts (see separate entry).

Services: mail order, special order
Catalogue: Academy Editions list
Publications: Academy Editions publishes books about architecture and fine and applied arts

The London Toy and Model Museum   *(Paddington)*
23 Craven Hill W2
262-7905/9450

Tue–Sat 10:00–5:30   Sun and Bank Holiday Mondays 11:00–5:30

The bookshop here is at the entrance to the museum, so you can browse without visiting the museum, or use it as an interesting postscript to the museum itself. The collection of books covers toys and juvenalia, the history of toys and toy makers, and there is a range of children's classics. They also stock New Cavendish publications.

Non-book material: items related to the museum, models, toys
Services: mail order
Catalogue: catalogue for the museum's own publications, lists for the entire shop
Publications: White Mouse publications

Music Book Centre   *(Goodge Street)*
78 Newman Street W1
636-7777

M–F 9:30–5:30

This small, modern shop is part of the publishing concern, Music Sales Ltd, and about 80% of the titles (all of which are new) are their own. The shop does, however, carry music books from other publishers. All the books and song books deal with contemporary music and music personalities – rock, jazz, blues, popular, contemporary classics.

Services: mail order
Catalogue: books and song books
Publications: music books by Music Sales Ltd, Wise Publications and Omnibus Press

John O'Callaghan   *(Bond Street)*
1-7 Davies Mews
Grays Antique Market W1
Stall J21-23
629-3788

M–F 10:00–6:00

ceramics / clocks and watches / fine arts / glass / jewellery / oriental

A collection of art and crafts reference books is stocked here. The stock is largely out-of-print books, with some new and second-hand titles.

Services: special order

The Open Book   *(Notting Hill Gate/Ladbroke Grove)*
15 Blenheim Crescent W11
243-1284

Tu–Sat 10:30–6:00

astrology / chess / Christianity / esoterica / maths and science / New Age consciousness / philosophy / psychology / self-awareness and improvement / sufism / yoga

This bookshop stocks books which it hopes will help people to make the most of their lives, by expanding their knowledge or consciousness – be it through learning chess or studying sufism. All spiritual traditions are included – hence the name 'Open Book'. Second-hand books are in the basement.

Non-book material: chess, computers, postcards, posters
Services: special order

Paddington & Friends   *(Edgware Road)*
22 Crawford Place W1
262-1866

M–Sat 10:00–5:00

This shop is entirely devoted to Paddington Bear. Paddington picture books and of course all the Paddington stories can be found here, as well as other works by Michael Bond, *Olga the Polga* and the Thursday books.

Non-book material: accessories, games, nursery china, nursery wear, wallpaper
Services: international mail order
Catalogue: comprehensive catalogue

Peters Music Shop   *(Oxford Circus/Tottenham Court Road)*
119 Wardour Street W1
437-1456

M–F 9:30–5:30

biography / counterpoint / dictionaries / harmony / history / instruments / opera / orchestration / theory

Peters Edition sells mostly sheet music and scores, but has a selection of new books about composers, performers, and music theory and history.

Non-book material: scores, sheet music
Services: mail order, special order
Publications: Peters Edition publishes books on music

Pilot Software Ltd   *(Tottenham Court Road)*
32 Rathbone Place W1
636-2666

M–F 9:30–6:00   Sat 9:30–5:00

This shop specializes in computer programs, so the books are all related to these programs. The manuals cover a wide range, from home computing to the IBM manual.

Non-book material: computer programs
Services: special order

Poland Street Publications Ltd   *(Oxford Circus)*
9 Poland Street W1
437-1984

M–F 9:30–6:00

charity information / cooperatives and small businesses / cultural politics / education / environment / media and communications / new technology / nuclear energy / social welfare / Third World / women's issues

The building here, which is wholly a subsidiary of the Joseph Rowntree Social Service Trust, houses a number of political and public interest groups each of whose publications are sold in this small shop on the ground floor. It contains new books plus studies, information booklets, newspapers and pamphlets, and also many remaindered titles. The organizations represented are: Acton Society, Campaign for Press and Broadcasting Freedom, Comedia Publishing, Counter Information Services, EIRIS, Job Ownership, LCC, Socialist Environment and Resources Association, 300 Group, TNIC, Unemployment Unit, Youth Aid.

Non-book material: badges, postcards
Services: special order
Publications: from the organizations listed above

Pollock's Toy Museum   (*Goodge Street*)
1 Scala Street W1
636-3452

M–Sat 10:00–5:00

The shop can be visited independently from the museum and its
stock caters for specialists and excited children leaving the
museum. There is a selective range of children's books, including
pop-up and cut-out books to recreate some of the museum's
exhibits. The specialist books cover studies of dolls' houses and
doll collections, toy theatre history and related subjects. You don't
have to be a child or a specialist to enjoy this shop – you could just
be an excited adult!

Non-book material: toy theatres in a range of sizes, a general
range of old-fashioned toys
Services: international mail order for the museum's own
publications and toy theatres
Catalogue: catalogue for Pollock's publications
Publications: specialist books related to the museum

Polonez   (*Shepherd's Bush*)
129/130 Shepherd's Bush Shopping Centre
Shepherd's Bush Green W12
749-3097/743-2391

M–F 9:00–5:00

Everything in Polonez is from, or about, Poland. Most of their
books are imported from Poland (in Polish), although titles
concerning Poland which might not be found in that country are
probably available here at Polonez (this odd situation arises
because books published in Poland often go out of print quickly,
becoming unobtainable behind the Iron Curtain, yet may sit on
Western booksellers' shelves for many months). Western classics
in translation and English language books about Poland are the
spheres of Western influence in this shop. In the areas of
out-of-print and antiquarian books, Polonez is able to obtain

books through the antiquarian department of Poland's national book distributor. The shop can order periodicals from a list of over 200 Polish publishers.

Polonez is also a gift shop featuring imported items from Poland including prints, records, crafts, folk art and Polish pianos.

Non-book material: see above
Services: mail order, special order, search service in field
Catalogue: specialized lists are produced frequently

RIBA Bookshop   *(Great Portland Street)*
66 Portland Place W1
251-0791

M–F 9:30–5:30

building types / carpentry / construction and structure / design data / energy conservation / estimating / gardens / history of architecture / history of design / interior design / interiors / land and leisure / legal and contracts / planning: city, town, country / planting / reference / rendering / specifications / surveying

This is a small (but complete) shop, off the foyer of the RIBA building, specializing in new books on architecture, design and construction. Most of the material is geared toward professionals working in these fields, though there are some illustrated books for the lay reader.

Services: mail order, special order
Catalogue: complete list annually
Publications: RIBA Publications publishes books on: architects, buildings, crafts and the visual arts; reports; building contracts and forms

Reader's Digest   *(Green Park)*
22 Berkeley Square W1
629-8144

M–F 9:00–5:30

art / cookery / DIY / gardening / household / language teaching / motoring / natural history / reference / Time Life / transport / travel guides

The majority of books here are new Reader's Digest titles, although other UK publishers are carried, particularly Time Life Books as their offices are just round the corner. Some of the more useful sections are those devoted to English language teaching, travel guides, cookery and the home.

Non-book material: calendars, cards, language cassettes, posters, records
Services: mail order, special order of Reader's Digest titles
Catalogue: Reader's Digest publications
Publications: see above

Walter Rodney Bookshop   *(West Ealing – British Rail)*
5a Chignell Place W13
579-4920

M–F 10:00–6:00

Africa / Afro-American / art / biography / children's books / cookery / crafts / drama / economics / education / fiction / folk tales and legends / history / imperialism / individual rights / music / myths / poetry / politics / religion / sociology / Third World development / West Indies / women

The name of the Walter Rodney Bookshop commemorates a scholar and political activist from Guyana. The shop specializes in new books about and by black people and is committed to literature with a multiracial perspective on the world – the primary concern of Walter Rodney in his lifetime.

Non-book material: cards, crafts, posters, records and tapes
Services: mail order, special order, exhibitions
Catalogue: Bogle-L'Ouverture Publications, general catalogue available
Publications: Bogle-L'Ouverture Publications publishes books about and by black people, including the work of Walter Rodney

Royal Academy of Arts   *(Piccadilly Circus)*
Burlington House
Piccadilly W1
734-9052

M–Sun 10:00–5:45

The shop in the Royal Academy of Arts carries books on the fine arts, art history, architecture, designs and practical manuals, many of which are related to current exhibitions. On hand, as well, are exhibition catalogues.

Non-book material: postcards, glassware and pottery, posters, prints, products designed for artists, art material
Services: mail order, special order, framing service
Publications: exhibition catalogues

St Paul Book Centre   *(High Street Kensington)*
199 Kensington High Street W8
937-9591/2

Tu–Sat 9:30–5:30

bibles and missals / children's / Christian life / justice and peace / liturgy / marriage and family / scripture / theology / world religions

This is a small bookshop with a large selection of paperbacks of Christian interest in addition to both hard and paper in the above subjects.

Non-book material: records, cassettes, audio-visuals, videos
Services: video library, mail order
Catalogue: selected lists for Advent, Christmas, Lent and Easter; video catalogue; audio-visual catalogue

Schott & Co. Ltd   *(Oxford Circus)*
48 Great Marlborough Street W1
437-1246

M–F 9:00–5:00

biography / classical music / counterpoint / dictionaries / harmony / musical instruments and teaching / opera / theory

A small portion of the stock of Schott & Co. consists of new books about music, though their primary business is selling classical and opera scores, and musical instruments. They also incorporate the Early Music Shop in their basement. They sell early musical instruments only.

Non-book material: see above
Services: mail order
Catalogue: Schott & Co. publications listed six times yearly
Publications: Ernst Eulenburg Ltd publishes books and sheet music

Scripture Union Bookshop   *(Bond Street)*
5 Wigmore Street W1
493-1851

M–Sat 9:00–5:30   Th 9:00–7:00

apologetics / bible characters and background / bibles / biography / children's books / Christian life / Christian service / the church / church history / commentaries / C.S. Lewis / daily readings / devotional / doctrine / ethics / evangelism / fiction / healing / Holy Spirit / life of Christ / music / morality / Old and New Testament / prayer / prophecy

Scripture Union is a religious bookshop with an emphasis on evangelical titles and subjects, though many of the books are concerned with practical approaches to daily Christian life. A corner of the shop is devoted to material for children, including teaching aids, prayer and assembly books, and bible games and puzzles.

Non-book material: audio-visual material, cards, cassettes, records, teaching material
Services: mail order (infrequent), special order, bookstalls
Catalogue: Scripture Union publications
Publications: Scripture Union publishes books about the church and Christian life

B. A. Seaby Ltd   *(Oxford Circus)*
8 Cavendish Square W1
580-3677

M–F 9:30–5:00

bibliography / history / military decorations and medals / mint reports / naval decorations and medals / numismatic handbooks / numismatic history: worldwide / private collections' catalogues / uniform history

Seaby specializes primarily in new books and journals, in a variety of languages, on all aspects of coins and paper money from ancient to modern times. Seaby's main activity, in fact, is the buying and selling of coins.

Non-book material: coins, medals
Services: mail order, special order (out of field as well)
Catalogue: new book lists are produced bi-monthly
Publications: B. A. Seaby Ltd publishes new books, semi-annuals and reprints exclusively on coins and medals

Shorouk International   *(Oxford Circus)*

316-318 Regent Street W1
637-2743/4   580-9819

M–Sat 9:30–6:00

Two floors of books cover a huge range of books in Arabic and books in English specializing in Islamic and Middle Eastern subjects. The books in both languages include literature, reference of all kinds and a section for children. There is a language section for both English- and Arabic-speaking customers, and a selection of papers and magazines.

Non-book material: arts and crafts from the Islamic world, cassettes, records, videos
Services: international mail order
Publications: books in Arabic and English

Soma Books   *(High Street Kensington)*

Commonwealth Institute
Kensington High Street W8
603-0754

M–Sat 10:00–5:30   Sun 2:00–5:00

art / children's / comparative literature / crafts / creative writing / decorative arts / economics / educational fiction / history / mythology / performing arts / poetry / politics / race and immigration / religion / sociology / women

This very special bookshop is situated inside the impressive Commonwealth Institute building. It stocks titles published in and about all the Commonwealth countries, including some bilingual textbooks. The shelves are organized by country, within which section you will find the subjects listed above. It does a roaring trade, particularly in term-time when about 300 children a day visit the shop – not the time to go in for a peaceful browse!

Non-book material: crafts, postcards, posters, records
Services: mail order, standing order

Note: There is another branch at Kennington Lane (see separate entry).

Star Books International   *(Warren Street)*
112 Whitfield Street W1
388-9832

M–Sat 10:00–5:30

art / culture / fiction / folklore / history / language teaching / literature / philosophy / poetry / politics / religion / sociology

This shop specializes in Asian language books from the Indian subcontinent. The political section is quite good, and there is a solid selection of language teaching books from India, Pakistan and Bangladesh. Also available are a variety of journals and magazines published in India.

Non-book material: cassettes, records, videos
Services: mail order, library and school supply
Catalogue: complete annual list with supplements every three months free of charge
Publications: Star Publications, one of the largest publishers in India, produces bilingual children's books

Stud Bookshop   *(Notting Hill Gate)*
57 Pembridge Road W11
727-1614

M–Sat 10:00–7:00

On the corner of Pembridge Road and Portobello Road is this bookshop specializing in gay literature and magazines for men and women. They also stock what are described as gay 'toys' and there is a gallery on the same premises.

Non-book material: cards, pictures

Tradition   *(Green Park)*
5 Shepherd Street W1
493-7452

M–F 9:30–5:30   Sat 9:30–3:30

Tradition carries solely books on military history, uniforms, equipment, weapons and campaigns. They have new titles on uniforms, especially, as well as out-of-print and antiquarian books about the military, such as 18th-century army lists.

Non-book material: new and antique military figures
Services: mail order, special order in field

Trailfinders   *(High Street Kensington)*
42-48 Earls Court Road W8
938-3444

M–Sat 9:00–6:00

This is a travel agency with a huge variety of books, maps and guides covering all the exotic destinations you dream of visiting. They stock the *Lonely Planet* series for the budget traveller as well as more up-market guides like the *Insight* series. Berlitz guides and Bartholomew maps are also included in their extensive range. All the subsidiary Trailfinders' services are open to the general public and it is only the travellers' library that is exclusively for the use of people booking their holiday on the premises.

Services: special order; travellers' information centre dealing with visas, immunization, etc.; insurance; American Express foreign exchange; travellers' library
Publications: *The Trailfinder*, free magazine including book reviews

The Travel Bookshop Ltd   *(Ladbroke Grove)*
13 Blenheim Crescent W11
229-5260

M–F 10:00–6:00   Sat 10:00–5:00

This delightful shop has a well deserved reputation for the scope and range of its titles, all of which are to do with travel in some form or other, and the charm and knowledge of its proprietor. Books are arranged by country and within each section are not only travel guides, but cookery, crafts, architecture, fiction and history relating to that particular area. If you find all this too exhausting you can always relax for a moment on an ancient but welcoming sofa in the front shop, before renewing your browsing.

Non-book material: maps
Services: mail order, special order, search service
Catalogue: selected lists two to three times yearly

Turf Newspapers Ltd   *(Green Park)*
25 Shepherd Market W1
499-4391

M–F 9:00–5:30   Sat 9:00–12:00

biography / breeding / courses / fiction / horses / Jockey Publications / Raceform / racing / sale figures / statistics / Timeform / Trainers' Record / training

This retail bookshop sells new titles about horse breeding and racing with a few related equestrian subjects. Much of the material is statistical, concerned with the present racing season, but the shop also stocks less utilitarian books, like all of the Dick Francis mysteries.

Non-book material: calendars, cards, diaries, prints, table mats, video films of horses and horse races
Services: mail order, special order
Catalogue: selected list
Publications: Turf Newspapers Ltd publishes reference books and other books about racing

Ukrainian Bookshop   *(Notting Hill Gate)*
49 Linden Gardens W2
229-0140

M–F 9:00–6:00 (closed 12:30–1:30)   Sat 2:00–6:00

children's books / history / language / literature / reference / religion / school books

This is primarily a Ukrainian language bookshop and it is a part of the Association of Ukrainians in Great Britain. The Ukrainian books cover a wide range of subjects and there are some books in English about Ukrainian history and culture and a stock of dictionaries for both languages. The books are new and second-hand. This is a residential street, so do not expect a large sign indicating the presence of the shop – there is a small notice for the Association outside number 49 so you have to look carefully to find it.

Non-book material: cards, carvings, cassettes, ceramics, records, T-shirts
Services: mail order
Catalogue: lists are available for the entire book stock and the records and cassettes
Publications: official weekly newspaper *Ukranian Thought*

Under Two Flags   *(Bond Street)*
4 St Christopher's Place W1
935-6934

Tue–Sat 10:00–5:00

military campaigns / military equipment / military history / models and miniatures / model soldier painting / uniforms / weapons

Under Two Flags is a charming small shop in the shopping precinct at St Christopher's Place. The shop specializes in new books on military uniforms and model soldiers and stocks titles in the related subject areas of military history and weapons. Only a portion of the shop is concerned with books, though, as model soldiers and prints are also sold.

Non-book material: see above
Services: mail order, special order in field

Virgin Megastore   *(Tottenham Court Road)*
28-30 Oxford Street W1
631-1234 ext. 266

M–Sat 10:00–9:00

art / biography / fiction / film / humour / music

Within this enormous record store is a correspondingly large section of books on rock music, biographies of rock stars and the music industry in general. The selection of jazz books is good and album sheet music also forms an important part of the stock. There is a smaller range of titles on fantasy, art, humour and film.

Non-book material: as above, and music magazines and weekly magazines

Roland Ward's at Holland & Holland   *(Green Park)*
33 Bruton Street W1
499-4411

M–F 9:00–5:30   Sat (November and December only) 9:30–5:00

Africana / arms and weapons / field sports / natural history / ornithology / shooting / travel

The books here fall into two main categories. There are those connected with Holland & Holland, the gun manufacturers who have their showroom in these premises, and the stock covered by Rowland Ward. Shooting, arms and weapons books come under Holland & Holland, while Africana, natural history, travel, ornithology and field sports are subjects concerning Rowland Ward. They also stock books published in association with the Quiller Press. The range includes new and second-hand books.

Non-book material: new, second-hand and antique guns; country clothing; pictures on sporting subjects
Services: mail order
Catalogue: a bi-annual catalogue covers the entire stock, both new and second-hand
Publications: publications include a history of the gunmakers W. & C. Scott and facsimile reprints of big game hunting books

Captain O.M. Watts Ltd   *(Piccadilly Circus)*
45 Albermarle Street W1
493-4633

M–F 9:00–6:00   Th 9:00–7:00   Sat 9:00–5:00

Captain Watts is one of the largest and most well-known chandlers in London, selling everything for the yachtsman and his yacht – sailing clothing, nautical giftware, flags, charts, instruments and nautical books. These you will find on both sides of the shop near the entrance.

Non-book material: see above
Services: mail order, special order
Catalogue: yes

Wholefood of Baker Street   *(Baker Street)*
24 Paddington Street W1
935-3924

M 8:45–6:00   T–F 8:45–6:30   Sat 8:45–1:00

organic agriculture / cookery / ecology / farming / gardening / natural childbirth / nutrition / therapies / vitamins / yoga

Wholefood is a bookshop as well as greengrocer, grocery shop and butcher. Most of the books are new though they have a shelf full of out-of-print titles, and all of the titles are concerned with nutrition, agriculture and horticulture.

Non-book material: see above
Services: mail order, special order in field
Catalogue: selected list

Wisdom Publications   *(Bond Street)*
23 Dering Street W1
499-0925

M–F 9:00–6:00

This bookshop on the second floor doubles as the offices of the Wisdom Publishing Company. Their own publications are all concerned with Buddhism and related subjects. Translations of Buddhist texts, studies on the theory and practice of Buddhism and a series on Buddhism and its relation to Western ideas and philosophy are just some examples of the range covered by Wisdom Publications. They also stock a variety of other publisher's books on Buddhism.

Non-book material: cards, posters, prints, Tibetan calendars
Services: international mail order, library supply
Catalogue: trade catalogue, mail order catalogue including titles from other publishers
Publications: Wisdom Publications

Young World
(High Street Kensington)
(Children's Book Centre Ltd)
229 Kensington High Street W8
937-6314

M–Sat 9:30–6:00   Sun 12:00–6:00

arts and religion / Beatrix Potter / crafts / Dr Seuss / fairy tales / fiction (ages 5–8) / fiction (ages 8–11) / geography / ghosts / history / humour / Ladybird / natural history / new recommended fiction / non-fiction series / nursery rhymes / picture books / poetry / pop-up books / reference / science / science fiction / sports and hobbies

With new toys on the ground floor and books downstairs, this brightly decorated, slightly crowded shop should delight any child who happens in for a look round. Books are categorized according to age group – from one to five years, through to fourteen to one hundred years! – and within each section is a range of fiction and non-fiction titles. All the old favourites, Winnie the Pooh, Thomas the Tank Engine, etc., are here together with today's favourites like Postman Pat, Spot, and Fungus the Bogeyman. There are frequent in-store promotions, author visits, and activity days (usually a Saturday) when colouring competitions and similar events are organized.

Non-book material: cards, games, posters, presents, story cassettes, toys
Services: mail order, special order
Catalogue: occasional book lists.

Note: There is another branch of Young World at:
The Trocadero Centre
15 Coventry Street W1
437-8336

Antiquarian and Second-hand Bookshops

Any Amount of Books   *(Hammersmith)*
103-105 Hammersmith Road W14
603-9232

T–Sat 11:00–7:00

ground floor:
architecture / art / classics / cookery / education / fiction / film / gardening / history / illustrated books / language teaching / law / legends / literature / memoirs / music / myths / non-fiction / Penguin / philosophy / photography / plays / poetry (first editions) / politics / psychology / religion / science fiction / sociology / sports / theatre / travel

basement:
arts / children's books / foreign language / literature / history / medicine / novels / thrillers / travel

Any Amount of Books is a cut above most general second-hand bookshops. Two floors house a general stock of titles, with particularly good sections of literature, poetry and travel books. Prices are extremely reasonable, and scattered among the second-hand books are a few new titles at reduced prices, including review copies and remainders.

Non-book material: a gallery next door has been opened selling prints, lithographs and book-plates
Services: mail order, wants lists accepted
Catalogue: art, first editions and literature twice a year

Brian L. Bailey   *(Notting Hill Gate)*
Westbourne Antique Arcade
113 Portobello Road W11
229-1692 (home number)

Sat 9:00–4:00

art / collecting / fiction / French literature / illustrated books / literature / natural history / poetry / reference / topography / travel

Brian Bailey specializes in antiquarian illustrated books, although the stock in his stall in Portobello Road has a selection of general second-hand and antiquarian titles.

Non-book material: maps, prints
Services: mail order

Book Bargains   *(Shepherd's Bush)*
14 Shepherd's Bush Market W12
740-0873

M–Sat 10:00–5:00 (closed Thursdays)

This stall in the market has a large range of second-hand paperbacks and welcomes exchange.

The Book Gallery   *(Bond Street)*
Grays Antique Market
B.12 Gray's Mews, W1
408-1239/452-7243

M–F 10:00–6:00

The Book Gallery is a small shop in this charming market just off Oxford Street. It is run by Sarah Fabian Baddiel who deals in anything to do with golf including books, clubs, jewellery, silver, paintings and ceramics. She also has many books in the field of motoring and transport and some juvenile titles.

Non-book material: prints, motoring and golf ephemera, tin and die-cast toys
Services: mail order, gift tokens
Catalogue: occasional golf

Books and Things   *(Notting Hill Gate)*
Dolphin Arcade (Upstairs)
157 Portobello Road W11

Sat 9:00–2:00

Almost overflowing into the snack bar area are the second-hand books of Books and Things. Late 19th-century and 20th-century books on the decorative and fine arts are the speciality of the shop. Also available are modern first editions and a smattering of general fiction and non-fiction.

Non-book material: ephemera, original posters and book illustrations
Services: mail order, wants lists accepted
Catalogue: twice-yearly list of general titles, art and illustrated books and modern first editions
Note: Books and Things can also be found at the PBFA London book fairs.

Demetzy Books   *(Notting Hill Gate)*
Westbourne Antique Arcade
113 Portobello Road W11

Sat 7:30–3:30

architecture / art / classics / collecting / cookery / crafts / illustrated books / medical literature / 19th-century first editions / natural history / science / travel

Demetzy carries second-hand and antiquarian books. Illustrated books and literature comprise most of the stock. He also has some fine leather bindings and sets of miniature books.

Non-book material: a few paintings
Services: mail order, wants lists accepted

Peter Eaton (Booksellers) Ltd   *(Holland Park)*
80 Holland Park Avenue W11
727-5211

M–Sat 10:00–5:00

first floor: antiquarian

ground floor: collectors items
antiques / architecture / art / classics / cookery / economics / heraldry / history: general, naval and military / literature / medicine / music / natural history / occult / religion / sets / science / sport / travel

basement: second-hand
anthropology / architecture / art / biography / British topography /
drama / economics / fiction / film / foreign literature / history /
literary criticism / literature / London history / music / occult /
philosophy / poetry / psychology / reference / science / sociology /
theatre / theology / travel

Peter Eaton is a lovely light and airy shop in which the cheapest
stock is kept in the basement, and rises in price – always
reasonable – as one ascends. 'General' is the only word to describe
the range of stock on all floors, all of which is in good condition
and well labelled. 'Distinctive' is hardly too strong a word for the
interior of this shop, with a multi-level ground floor and soft,
natural lighting throughout. The atmosphere is serene, and
spending a few hours here with the shop's diverse stock is
certainly pleasurable.

Non-book material: manuscripts, old photo albums
Services: mail order
Catalogue: occasional specialized lists
Publications: Peter Eaton has published bibliographies in the past

Andrew Edmunds   *(Oxford Circus/Piccadilly Circus)*
44 Lexington Street W1
437-8594

M–F 10:00–6:00

This shop specializes in 18th- and early 19th-century prints of
social and political caricatures and decorative and architectural
prints. There is a small selection of antiquarian books, as well as a
few modern editions, relating to the history of prints and
printmakers.

Non-book material: see above
Services: mail order, wants lists accepted in field of art

W.A. Foster   *(Turnham Green)*
134 Chiswick High Road W4
995-2768

M–Sat 10:00–6:00 (occasionally closed for lunch)   Th 10:00–1:30

archaeology / architecture / art / biography / British topography / children's books / cinema / classics / collecting / cookery / economics / fiction / fine bindings / first editions / gardening / geology / health / humour / illustrated books / limited editions / literary criticism / literature / music / mysteries / natural history / plays / poetry / psychology / railways / reference / religion / sailing / social sciences / sport / stage history / travel accounts and guides

This bookshop carries a general selection of second-hand books, as well as a few antiquarian titles, with particularly good sections of literature and children's books. They also have another shop at number 183 which specializes in engravings, prints and framing.

Non-book material: cards, engravings, prints

M. & R. Glendale   *(Bond Street/Baker Street)*
9a Cavendish Street W1
487-5348

M–F 10:00–6:00

Walking into the shop of M. & R. Glendale is like walking into a world of fine detail and precise decorative purposes. Their beautifully bound and arranged books are mainly for children and collectors of (Victorian) children's books and ephemera, but they also carry titles on women's rights, cookery, domestic history, colour plate and illustrated books, and such obscure subjects as flush toilet construction! Also featured are entertainment items – games, puzzles, etc. – made of paper. More second-hand books in fairly good condition are to be found in the basement.

Non-book material: paper ephemera
Services: mail order, search service, will respond with offers to specific book(s) requests

Hosains Books   *(Marble Arch)*
25 Connaught Street W2
262-7900

T–F 10:30–5:30   Sat 10:30–1:00

art / biography / culture / history / literature / religion / travel

Hosains specializes in second-hand, antiquarian and rare books about the Middle East, Central Asia, North Africa, India and Islam, most of which are in English. A few of the titles are set apart by cards with detailed explanations of their history and significance. Art, travel and illustrated books and literature form the largest portion of the stock, while the basement houses additional books, as well as Persian and Indian miniatures and oriental prints.

Non-book material: see above
Services: mail order, search service in field
Catalogue: selected lists four or five times a year
Publications: Nash Publications plans to publish oriental works

E. Joseph   *(Bond Street)*
(in association with Chas. J. Sawyer)
1 Vere Street W1
493-8353

M–F 9:30–5:30 (phone for Saturday hours)

Churchill / colour plate books / early printed books / English literature / fine bindings / natural history / original works of book illustration / private press books / rare Africana / sporting

E. Joseph sells fine and rare books with some emphasis on illustrated works, press books, fine bindings, colour plate books, as well as Victorian and early twentieth-century watercolour paintings. It is perhaps the first place to try for sets of standard authors, such as the *Waverley* novels, bound in cloth or leather. There is also an interesting stock of general literature. One of Mr Sawyer's specialities is books by, about and owned by Churchill. Africa, especially South Africa, is another area of interest.

Non-book material: see above
Services: mail order, search service
Catalogue: various always available

Maggs Bros Ltd   *(Green Park)*
50 Berkeley Square W1
493-7160

M–F 9:30–5:00

Maggs Bros, bookseller by appointment to the Queen, is the last of London's grand 19th-century antiquarian booksellers still to be family-run (it now has a fifth generation at work here). The shop on Berkeley Square is a listed, blue-plaque house with five floors of medium- to high-priced antiquarian books in all subjects.

Each general department is run by a seasoned book buyer and scholar in the field, each of whom seems to be more than happy to spend time with any customer who shows genuine interest in books. Somehow amid the grandeur of lovely bookcases filled with (almost) priceless volumes, the shop maintains an atmosphere of friendliness which always makes me feel as though I'm walking into someone's home. And chances are, you will run into one member of the Maggs family if more than a half hour passes by before you leave.

The special interest of one of the family is the literature of exploration and travel, especially the voyages of Captain Cook, and there are also beautiful books in the area of natural history and military history.

Non-book material: ephemera, engravings, maps, prints, autographs, Indian miniatures, illuminated manuscripts
Services: mail order, search service, valuations, bid on commission
Catalogue: numerous specialized catalogues
Publications: Maggs Bros Ltd has published reprints on exploration, natural history and bibliography and other areas

Marlborough Rare Books Ltd   *(Piccadilly Circus)*
35 Old Bond Street W1
493-6993

M–F 9:30–6:00

Marlborough, which has now expanded into more general books as well, specializes in antiquarian books on fine and graphic arts, including architecture, calligraphy, bibliography and illustrated books. The stock ranges from the rarest specimens of early printing to mid 19th-century illustrated books. The staff are knowledgeable and gracious.

Services: mail order, search service in fields, binding repair, valuation, bid on commission
Catalogue: separate lists on architecture, bibliography and calligraphy, illustrated books, fine and applied arts; regular lists of new acquisitions

Notting Hill Books   *(Notting Hill Gate)*
132 Palace Gardens Terrace W8
727-5988

M–Sat 10:15–6:00   Th 10:15–1:00

Africa / ancient world / architecture / art / biography / British topography / China and South-East Asia / cinema / cookery / crafts / education / English literary criticism / French literature / gardening / general history / German literary criticism / German literature / Latin America / London / Middle East / music / natural history / philosophy / plays / poetry / politics / psychology / Russian literary art / Russian literature / sociology / theatre / travel / USA / USSR / women

Publishers' remainders, review copies and a few second-hand titles comprise the stock of this friendly shop where the speciality subjects are art, history, poetry, literature and literary criticism. Half-price paperbacks are available, and here the selections of literature and literary criticism offer especially good choice and value as the cover price, rather than the current price, is the basis for the reduction.

Oxfam Books   *(Baker Street)*
91 Marylebone High Street W1

M–Sat 11:00–5:00

This is the first of the Oxfam shops to be entirely devoted to books. They sell what people bring them and the stock therefore ranges from paperback fiction to hardback non-fiction – most is second-hand though some are in new condition being review copies or unwanted presents. The shop is staffed by volunteers.

Non-book material: Christmas cards

Popular Book Centre   *(Leicester Square)*
218 Shaftesbury Avenue W1
240-2210

M–Sat 10:00–5:30

This is a small, general, second-hand bookshop. It also sells a few comics and half of the shop has shelves of adult material.

Jonathan Potter Ltd
159 New Bond Street W1
491-3520

M–F 9:30–5:30   Sat 9:30–11:30

This shop, which specializes in prints of London, maps and atlases pre-1850, has an excellent selection of more modern reference books on all aspects of cartography. Many of these are out-of-print and modern first editions. In temporary accommodation, so please ring before visiting.

Non-book material: see above
Services: mail order, special order
Catalogue: comprehensive list issued once a year

Bernard Quaritch Ltd   *(Piccadilly Circus)*
5 Lower John Street W1
734-2983

M–F 9:30–5:30   Closed 1:00–2:00

Arabic / art, colour plate and illustrated books / bibliography and palaeography / early printed books and manuscripts / English literature / natural history / philosophy and human sciences / Quran / science, medicine and technology / travel

Quaritch is one of the grand old antiquarian booksellers in London. The shop was founded in 1847 by Bernard Quaritch who built his business into the largest bookselling enterprise in the world. The vast collection of catalogues he produced from his stock during his 50 years as a bookseller carried the stamp of his interests in natural history, oriental learning, fine art, incunabula, illustrated manuscripts, early English literature and cartography – to name but a few areas. They also have a considerable stock of books in Arabic.

Today, the staff, though no longer all in the family, are still producing up to 10 catalogues yearly, reflecting an extensive stock of general antiquarian books. The layout of the shop does not encourage browsing, as most of the books are kept out of sight or locked in cases. The staff, however, are happy to attend to 'specific' browsers and willingly spend an afternoon with serious bibliophiles.

Services: mail order, auction service, sale by consignment, appraisal
Catalogue: many on specialized subjects

Quinto
(Baker Street)

83 Marylebone High Street W1
935-9303

M–Sat 9:00–6:00

anthropology / art / Australasia and Pacific / biography / British history / children's / classics / cookery / crafts / Eastern Europe / Eastern religions / economics / education / exploration and travel / Far East / fiction / foreign literature / history / humour / journalism / Judaica / literary criticism / medicine / Middle East / military history / modern first editions / North America / occult / Penguin / performing arts / philosophy / politics / psychology / science / South America / sports and pastimes / technology / theology / Virago

Quinto is a very attractive shop selling second-hand books downstairs and housing the famous Francis Edwards naval and military department upstairs. Prices are reasonable and staff helpful. There is a new acquisition shelf where any newly arrived books are kept for three weeks before being classified.

Non-book material: records
Services: mail order, search service
Catalogue: four naval and military catalogues yearly

Red Lion Books
(Notting Hill Gate)
(Richard H. Wilmott)
Red Lion Arcade (Upstairs)
169 Portobello Road W11

Sat 8:00–5:00

This is a small stall selling second-hand and antiquarian books. They have a selection on antiques and travel plus a range of general titles.

Seal Books
(South Ealing)
2 Coningsby Road W5
567-7198

W–Sat 10:00–5:30

Africana / archaeology / art / astronomy / biography / children's books / classics / cookery / crafts / economics / education / fiction / French literature / gardening / health / history / literature / music / natural history / philosophy / photography / poetry / politics / psychology / reference / religion / sociology / topography / translations / travel

Seal Books is one of Ealing's little treasures. Second-hand books pack the shelves of this rambling but cosy bookshop. English literature, modern first editions and Africana are the specialities of the shop, and they also have large sections of cookery books, French literature and titles on religion. The woman who runs the shop also has a nearby bookroom which she opens by appointment.

Services: mail order

Charlotte Robinson Bookshop   *(Piccadilly Circus)*
35 Great Pulteney Street W1
437-3683

M–F 11:00–6:00

Amid the encircling gloom and glitter of the surrounding area the Charlotte Robinson Bookshop is most welcome. Run in a cooperative with Peter Jolliffe Clearwater Books and Unicorn Books, the shop brings together an excellent, beguiling collection of modern first editions and illustrated books as well as a fair proportion of children's illustrated. Much of the stock is fiction (including some detective stories), but poetry, biography and literature are covered as well. Notable is the section of books by the increasingly-popular Henry Williamson, and the collection of titles concerning the First World War. Many of the book have their original dust-wrappers and if the prices at first might seem a little expensive it should be remembered that the first-edition market is continuing to grow, and that even original issues by post-war writers fetch high prices, the first printing of so recent a novel as Martin Amis's *Other People* realizing more than the cover-price.

Non-book material: none
Services: mail order
Catalogue: all the partners issue regularly

Thomas E. Schuster Antiquarian Books   *(Oxford Circus)*
14 Maddox Street W1
491-2208

M–F 10:00–5:30   Sat 10:00–1:00

architecture / atlases / birds / flowers / topography

Thomas Schuster's bookshop in Gillingham Street has now moved to Maddox Street where it shares the ground floor of the building with the Schuster Gallery. He is a specialist in illustrated antiquarian books covering a carefully selected range of subjects. The gallery at the front of the shop has continuous exhibitions of antiquarian prints concerned with similar subject matter and a range of decorative prints on any subject is available.

Non-book material: antiquarian print gallery
Services: mail order
Catalogue: the catalogues usually cover the print stock, but there are occasional issues on selected book stock

Bernard Shapero   *(Bond Street)*
125 Grays Antique Market
58 Davies Street W1
493-0876

M–F 10:00–6:00

Downstairs in Grays Antique Market will be found what is perhaps the UK's largest dealer in second-hand Baedeker travel guides. Bernard Shapero's shop has a marvellous selection of second-hand and antiquarian travel and guide books, general illustrated books, natural history and shelves of rare Baedekers.

Services: mail order
Catalogue: annual guidebook list

Sky Books   *(Hammersmith)*
119 Shepherd's Bush Road W6
603-5620

M–Sat 10:00–6:00

crime / fiction / horror / romance / science fiction / thrillers

Sky Books is one of the book exchange shops in London. Any books bought at the shop can be returned for a 50% credit towards your next purchase. Second-hand paperback science fiction, horror stories and thrillers comprise most of the stock of Sky Books. There are also UK and US comics and science fiction magazines.

Non-book material: see above
Services: search service for American comics

Henry Sotheran Ltd   *(Piccadilly Circus)*
2-5 Sackville Street W1
734-1150

M–F 9:00–5:30

art and architecture / bibliography / biography / children's books / cookery and wine / English literature / fine bindings / first editions / history / natural history / ornithology / rare bibles / sport / travel and topography

Sotheran's was founded in 1761 in York, which makes it the country's oldest surviving booksellers, and moved to London in 1815. It has an illustrious history behind it. H. C. Folger of New York acquired much of his renowned Shakespeare Collection with Sotheran's help. Charles Dickens was a regular customer of the shop and, on his death, Dickens's library was purchased by Sotheran. Many of the items are still in the shop's possession.

No business can rest on past laurels though, and Sotheran's continues to sparkle in this century. They are London's leading stockists of ornithology books and carry new, remaindered, second-hand and antiquarian books, so it is possible to find a 50p book next to a rare £2,500 bible.

Whatever the price, each book is there to be looked at, taken out of their beautiful bookcases, leafed through and appreciated. To me, this is the wonder of Sotheran – books aren't locked away, prices are marked on the back flyleaf (a custom once general but now unique to Sotheran) and the staff are happy to let people wander around.

The shop also has an extensive collection of prints and maps, and English hand-coloured engravings in all subject areas.

Not too many book lovers could walk by the lovely, tall windows of this shop front and pass by the contents.

Non-book material: see above
Services: export dept, catering for libraries and institutions and acts as an agent for periodicals, mail order, special order anything in print, search service, framing service, binding and restoration
Catalogue: numerous lists on specialized topics
Publications: Henry Sotheran Ltd publishes fine books on natural history

Harriet Truscott Books   *(Notting Hill Gate)*
Portobello Antiques Arcade
139-149 Portobello Road W11

Sat 7:00–3:30

Harriet Truscott has a medium-sized stall in the Portobello Antique Arcade which is stocked with antiquarian and second-hand books. Natural history, travel, art and a general stock of non-fiction are the specialities of the stall.

Services: mail order, search service

The Vintage Magazine Shop   *(Piccadilly Circus)*
39-41 Brewer Street W1
439-8525

M–Sat 10:30–7:00   Sun 2:00–6:00

This is the place to go if you are suddenly gripped with nostalgic yearnings in the heart of London's big budget movie land. The ground floor of the shop stocks cinema stills and photographs, and pop posters of all periods as well as a selection of pop and fashion magazines. In the basement you will find a large collection of vintage magazines covering every subject imaginable and going back 150 years or more. Glamour magazines of the 1950s, *Vogue* from the 1930s onwards and the earliest comic publications are just some examples of the extensive stock. They also stock second-hand film books, old comic book annuals and football annuals.

Services: mail order for the film stills and posters; a special department supplies pictures for pubs, clubs and restaurants
Catalogue: a limited catalogue is available for the film stills and posters only

Wyvern Bookshop   *(Turnham Green)*
148 Devonshire Road W4
995-6769/5005

Th–Sat 10:00–5:30

extensive railway collection (by appointment only) / transport

This is a small antiquarian and second-hand bookseller specializing in railways, tramways, buses and trolleybuses. It is the London branch of Robert Humm & Co., Station House, Stamford, Lincs., from where all their mail order and catalogue business is handled.

Catalogue: railways, buses, trams and trolleys

South West London

General Bookshops

Army & Navy *(Victoria)*
101-105 Victoria Street SW1
834-1234 ext. 463

M–Th 9:00–5:30   Tue 9:30–5:30   F–Sat 9:00–6:00

antiques / art / biography / children's books / classics / cookery / crafts / fiction / film / gardening / history / humour / illustrated books and special editions / languages / literature / natural history / naval and military / reference / sport / theatre / transport / travel accounts and guides

This is quite a large and complete book department for a general department store. Hardcover and paperback fiction and non-fiction are carried, with illustrated and gift books overflowing out of the shelves onto tables.

Non-book material: department store
Services: mail order, special order

Balham Food and Book Co-op *(Balham)*
92 Balham High Road SW12
673-0946

M–Sat 9:30–5:30   W 11:30–5:30

anarchy / animals and pets / anthropology / black writers / child raising / children's books / cosmic solutions and theory / essays / fantasy / feminist fiction and poetry / fiction / health / history / homeopathy / Irish fiction and politics / literature / Marxism / media / mysticism / nutrition / occult / photography / poetry / politics / psychology / racial politics / religions / self-sufficiency / sexual politics / sociology / stress / Third World fiction and politics / women's issues / yoga

If the variety of current titles at the Balham Food and Book Co-op have any one thing in common it is that they are all non-racist and non-sexist, including the wide selection of children's books. Different areas of radical politics figure prominently in the stock, as do titles on alternative medicine, Eastern philosophies and general nutrition. Good selections of feminist, Irish and Third World fiction are available, as well as journals and newspapers on politics and community issues.

Adjoining the bookshop is a food shop and a vegetarian café.

Non-book material: badges, cards
Services: special orders

Barnes Books   *(Barnes – British Rail)*
60 Church Road SW13
741-0786

M–Sat 9:30–5:30 (closed 1:00–2:00)

A small but well stocked shop, covering a range of general subjects. There is a particular emphasis on art, biography and travel and a good children's room with toys on hand if the adults' section proves to be too alluring.

Non-book material: cards, children's tapes, wrapping-paper
Services: special order

Battersea Arts Centre Bookshop   *(Clapham Junction*
Old Town Hall   *– British Rail)*
Lavender Hill SW11
223-6557

Tue 10:00–6:00   W–Sat 10:00–8:00   Sun 11:00–8:00

alternative medicine / architecture / art / biography / children's classics / cookery and food / crafts / feminism / fiction / film / history / humour / literature / music / philosophy / photography / poetry / politics / psychology / reference / sociology / theatre and stage / travel / women's presses

Although Battersea has been acquiring something of an overspill population from Chelsea in recent years it still lacks bookshops, which makes this good one in the Battersea Arts Centre (in the Old Town Hall, at the top of Theatre Street, where Bertrand

Russell delivered 'Why I am not a Christian' in 1927) all the more useful. Its general stock, which is largely in paperback, has a large children's section as well as an emphasis on the arts and stage, literary fiction, poetry and the various women's presses. They are particularly keen on anti-sexist and anti-racist books. Run highly knowledgably and enthusiastically, it is very much a part of the Arts Centre, organizing, for example, a stall of books outside the cinema and holding a literary festival.

Non-book material: cards, a good range of literary and political magazines, maps, postcards, wrapping-paper
Services: mail order; special order; travelling bookshops to schools, etc.; school supply; mailing list sent to members of Battersea Arts Centre

Berger & Tims   *(Victoria)*
7 Bressenden Place SW1
828-8322

M–F 9:30–5:30

art / biography / classics / collecting / cookery / fiction / gardening / health / history / hobbies / literature / music / natural history / poetry / reference / sports / thrillers / travel guides

Berger & Tims is a very nicely stocked general bookshop carrying a range of paperback and hardcover fiction and non-fiction, conveniently located just around the corner from Victoria Station. The books here certainly offer an excellent range of new titles which makes for a better choice than the usual station kiosk fare.

Non-book material: video, classical compact discs
Services: mail order, special order, library suppliers

Bolingbroke Bookshop   *(Clapham South)*
147 Northcote Road SW11
223-9344

M–Sat 9:30–5:30   W 9:30–12:30   Th 9:30–7:00

antiques / art / architecture / biographies / children's / classics / cookery and food / crime / essays / fiction / gardening / health / history / humour / languages / natural history / poetry / reference / travel

A welcome addition to the largely bookless Battersea and Clapham is this shop close to the excellent Northcote Road market. Its stock is concentrated on paperbacks, but a range of hardbacks, especially in new titles, is also kept. It also has some second-hand titles.

Non-book material: cards, maps, wrapping-paper, classical cassettes
Services: mail order, prompt special order (also by telephone)

Books Etc. *(Victoria)*
66/74 Victoria Street SW1
828-8849

M–F 9:00–6:30   W 9:00–7:30   Sat 10:00–6:30

antiques / art / biography / business / children's / classics / computers / cookery / crafts / crime / film / games / gardening / health and child care / history / humour / literature / mythology / natural history / photography / plays / poetry / politics / psychology / reference / sex / sociology / sports / travel / women

This branch of Books Etc. always seem to be extremely busy. The business section is strong, reflecting the lunchtime office trade, and there are good displays of fiction, biography, current affairs and other hardbacks as well as a wide range of paperbacks in all subjects. At the back of the shop is a raised platform with racks of greetings cards and postcards.

Non-book material: calendars, cards, diaries, wrapping-paper
Services: special order

Bookstop *(Fulham Broadway)*
36 Vanston Place SW6
381-8764

M–F 9:30–6:30   Sat 9:30–6:00

This is a general bookshop situated just off the lower end of the Fulham Road. It is light and friendly and its stock well organised and signposted. Paperbacks are most popular here though some new hardbacks are also stocked.

Non-book material: cards, book tokens
Services: special order, gift wrapping

Broadway Books   *(Fulham Broadway)*
15 Jerdan Place SW6
385-8334

M–Sat 10:00–6:00

antiques / art / architecture / biography / children's books / cinema /
cookery / crafts / fiction / gardening / history / humour / illustrated /
nature / photography / reference / sport / transport / travel / wine

This remainder shop belongs to West London Books, a firm which
specializes in taking quantities of books for sale at offices and
factories. The turnover, both in paperback and hardback, is
therefore rapid. While some of the books are the sort that are only
published to be remaindered, there are a number of interesting
titles to be found. They also stock a limited number of new books
in the popular range.

Elys Ltd   *(Wimbledon)*
16 St George's Road SW19
946-9191

M–F 9:00–5:30   Sat 9:00–6:00

autobiography / cookery / fiction / reference / sport

There is a general range of popular fiction and reference books in
this section within Elys department store.

Non-book material: department store

Fielders   *(Wimbledon)*
54 Wimbledon Hill Road SW19
946-5044

M–Sat 9:00–5:30

antiques / art / BBC publications / biography / biology / business /
chemistry / children's books / classics / collecting / cookery / crafts /
economics / fiction / film / gardening / geography / geology /
history / law / literature / military history / music / natural history /
paperbacks / photography / physics / plays / poetry and verse /
reference / science fiction / sports / travel guides

283

Fielders carries current paperback and hardcover titles and has particularly good sections of children's books, travel guides and paperback fiction. It also stocks a range of academic books. The ground floor is completely given over to stationery, maps, artist's materials, newspapers and magazines, and cassettes.

Non-book material: stationery, artists' materials, maps
Services: mail order, special order
Catalogue: Christmas

General Trading Company   *(Sloane Square)*
144 Sloane Street SW1
730-0411

M–F 9:00–5:30   Sat 9:00–2:00

Within this up-market general store (once dubbed the Sloane Ranger's paradise) are several areas where books may be found. The children's department at the rear of the ground floor has an excellent selection of top-of-the-range classics, pop-ups and new publications. More general glossy books are displayed near one of the entrances with gift items, a few cookery titles are sold in the kitchen department on the lower ground floor and similarly gardening books in the gardening department

Non-book material: see above
Services: special order
Catalogue: general catalogue for Christmas

Harrods Book Department   *(Knightsbridge)*
Knightsbridge SW3
730-1234

M–F 9:00–5:00   W 9:30–7:00   Sat 9:00–6:00

general:
antiques / archaeology / architecture / art / bibles / biography / business / classics / collecting / cookery / crafts / drama / fiction / film and TV / fishing and yachting / French texts / gardening / health and childcare / history / humour / language teaching / literature / London / medicine / military history / music / natural history / pets / photography / poetry / politics / prayer books / reference / religion / science fiction / sports / teach yourself / theatre / thrillers / transport / travel guides / wine

children's books:
Beatrix Potter / cartoon books / classics / fairy tales / fiction up to nine / fiction over nine / first readers / foreign languages / general knowledge / geography / history / hobbies / Ladybird / music / nature / nursery rhymes / painting / poetry / pre-school reference

Harrods has a very large book department on the second floor with new paperback and hardcover titles. Children's books have an entire room of their own with a range of books for all ages and reading levels and wonderful in-store displays. For adults there is a wide selection of illustrated books about Britain, art, antiques, food, wine and sports, a section of Penguin classics and new fiction, as well as sections of recent hardcover titles in politics and bestselling fiction, and a large selection of Michelin guides.

Britain's largest private library is located on the fourth floor at Harrods through which, for an annual subscription fee, customers can borrow newly published books, especially in the areas of biography, history, travel and fiction.

Non-book material: department store
Services: mail order, special order, library lending
Catalogue: selected titles are featured in the Harrods store catalogue at Christmas

Hatchards   *(Sloane Square)*
150-152 King's Road SW3
351-7649

M–Sat 9:30–6:00

ground:
biography / fiction / music / theatre / travel and maps

basement:
antiques / architecture / art / children's / classics / cookery / design / gardening / history / philosophy / photography / poetry / psychology / reference / religion / science / social / sport

This branch of Hatchards is, like the others, an excellent bookshop. It differs greatly in the way it has been set up though, as it shares premises with the office stationery suppliers Rymans. This was an experiment which seems to be working, as the two businesses maintain their own separate identities and floor space.

Once inside the bookshop the proximity of Rymans does not impinge too greatly on one's consciousness, which some may feel to be a good thing. Attractive window displays are a feature of this shop and the staff are extremely knowledgeable and helpful. This together with the range and depth of titles makes it one of the best general bookshops in London. (The children's department is especially well run and stocked with a good choice of hardbacks.)

Services: mail order, special order
Catalogue: Spring and Autumn catalogues, monthly review, gardening and art catalogues

The Hill Bookshop   *(Wimbledon)*
87 High Street Wimbledon SW19
946-0198

M–Sat 9:30–5:30   W 9:30–1:00

art / biography / child care and pregnancy / children's books / classics / cookery / fiction / gardening / health / history / humour / literature / military history / mysteries / naval history / poetry and verse / reference / religion / sports / travel guides

The Hill Bookshop is an old and established general bookseller with a somewhat up-market stock of current paperback and hardcover titles, much of which is fiction, literature and art. At the rear of the shop is a children's room with books including Asterix and Tintin titles, as well as some BBC educational materials. They are very strong on books for the pre-school age.

Services: special order

The Little Bookshop   *(Wimbledon)*
39b The Broadway SW19
543-1031

M–Sat 9:30–6:00

A general bookshop with a good selection over a wide range of subjects including children's books and the latest paperback publications.

Services: special order

286

Martin the Newsagent   *(Clapham Junction – British Rail)*
66-68 St John's Road SW11
223-9415

M–Sat 7:30–6:00   Sun 8:00–1:00

children's books / cookery / education / fiction / hobbies / reference

A general range of reference books and the bestselling fiction can be found in the books section of this newsagent.

Non-book material: newsagents

Martin the Newsagent   *(Clapham Junction – British Rail)*
38-39 The Arndale Centre SW18
874-5110

M–Th 7:30–5:30   F 8:30–7:30   Sat 8:30–5:00

This branch of the newsagency chain has a small stock of general reference books, children's books and bestselling paperback fiction.

Non-book material: newsagents

John Menzies Ltd   *(South Kensington)*
50/52 Old Brompton Road SW7
589-3769

M–F 7:00a.m.–8:00p.m.   Sat–Sun 7:00a.m.–6:00p.m.

This is a small section including children's books and bestselling fiction.

Non-book material: stationery

Oppenheim & Co. Ltd   *(South Kensington)*
7-9 Exhibition Road SW7
584-5641

M–Sun 9:00–7:30

antiques / architecture / art / British monuments and cathedrals / Buddhism and Eastern religions / classics / cookery / crafts / decorative arts / Everyman / fiction / film / gardening / history / literature / military / natural history / philosophy / photography / psychology / transport / travel guides

With a general selection of current paperback fiction and non-fiction, Oppenheim particularly concentrates on books in the field of art. Not only are full-price art books available, but the shop has two large tables full of reduced-price art books, some of which are remaindered, but many of which are the last few copies of current titles. There is always a good stock of Everyman titles at half-price or less. A section has been opened upstairs devoted to military and transport books.

Non-book material: cards, prints
Services: mail order, special order (when possible)

Pages of Fun   *(Victoria)*
16 Terminus Place SW1
834-7747

M–Sat 9:00a.m.–10:00p.m.

The range of magazines and paperbacks here includes science fiction, horror, gay magazines and 'girlie' magazines.

Non-book magazines: London guides, postcards

The Pan Bookshop   *(South Kensington)*
158-162 Fulham Road SW10
373-4997

M–Sat 10:00–10:00   Sun 2:00–9:00

art / art history and criticism / biography / children's books / cinema / classics / cookery / crime / drama / economics / feminism / fiction / gardening / health and sex / history / humour / literary criticism / literature / music / natural history / occult / philosophy / poetry / politics / psychology / reference / religion / science fiction / sociology / teach yourself

This bookshop is owned by Pan Publishers and occupies the ground floor of their offices on the Fulham Road. Its cosmopolitan New York image, attractive red awnings, and late opening hours reflect the fashionable character of this part of Fulham with its pasta joints and cinemas. Pan is a general bookshop which stocks a wide range of paperback literature and poetry, among other subjects. In addition to these areas, however, are excellent selections of hardcover and paperback books on the fine and visual arts.

Non-book material: cards, magazines
Services: mail order, special order

Paperback Centre   *(Brixton)*
10 Atlantic Road Brixton SW9
274-8342

M–Sat 9:00–5:30   W 9:00–2:00   F 9:00–6:00

Africa and Caribbean / biography / children's books / China / cookery / education / fiction / health / humour / labour history / Latin America / Lenin / literary criticism / Marxism / philosophy / plays / poetry / politics / psychology / reference / science fiction / sciences / sexual politics / sociology / Soviet Union

As with the other two shops in this group the Paperback Centre has an emphasis on left-wing and socialist literature, while this branch has rather more stock of children's books and those about the Caribbean and much of the stock is in paperback. The shop also sells a wide range of newspapers and magazines.

Non-back material: see above, maps, posters
Services: mail order, special order

The Penguin Bookshop   *(Sloane Square)*
157 King's Road SW3
351-1915

ground floor:
art / crime / fiction / music / new titles / photography / science fiction / travel

basement:
biography / business / children's / classics / cookery / crafts / drama /
education / feminism / health and medicine / history / humour /
languages / literary criticism / literature / natural history /
philosophy / poetry / politics / recreation / reference / science /
sociology

Like its sister in Covent Garden, this shop stocks mainly
paperbacks, though not exclusively from the Penguin, Pelican
and Puffin imprints, most of the titles from which are on the
shelves. Those that are not can be ordered in up to two days.

Non-book material: greeting cards and postcards,
wrapping-paper
Services: special order
Catalogue: Penguin monthly stocklist

Plus Books   *(Colliers Wood)*
19 Abbey Parade
Merton High Street SW19
542-1665

M–Sat 9:00–6:00

This branch of Plus Books has a wide range of new and
second-hand books, mostly fiction, with a selection of general
magazines and comics. Exchange is welcomed.

Pulteney & Co.   *(South Kensington)*
22 Thurloe Street SW7
589-0522

M–F 9:30–5:30   Sat 10:00–2:00

antiques / applied art / art history / classics / collecting / cookery /
crafts / decorative arts / drama / fiction / history / literature / music /
natural history / philosophy and religion / poetry / psychology /
sports / UK monuments and cathedrals

Pulteney carries new paperback fiction, as well as a large selection
of art books, in the fine and applied arts. An interesting frequently
changing number of remaindered books fills much of the shop.

Non-book material: posters, prints

Razzall's Riverside Books   *(Barnes – British Rail)*
36a High Street SW13
878-7859

M–Sat 9:00–6:00   Th 9:00–5:00

biography / children's / cinema / cookery / fiction / gardening / history / humour / music / reference / sport / travel / wildlife

It is good to see another bookshop catering for literary Barnes. Razzall's sells both hard and paperbacks in the above subjects, and it also has books by local authors.

Services: special order

Response Community Bookshop   *(West Brompton/*
300 Old Brompton Road SW5   *Earls Court)*
370-4606

M–Sat 12:00–7:00

new:
around Earls Court / art / biography / British history and politics / children's books / China / Earls Court authors / education / feminism / fiction / food and drink / gay books / health / humour / Irish history and politics / Middle-East / natural history / philosophy / photography / popular science / psychology / sexuality / sociology / supernatural / Third World / US history and politics / USSR

second-hand:
biography / cookery / history / hobbies / language teaching / literature / philosophy / poetry / religion / society / travel guides

Response is a small community bookshop with a welcoming, living-room atmosphere. While the selection of books is limited, the shop has acquired funds to expand the already well-chosen stock of alternative and community-oriented literature. In the front room of the shop are current titles, including a nice range of fiction with authors like Tom Sharpe and Muriel Spark. Non-fiction is stocked with its usefulness to the neighbourhood in mind, so instead of the Michelin guide to France, there is *The Hitchhiker's Guide to Europe*. Second-hand books are in the rear of the shop, and include some children's, as well as general fiction.

Tea and coffee are available for browsers.

A printing workshop downstairs is available for community use, as is the meeting room upstairs. A free community newspaper, Response, is published by the shop and the back page of the paper is devoted to news about books and the Response project. It is hoped to open a darkroom.

Non-book material: postcards
Services: special order
Publications: Response publishes a community newspaper

John Sandoe Books   *(Sloane Square)*
10 Blacklands Terrace SW3
589-9473

M–Sat 9:30–5:30

ground floor:
antiques / antiquities / architecture / art / biography / classics / collecting / cookery / Eastern religions / fiction / furniture / gardening / history / literature / natural history / pottery / textiles / travel guides

basement: children's
classics / dance / fairy tales / fiction / games and sport / history / music / nursery rhymes / story books / verse

adult
health / psychology

first floor: paperbacks
classics / drama / drama criticism / fiction / history / literature / literary criticism / philosophy / poetry / psychology / religion / sociology / stage history / Virago

John Sandoe is a complete general bookshop, set back from the King's Road in a lovely low-slung cottage. With three floors of books, the shop has a large children's section, an unusually wide range of hardcover books in all subjects with particularly large sections of biography and literature, and an excellent range of paperbacks. The friendly staff are highly knowledgeable.

Services: mail order, special order
Catalogue: Christmas selections

Slaney & Mckay   *(Sloane Square)*
263 King's Road SW3
352-7123

M–Sun 10:00–6:00   Sat 10:00–10:00

ground floor:
antiques / art / cookery / design / fiction / gardening / gay
literature / interior decorating / popular culture / travel

basement:
astrology / biography / children's / crime / drama / health /
mysticism / paperback fiction / poetry / psychology / reference /
women's issues

This is a charming bookshop on two floors with a good selection of
paperbacks, children's books, new biographies and hardback
bestsellers. They have developed a loyal clientele largely from the
local Chelsea area and the window displays and in-store
promotions make the shop very appealing. They have a strong
section on design and decorative finishes, and it shows.

Non-book material: address books, cards, diaries, postcards,
wrapping-paper
Services: special order
Catalogue: first one due in 1987

W.H. Smith   *(Sloane Square)*
36 Sloane Square SW1
730-0351

M/Th/F 9:00–6:30   Tue 9:30–6:30   W 9:00–7:00   Sat 9:00–6:00

There is a thriving book department in this branch of W.H. Smith.
They sell a range of general hardback titles, doing well with
biographies, the latest fiction and homecare titles. The paperback
department also sells fiction and travel particularly well.

Non-book material: stationery, cards, paper, news, magazines,
etc.
Services: special order, post-a-book, tokens
Catalogue: *Bookcase* review of books twice yearly

W.H. Smith
(Victoria)

Eastern Shop
Victoria Station SW1
828-2853

M–Sat 6:30a.m.–9:30p.m.   Sun 7:00a.m.–7:00p.m.

There are two branches of Smith's in Victoria Station and this one is near platform 1, where the trains for the Continent leave. The book department covers the standard range of subjects, including a section of new hardback titles. They have an extensive range of language books both for the English holidaymakers and those arriving from overseas in the station. These, and holiday guides, make up a large part of their summer trade.

Non-book material: stationery, cards, paper, news, magazines, etc.
Services: special order, tokens
Catalogue: *Bookcase* review of books twice yearly

W.H. Smith
(Victoria)

Western Shop
Victoria Station SW1
834-2534

M–Sat 7:00a.m.–10:00p.m.   Sun 8:00a.m.–9:00p.m.

This is one of two branches of W.H. Smith in the station and it is near the local lines. The books cover the usual range of subjects, including new hardback titles and a wide range of bestsellers, with occasional bargain selections.

Non-book material: stationery, cards, paper, news, magazines, etc.
Services: special order, tokens
Catalogue: *Bookcase* review of books twice yearly

W.H. Smith
(Earls Court)

266 Earls Court Road SW5
370-3201

M–Sat 9:00–6:00

The book department here stocks a range of fiction, children's books and the standard selection of general interest books including cookery, maps and guides. New hardback titles are carried.

Non-book material: stationery, cards, paper, news, magazines, etc.
Services: special order, post-a-book, tokens
Catalogue: *Bookcase* review of books twice yearly

W.H. Smith   *(Putney – British Rail)*
111 Putney High Street SW15
788-2573

M–Sat 8:30–5:30   Tue 9:30–5:30

The book department in this large branch of W.H. Smith covers most of the first floor and it has an extensive range including fiction, general and special interests and children's books. One section of the refreshingly thorough collection keeps new titles in hardback.

Non-book material: stationery, cards, paper, news, magazines, etc.
Services: special order, post-a-book, tokens
Catalogue: *Bookcase* review of books twice yearly

W.H. Smith   *(Streatham Hill – British Rail)*
180-182 Streatham High Road SW16
677-3031/2

M–Sat 8:30–5:30

This is a reasonably large book department, with a standard range of subjects and a section for new hardback titles.

Non-book material: stationery, cards, paper, news, magazines, etc.
Services: special order, post-a-book, token
Catalogue: *Bookcase* review of books twice yearly

W.H. Smith   *(Wimbledon)*
Wimbledon Station SW19
946-6143

M–F 6:30a.m.–6:30p.m.   Sat 8:00–5:00

This is a small shop just outside Wimbledon station and so the space for books is limited. However, there is the standard range of subjects here and a selection of new hardback titles.

Non-book material: cards, stationery, paper, news, magazines
Services: special order, tokens
Catalogue: *Bookcase* review of books twice yearly

Tetric Bookshop   *(Clapham Common)*
116 Clapham High Street SW4
622-5344

M–F 10:00–6:00   Sat 10:00–5:30

Africa / anthropology / art / biography / business and management / child care / children's books / classics / cookery / crime / DIY / drama / economics / education / feminism / fiction / film / games / gardening / humour / literature / medicine / music / natural history / occult / philosophy / poetry / politics / psychology / reference / science / short stories / sociology / sports / study aids / transport / travel guides

Though it is a general bookshop, the shop specializes primarily in books on the social sciences, especially those on local and national political issues, black studies and sociology, as well as contemporary literature. They have a good deal of paperback fiction and current literary hardbacks.

Non-book material: cards, wrapping-paper, protective plastic book-jackets
Services: special order

Truslove and Hanson   *(Knightsbridge)*
205 Sloane Street SW3
235-2128

M–F 9:00–8:00   Sat 9:00–6:30

ground floor:
biography / children's books / cookery / fiction / games / gardening / history / humour / natural history / sports / travel guides

basement: hardbacks:
antiques / architecture / art / crafts / philosophy / poetry / psychology / reference
paperbacks:
biography / classics / crime / fiction / history / science fiction

With an interior as smart and sparkling as the rest of Knightsbridge, Truslove and Hanson, part of the Sherratt & Hughes group of bookshops, stock current titles which also reflect the tastes of their well-heeled 'neighbourhood' clientele. Extensive sections of travel guides, children's books and current fiction mark the general stock of this two-floor bookshop.

Non-book material: cards; photo albums; printed and engraved personalized writing paper, business cards, etc.; stationery; visitors' books; wrapping-paper
Services: mail order, special order
Catalogue: Christmas, Spring and Autumn lists

Village Books   *(Streatham/Streatham Common – British Rail)*
17 Shrubbery Road SW16
677-2667

M–Sat 10:30–7:00   W closed

academic textbooks / art / business / child care and education / children's books / cinema / classics / cookery / crafts / DIY / fiction / gardening / health / history / humour / literature / local history and authors / natural history / occult / philosophy / poetry / politics / psychology / reference / religion / science fiction / sociology / sports and games / travel guides / women's studies

This small shop, a few yards from Streatham High Street, carries mostly current titles; in its small space it contains a remarkably wide stock owing to a system of keeping one copy of most titles and replacing them within a few days. There is a special antiquarian and second-hand section and some of the rest of the stock includes 'alternative' literature and politics. However, as the owner of this friendly, enterprising shop remarks, he is willing to take any book that looks interesting and, as a result, this shop draws customers from all over London. Certainly, it is a refreshing change from the bland chain-stores which fill much of the High Street. On the first Sunday of the month a book fair is usually held in the shop.

Non-book material: cards, comics, posters, South American crafts
Services: mail order, special order, school and library supply
Catalogue: occasional

Waterstone's   *(South Kensington)*
99-101 Old Brompton Road SW7
581-8522

M–F 9:30a.m.–10:30p.m.   Sat 9:30–7:00   Sun 12:00–7:00

art and antiques / biography and memoirs / children's books / cookery and diet / drama / gardening / health / history / literature / military / natural history / poetry / reference / religion and philosophy / travel and guides / twentieth-century fiction

This was the first Waterstone's to open, in 1982. Each branch tries to cater to a particular market, and this one is very much a neighbourhood bookstore, taking a lot of special orders from local people. They do well with a range of subjects from biography to cookery and the latest fiction. The staff are friendly young booksellers who do a good deal of their business in the latter part of the evening when people wander in on their way to or from nearby restaurants or cinemas.

Non-book material: maps, postcards, literary magazines
Services: mail order, search service and selective lists for account holders, Waterstone's credit card which can be used in all branches and by telephone

Richard Worth Booksellers   *(Putney Bridge)*
7-9 Lower Richmond Road SW15
788-9006

M–Sat 10:00–6:00

animals and pets / art / biography / Buddhism / business / child care / children's books / classics / cookery / crafts / current affairs / dance / drama / Eastern religions and philosophies / fiction / gardening / health / history / literary biography and criticism / literature / magic / music / natural history / philosophy / plays / poetry / politics / psychology / reference / science fiction / Shakespeare / sports and games / transport / travel guides / war novels

Richard Worth is a general bookshop specializing, in their words, in 'better books', all of which are new. There is a wide selection of books on fine, modern and visual arts, Eastern religion, politics, fiction, poetry and biography, with smaller sections in other areas.

Non-book material: stationery, greetings cards, postcards
Services: mail order, special order

Speciality Bookshops

J. A. Allen & Company
(Victoria)
(The Horseman's Bookshop)
1 Lower Grosvenor Place SW1
828-8855   834-5606/7

M–F 9:00–5:30   Sat 9:00–1:00

anatomy / Arabians / betting / breeds and breeding / driving / equitation / events / fiction / general equestrian / hunting / nutrition / polo / racing / reference / stable management / training / veterinary medicine

J. A. Allen is London's leading bookshop for people interested in horses. New, second-hand and antiquarian books are available on all aspects of horse training, breeding, riding and racing.

Non-book material: anatomy charts, cards, calendars
Services: mail order, special order
Catalogue: new title lists, specialized lists, J. A. Allen publications catalogue
Publications: J. A. Allen & Co. publishes a wide range of books about horses

At the Sign of the Dragon
(Mortlake – British Rail)
131 Sheen Lane SW14
876-3855

M–Sat 10:00–6:00   W 10:00–1:30

antiques / children's books / classics / cookery / detective fiction / fantasy / fiction / film / gardening / humour / language teaching / psychic world / religion / science fiction / war novels

Although a portion of the stock is devoted to current fiction and non-fiction titles, this shop specializes in affordable children's books and current science fiction and fantasy titles. The owner has a special interest in science fiction and is, therefore, extremely knowledgeable in the field and very helpful. The commitment to children's books is realized in a range of fiction and non-fiction titles, mostly paperback, for all age levels (there is also a section of science fiction books for children).

A wonderfully chatty catalogue on science fiction titles is put out every three months, and the shop stocks a range of science fiction and fantasy magazines.

Non-book material: badges, cassettes, science fiction records, fantasy games
Services: mail order, special order
Catalogue: science fiction and fantasy lists quarterly (includes books on science facts versus fiction)

Bayswater Books   *(Putney)*
21 Gwendolen Avenue SW15
788-4029

By appointment

dyeing / spinning / weaving

Bayswater Books have no retail outlet as such, but will see potential customers by appointment. Otherwise they operate quite satisfactorily as a mail order only concern, supplying books in their special field. They do not have any second-hand publications.

Services: mail order
Catalogue: booklist available, sae required

Benedicts Bookshop   *(Fulham Broadway)*
92 Lillie Road SW6
385-6798

M–F 9:30–6:00   Sat 10:00–3:00

Benedicts specializes in language books and this includes both English as a foreign language and a range of books for English speakers learning another language. There is some foreign literature, a small general section and a second-hand department.

Non-book material: language teaching aids, including cassettes, computer programs and videos
Services: mail order, comprehensive lists of teaching materials for particular languages on request

The Bookshop   *(Tooting Bec)*
15 Trinity Road SW17
767-5356

M–Sat 10:00–6:00

The Bookshop, formerly called Bec Business Books, specializes in business and professional studies books, though they have recently increased their general stock.

Services: deliveries within three miles, school and college supply, mail order

Bookspread   *(Tooting Bec)*
58 Tooting Bec Road SW17
767-6377/4551

M–F 10:00–5:00   Th 10:00–9:00   Sat 10:00–3:00

birth / death / divorce / fairy tales / fiction / films and TV / history / literature / marriage / music / myths / natural history / picture books / poetry / reference / story books

Current titles for and about children are the specialities of Bookspread, located on the ground floor of a building in a residential area of Tooting Bec. The staff is concerned with making books and reading fun. Titles are arranged according to age groups, so it is easy for mothers, playgroup leaders, teachers and children to find the most appropriate books. The shop which also carries books for adults about children and child care, organizes storytellings, talks about books, has visiting writers and runs an advisory service.

Non-book material: cassettes, cards
Services: mail order, special order in any field, boxes of books on sale or return for schools and children's organizations, mobile bookshop

British Travel Centre   *(Piccadilly Circus)*
12 Regent Street, SW1
846-9000

M–Sat 9:00–6:30   Sun 10:00–4:00

British Travel Centre stocks a comprehensive range of travel books, guides and maps covering the whole of Britain. The major guides are available in foreign-language editions and there are books for special interests and needs, such as staying in castles and taking children on holiday.

John Buckle Bookshop   *(Stockwell)*
170 Wandsworth Road SW8
627-0599

M–Sat 12:00–6:00

Engels / Hoxha / Lenin / Marx / Stalin

Specialists in revolutionary literature, who stock the works of the great leaders as well as Russian novels from the thirties. Cultural material from the Marxist-Leninist movement and a wide range of Marxist-Leninist foreign newspapers can also be found here.

Non-book material: cassettes and records of revolutionary works and revolutionary music.
Services: mail order
Publications: *Workers Weekly*, the newspaper of The Revolutionary Communist Party of Britain; Marxist-Leninist works

Catholic Truth Society   *(Victoria)*
Ashley Place SW1
834-1363

M–F 9:15–5:00   Sat 9:15–1:00

bibles / biography / children's books / comparative religion / death / family / marriage / meditation / Old and New Testaments / prayers / spiritual life / Sunday readings / travel guides

This shop sells new books relating exclusively to the Catholic faith, indeed mainly titles which carry the Imprimatur are in stock. Major Catholic newspapers and periodicals are also sold.

Non-book material: cards, crucifixes, rosaries
Services: mail order, special order
Publications: The Catholic Truth Society publishes religious pamphlets and books

Children's Bookshop   *(Wimbledon)*
66 High Street SW19
947-2038

M–Sat 9:00–5:30

Sister to the Muswell Hill Children's Bookshop, this shop in Wimbledon village largely shares its stock, which caters for 0–14-year-olds. Adult bestsellers are on sale too, to catch the bigger children.

Non-book material: birthday cards, bookmarks, story tapes, wrapping-paper
Services: special order, mail order, school supply

Church House Bookshop   *(Westminster/St James's Park)*
31 Great Smith Street SW1
222-9011

M–F 9:00–5:00   Th 9:00–6:00

bibles / biography / children's books / commentaries / comparative religion / doctrine / ecumenism / liturgy and worship / pastoral work / philosophy / prayer / religious education / study aids / vocations

This religious bookshop focuses on issues in Christianity, but also has a special section of books on Tolkien and C. S. Lewis. A variety of subject areas are covered, from daily religious life to church history, and the shop is the main outlet for publications of the General Synod.

Non-book material: calendars, church registers, posters, stationery, records, cassettes, video hire
Services: mail order, special order
Catalogue: *Booklines* lists new titles three times yearly, Church House Publishing catalogue
Publications: the shop is affiliated to Church House Publishing which publishes books and other materials on Christianity

Cook, Hammond & Kell Ltd   *(St James's Park)*
(The London Map Centre)
22 Caxton Street SW1
222-4945 (general)   222-2466 (O.S. sales)

M–F 9:00–5:00

This is the place for intrepid travellers – the main agents for Ordnance Survey maps. The shop is on two levels, with a more general range of maps and guides, including some coverage outside Britain, as well as the exhaustive stock of O.S. maps.

Non-book material: compasses, map measures
Publications: maps of nineteenth-century London, John Speed maps of fifteenth and sixteenth-century English counties, modern maps of Great Britain, Europe and the World

Paul H. Crompton Ltd   *(Parsons Green)*
638 Fulham Road SW6
736-2551

M–Sat 10:00–6:00

Most of this shop's business is wholesale, although the rather cramped quarters are open for retail customers. Their specialities are martial arts, Eastern religions and philosophies. The shop stocks new books and magazines from the UK, USA and East Asia, and the staff are friendly and helpful.

Non-book material: badges, posters
Services: mail order, special order in field
Catalogue: complete list
Publications: Paul H. Crompton publishes books on the martial arts and survival, with sixty titles in print

The Design Centre   *(Piccadilly Circus)*
28 Haymarket SW1
839-8000

M–Tu 10:00–6:00   W–Sat 10:00–8:00   Sun 1:00–6:00

architecture / children's books / cookery / crafts / design history / design sourcebooks / design theory / engineering design / environmental design / fashion / futures / gardening / general paperbacks / graphics / home design / interior design / London and Britain guides / photography

The Design Centre incorporates a large exhibition area and gift shop on the ground floor, a snack bar, stationery and household wares department on the first floor and at the back of the building, on a large mezzanine area, all to itself, a superb bookshop has been designed. It naturally specializes in all aspects of home and commercial design from DIY to publications on architecture for the professional. The general selection of books includes imaginatively designed children's books (e.g., pop-up, cut-out). With plenty of space the staff are able to show books to their best advantage and to create regular in-store displays.

Non-book material: see above
Services: mail order
Catalogue: general book list, three to four times yearly
Publications: Design Council Publications produces titles on all aspects of design, three magazines and a variety of design journals

The Faith House Bookshop   *(Westminster)*
7 Tufton Street SW1
222-6952

M–F 9:30–5:00

bible stories / bibles / biblical lands / children's books / Christian education / church history / church and politics / church and society / commentaries / doctrine / ethics / faith / liturgy / Marx and Christ / mysticism / poetry / prayer / religion / spirituality / theology / worship

This Christian bookshop is as quiet as the back streets of Westminster in which it is located. The shop's interior has the look and feel of a church and, indeed, the books here are about all aspects of Christianity and the church.

The most recent books on the role of the church in society are available, as well as a selection of children's books.

Non-book material: cards, church stationery, devotional articles, music and song books
Services: mail order, special order
Catalogue: CLA publications
Publications: The Church Literature Association publishes books about religion and related issues

Farlows of Pall Mall   *(Piccadilly Circus)*
5 Pall Mall SW1
839-2423

M–F 9:00–5:00   Th 9:00–6:00   Sat 9:00–4:00

Farlows specialize in the country pursuits of the gentlemen who dine in the Pall Mall clubs; shooting, fishing and hunting. Fishing tackle and shooting goods make up the bulk of their stock, but they do have some related literature.

Non-book material: fishing tackle and shooting goods
Services: mail order, special order

The French Bookshop   *(South Kensington)*
28 Bute Street SW7
584-2840

M–F 8:30–6:00 term time (9:30–6:00 holidays)   Sat 10:00–4:00

The French Bookshop is a friendly shop with a cool, blue and white interior lined with current titles, imported from France. Larousse classics, Gallimard Folio fiction, poetry, literary criticism, thrillers and drama are all here, in French. Michelin guides, language texts, a shelf of cookery books and a large range of children's books – including Tintin and Asterix – are also featured. A small section is given over to French translations. Students from the nearby Lycée are well served.

For a helpful and well-informed staff on French literature and dictionaries, this is the place to look.

Non-book material: cards, school satchels, wrapping paper, French stationery
Services: mail order, special order
Catalogue: specialized lists

Geological Museum Bookshop   *(South Kensington)*
Exhibition Road SW7
589-3444 ext. 298

M–Sat 10:00–5:30   Sun 2:30–5:30

geology / HMSO publications / land formation / mineralogy / minerals / palaeontology / petrology / rocks / UK regional geology / volcanoes

The small stock of books at the Geological Museum Bookshop are about geology and related subjects. Children's books, gift books, adult reading and museum catalogues are available, as well as a wide range of 'geological' gifts. The Geological Museum itself now forms part of the Natural History Museum.

Non-book material: cards, geological charts, jewellery, maps, plaster casts of fossils, posters, prints, slides, stones
Services: mail order
Catalogue: HMSO and map lists
Publications: The Institute of Geological Services publishes in the field of geological sciences

Girl Guides Association Shop   *(Victoria)*
17-19 Buckingham Palace Road SW1
834-6242

M–F 9:00–5:30   Sat 9:00–1:00

badges / camping / charts / games / guiding books / handicrafts / knotting books / sport

The book section is a small part of the Girl Guides Association Shop, containing new titles relevant to all aspects of guiding.

Non-book material: badges, camping equipment, uniforms
Services: mail order
Catalogue: complete list of Girl Guide Association publications annually
Publications: The Girl Guides Association publishes books and magazines about guiding

Han-Shan Tang   *(Parsons Green)*
717 Fulham Road SW6
731-2447

M–F 10:00–6:00

central Asia / China / Far East / Japan / Korea

This bookshop concentrates on antiquarian, out-of-print and new titles on all aspects of the above countries, with special emphasis on the arts.

Catalogue: 4–5 general lists and 1–2 specialist catalogues yearly

Heaven on Earth Books   *(Clapham South)*
126 Elms Crescent
Clapham South SW4
673-0962

Alexander technique / healing / metaphysical / natural childbirth / 'New Age' books / personal growth and development / rebirthing / spiritual

This specialist bookseller is a mail order account only.

Non-book material: cassettes, cards, incense
Services: mail order, acquire 'New Age' books from USA
Catalogue: twice yearly
Publications: *Heal Your Body – the Mental Causes for Physical Illness and the Metaphysical Way to Overcome Them*

Heraldry Today   *(Knightsbridge)*
10 Beauchamp Place SW3
584-1656

M–W 9:30–5:00

academic dress and insignia / coins, orders and medals / decorations / family heraldry and history / flags and arms / French heraldry / genealogy / heraldic design / Italian heraldry / peerage / reference / royal heraldry / school arms / symbols / topography / UK heraldry

Located at the rear of the building at 10 Beauchamp Place, Heraldry Today specializes in new, second-hand and antiquarian books on genealogy and heraldry. Despite the small size of the shop (which is a branch of a much larger shop in Wiltshire) there is a comprehensive selection of titles about heraldry and related subjects in the UK and on the Continent. Burke's Peerage and Debrett publications are here as well as rare and more obscure books on, for example, Italian military insignia or English flags. The shop keeps current and back issues of relevant journals as well.

Services: mail order, special order in field, search service in field
Catalogue: selected list of second-hand and antiquarian books every four months, complete list of new titles every January
Publications: Heraldry Today has published original books and reprints in the field of heraldry

ICA Bookshop   *(Charing Cross)*
Nash House
12 Carlton House Terrace SW1
930-0493

M–Sun 12:00–9:00

art / artists / biography / cinema: biography, genres, theory / ICA exhibition catalogues / individual rights / literature / Marx / philosophy / photography / politics / semiotics / sexual politics / USSR / women's issues and literature

The limited space available to the ICA Bookshop is unfortunate because in addition to having a good range of books on contemporary art and artists, the shop has the beginnings of an excellent selection of alternative literature, modern classics, film theory and political philosophy. There is a wide range of arts, crafts, photography, film and political magazines from the UK, US and the Continent. An extra tip – time your visit well and you can have a cheap, imaginative meal in the ICA self-service restaurant which is open to gallery visitors and extremely good value.

Non-book material: artists' cards, international selection of arts magazines (including back issues)
Services: special order

Imperial College Bookshop   *(South Kensington)*

223 Sherfield Building
Imperial College of Science and Technology
Exhibition Road SW7
589-5218

M–F 9:15–5:15

aeronautics / art / biology / chemical engineering / classics /
computers / cookery / fiction / geology / humanities / life sciences /
literature / management / mechanical engineering / mining /
Pelican, Penguin / physics / reference

The IC Bookshop is a source for a wide range of university level
textbooks, but about 40% of the titles are now general paperback
fiction and non-fiction. In the general subject areas, reference
books figure prominently, but there is also a selection of current
fiction and literary classics.

Non-book material: cards, drawing equipment, stationery
Services: mail order, special order

J. & G. Books   *(Streatham Common – British Rail)*

17 Streatham Vale SW16
764-4669

Tue–Sat 10:00–5:00   Th 10:00–1:00

One visit to Streatham will equip you not only with a rare reptilian
pet, but all the background information you need to care for it and
understand the species. This shop specializes in reptiles and
amphibians and the stock is both new and second-hand. There are
a few natural history books and a small collection of gemmology
reflecting the owner's recent interest in the subject. The pet shop
is next door to the book shop and there is access to the books via
the living half of this exotic entourage when the book shop is
closed.

Non-book material: pet shop
Services: mail order
Catalogue: book lists available

Peter Jones   *(Sloane Square)*
Sloane Square SW1
730-3434

M–Sat 9:00–5:30   Wed 9:30–7:00

The children's book department in Peter Jones is aimed at children up to ten years. The range moves from 'bath' books through to paperback fiction and reference books.

Non-book material: cassettes, department store
Services: special order

H. Karnac (Books) Ltd   *(Gloucester Road)*
58 Gloucester Road SW7
584-3303

M–Sat 9:00–6:00

ground floor:
architecture / art / biography / cookery / crafts / fiction / furniture / literature / memoirs / music / natural history / reference / travel guides

basement:
group analysis / general Freudian and Jungian literature / psychoanalysis / psychotherapy

Karnac specializes in psychoanalysis and psychotherapy while keeping some general books on its ground floor. The general stock is concentrated on recent fiction, art books and other non-fiction. Downstairs are books in the shop's speciality, psychoanalysis and psychotherapy; all aspects of the subjects are covered, making this the best-stocked shop of its sort in Europe.

Services: international mail order, special order, specialist conference bookstalls
Catalogue: books on psychotherapy and psychoanalysis listed every two years
Publications: Maresfield Library, original titles under Karnac imprint
Note: There is another branch at 118 Finchley Road – see separate entry.

Don Kelly   *(Sloane Square)*
Antiquarius Stand M13
135 King's Road SW3
352-4690

M–Sat 10:00–6:00

There are some 1,000 new and out-of-print books at this antique
stand in the King's Road, all of which deal with collecting and
antiques (e.g., dolls, furniture, brass, pottery, watches, silver and
porcelain).

Services: mail order, special order, search service

Kensington Music Shop   *(South Kensington)*
9 Harrington Road SW7
589-9054   581-3590

M–F 9:00–5:45   Sat 9:00–4:00

biography / composers / harmony / instruments / music history /
music teaching / orchestration / sight reading

Situated only a matter of yards from South Kensington tube
station, Kensington Music sells both musical instruments and
books. Titles cover composers, musicians, music theory and
history and are in both hard and paper covers. The shop has a
strong section of sheet music.

Non-book material: instruments and accessories
Services: mail order, special order, discount on scores and sheet
music to students, teachers, and colleges

London Visitor and Convention Bureau   *(Victoria)*
Victoria Station forecourt SW1
730-3450

M–Sat 9:00–7:00   Sun 9:00–5:00 (times may vary)

The London Tourist Board runs a bookshop on the first floor of its
Tourist Information Centre in Victoria Station which features
books about, and guides to, London. Londoners as well as

tourists are catered for, with books for visitors to London from overseas and the rest of Britain (e.g., accommodation and shopping guides, maps, picture books), and books for these taking day trips out of London. An exceedingly cordial staff make discovering our own city an enjoyable experience.

Non-book material: maps, posters, taped walking tours
Services: mail order
Catalogue: book list
Publications: LTB publishes *Where to stay in London, Children's London, Exploring Central London, Exploring Outer London*

Manna Christian Centre   *(Streatham – British Rail)*
147-149 Streatham High Road SW16
769-8588

M–Sat 9:30–5:30

There is a wide range of Christian literature here, covering bible commentaries, biographies, devotional handbooks and prayer. A coffee shop is attached to the bookshop so you can take your time and spend the whole morning here.

Non-book material: cards, cassettes, posters, records
Services: special order

The Medici Gallery   *(South Kensington)*
26 Thurloe Street SW7
589-1363

M–F 9:00–5:30   Sat 9:00–5:00

art / fashion / film / photography

The books here are all related to art in some shape or form.

Non-book material: artists' materials and supplies, gifts, Medici cards, Medici prints, stationery
Services: framing
Catalogue: a catalogue is available for the Medici publications
Publications: Medici publications

The Mothers' Union Bookshop   *(Westminster)*

Mary Sumner House
24 Tufton Street SW1
222-5533

M–F 9:30–5:00

bible stories / bibles / children's books / Christian faith / cookery /
crafts and hobbies / early learning / education / family and children /
literature / London maps / marriage / natural history / prayer /
social issues / worship / youth clubs and school assemblies

Mother's Union Bookshop has three main areas – children, the
family and religion. Their subject categories are now fairly easy to
find one's way around as they have big blue and white headings.

Non-book material: cards, wrapping-paper
Services: mail order, special order
Catalogue: Mothers' Union publications
Publications: The Mothers' Union publishes books about the
family and children

National Army Museum Bookshop   *(Sloane Square)*

Royal Hospital Road SW3
730-0717

M–Sat 10:00–5:30   Sun 2:00–5:30

The bookshop in this museum specializes in all things military, in
particular the history of the British army and its campaigns.
Children's educational books and introductory guides to military
history ranging from the Civil to the Falklands War are just some
of the publications on offer. The stock includes regimental
histories and facsimiles of Civil War army procedures.

Non-book material: calendars, cassettes, games, kits, posters, souvenirs, toy soldiers
Services: mail order
Catalogue: comprehensive catalogue available
Publications: *Army Museum* is the annual publication with news on exhibitions and special interest articles

National Poetry Centre Bookshop *(Earls Court)*
21 Earls Court Square SW5
373-7861/2

M–F 10:00–5:00   during evening events 7:00pm–9:30pm

anthologies / children's poetry / collected works / criticism / individual poets

One nice retail characteristic of modern poetry is that the volumes are usually slim enough to require little shelf space so, although this shop is a small book room, there is much poetry on display. The majority of the work is by contemporary British poets; there are also small press publications and poetry from the USA, Canada and the Continent. It is run with knowledge and enthusiasm and makes a visit well worthwhile for books so often shunned even by the largest shops.

Non-book material: poetry records and cassettes, magazines
Services: mail order, special order
Catalogue: periodic book lists
Publications: the NPC publishes a major poetry magazine, *Poetry Review*

Natural History Museum Bookshop *(South Kensington)*
Cromwell Road SW7
589-6323 ext. 285

M–Sat 10:00–5:40   Sun 2:30–5:40

birds / children's / conservation / countryside / evolution / fish / mammals / plants and gardening / rocks and fossils

This is a small shop in a row to the left of the museum entrance hall. It is next door to the gift shop and souvenir shop – all of which seem to be permanently thronged with excited children and harassed-looking parents and teachers. The bookshop obviously specializes in natural history subjects as outlined above, with much of the stock geared particularly towards the younger reader.

Non-book material: see above
Services: mail order
Catalogue: yes
Publications: The British Museum (Natural History) publishes many books and information bulletins which are all sold in the shop

Orbis Books (London) Ltd   *(Earls Court)*
66 Kenway Road SW5
370-2210

M–F 9:30–5:30   Sat 9:30–4:30

Orbis specializes in new books, magazines and journals about, and from, Eastern Europe, with particular emphasis upon Poland, the Ukraine, the USSR and Czechoslovakia. Most of the books are in the languages of Eastern Europe, although the shop stocks books published in English which are relevant to the region. Politics, art, religion, women's issues, labour, language teaching and literature are just a few of the subjects covered, though they carry everything from children's books to specialized academic texts. Orbis has a small antiquarian section and is quite willing to attempt to track down out-of-print titles.

Non-book material: cassettes, folk art, records
Services: mail order, special order
Catalogue: new titles list every four months
Publications: Orbis Books publishes books in Polish about Poland

Padre Pio Bookshop Centre   *(Victoria)*
10 Upper Tachbrook Street SW1
834-5363

M–Sat 10:00–5:30

This is a very special bookshop concerned with the life and works of Padre Pio, the stigmatized Capuchin monk of San Giovanni. The stock includes Padre Pio's writings and a wide variety of books about both Padre Pio and more general religious subjects.

Non-book material: cassettes, cribs, religious items, statues, videos
Services: mail order

Paperchase   *(South Kensington)*
167 Fulham Road SW3
589-7839

M–Sat 9:30–6:00   Wed 9:30–7:00

art / children's books / cookery / crafts / gardening / toy-making

The book department here concentrates on subjects related to the general stock, specializing in off-beat arts and crafts and ideas for the decorative arts in general.

Non-book material: artists' materials, gifts, stationery
Services: special order

Le Petit Prince Bookshop   *(South Kensington)*
7 Harrington Road SW7
589-5991

M–F 8:15–6:15   Sat 10:00–5:00

Le Petit Prince specializes in French books, and books in English about France. Current Penguin classics, literature, reference books and titles in general subject areas are also available in English. French literature, classics, philosophy, history, travel guides, language teaching texts – among other subjects – are available in French. Publishers include Glenat, Gallimard, Garnier-Flammarion, Hachette, Dargaud, Dupuis and many British publishers. There is French literature in translation and a special children's book section in French. International *bandes dessinées* and journals from France are carried, and the shop gives a 10% discount to students.

Non-book material: cards, maps, posters, stationery, wrapping-paper, pen-repair service, story cassettes, satchels
Services: mail order, special order, photocopying
Catalogue: monthly book list and catalogue

Planning Bookshop   *(Charing Cross)*
17 Carlton House Terrace SW1
930-88903/4/5

M–F 10:00–5:30

architecture / conservation / design energy / environment / environmental education / general planning / history of planning / housing / impact assessment / land use: derelict and inner city / leisure / new towns / planning in developing centres / planning in Europe / planning law and procedures / psychology / public participation / regional planning / resources technology / rural planning / sociology / transport / urban and city planning

This is the bookshop of The Town and Country Planning Association carrying only new, second-hand and antiquarian books in the above subjects. The shop may be moving in 1987, so it is best to telephone first to check whether it is still at the above address.

Services: mail order, special order
Catalogue: annual list updated quarterly
Publications: The Town and Country Planning Association publishes two magazines and an occasional book

The Puppet Centre   *(Clapham Junction – British Rail)*
Battersea Arts Centre
Old Town Hall
Lavender Hill SW11
228-5335

M–F 2:00–6:00 (and also by appointment)

Upstairs at Battersea Arts Centre is a thriving place for all aspects – practical and theoretical – or puppetry; it forms London's most specialized shop for books, new and second-hand, on the subject, together with an excellent reference library with many long-out-of-print titles. The Puppet Centre acts very much as an information bureau, able, for example, to provide a directory of all the puppeteers around the country.

Non-book material: postcards (lists available)
Services: see above, mail order, special order, courses,

exhibitions, school and educational work, etc.
Catalogue: regular lists issued
Publications: many pamphlets (lists available) on all aspects of puppetry, a bi-monthly magazine, *Animations*, on worldwide puppetry

John Randall – Books of Asia   *(Pimlico)*
47 Moreton Street SW1
630-5331

M–F 10:00–6:00 (Wed 10:00–8:00)

John Randall specializes in new, second-hand and antiquarian titles on the Middle East, India and South East Asia. He does not deal in books on China and Japan – these are now the province of Han Shan Tang (see separate entry). His section on anthropology worldwide is also very strong.

Services: mail order, special order
Catalogue: three times yearly

Ruposhi Bangla Ltd   *(Tooting Broadway)*
220 Tooting High Street SW17
672-7843

M–Sat 10:00–5:30

This bookshop specializes in Bengali publications, mostly published in India and Bangladesh. They cover a wide range of subjects including children's books, literature and all kinds of reference books. You should be able to find almost anything you want in Bengali or about Bangladesh in this shop. Some bi-lingual books and a variety of periodicals in English and Bengali are also in stock. The main trade is to retailers.

Non-book material: handicrafts, maps, paintings, posters, typewriters (Bengali, Urdu and Arabic)
Services: mail order; school and library supply; supply for retailers; translation service, often used by metropolitan councils
Catalogue: price lists for the books are available

Russian Orthodox Cathedral Bookshop
(South Kensington/ Knightsbridge)

67 Ennismore Gardens SW7
485-8102

Sat 5:00–5:30   7:15–7:45   Sun 10:00–10:30   12:15–1:00

Although it is only open for these short periods the cathedral's bookshop is useful for being one of the few places to stock Orthodox books, prayer-books and Russian bibles as well as American and English theology in English by Russian and Greek church authorities. Notable too is the section of Orthodox art books.

Non-book material: gramophone records and tapes of Orthodox church music, cards, Greek postcards, original hand-painted icons and reproduction icons
Services: mail order, special order
Catalogue: a book-list is available

S.T.A. Travel
(South Kensington)

74 Old Brompton Road SW7
581-4751

M–F 9:00–6:00   Sat 10:00–4:00

This is a travel agency with a range of books, maps and guides to help their intrepid customers plan their holidays. It is largely a student market and they stock the *Lonely Planet* series, aimed at the more independent traveller. The areas covered include South America, India, China, Thailand, Tibet and Australia.

Non-book material: travel agency

St George's Gallery Books Ltd
(Piccadilly Circus)

8 Duke St St James's SW1
930-0935

M–F 10:00–6:00   Sat 10:00–1:00

St George's is a small but classy art bookshop set amidst many well-known art galleries in fashionable St James's. It specializes in new and second-hand academic and scholarly books on fine art, antiques architecture, glass, furniture and related subjects. The range of the stock and the owner's knowledge are extremely wide, combining to make this an essential visit for those interested in such subjects.

Services: mail order, special order worldwide of art exhibition catalogues
Catalogue: new titles lists

Science Museum Bookshop *(South Kensington)*
Exhibition Road SW7
589-3456

M–Tue 11:00–5:40   W–Sat 10:00–5:40   Sun 2:30–5:40

astronomy / clocks and time / computers / farming / lasers / photography / space / telecommunications / transport

The bookshop in the Science Museum is divided into two sections. At the front of the shop are the more general books for children and unscientific adults, while the more specialized stock can be found towards the back of the shop. There is a wide range of subjects here, covering current thought and historical background to all aspects of science and technology.

Non-book material: general souvenirs, educational cassettes, recording of man landing on the moon
Services: special order, mail order for HMSO publications
Catalogue: catalogue covers HMSO publications

Spink and Son *(Green Park)*
5-7 King Street St James's SW1
930-7888

M–F 9:30–5:30

Spink and Son is a large, elegant Oriental and Islamic art dealer which has a relatively small book department on the third floor of the building on King Street. As part of the numismatic department at Spink, the book department specializes in new, second-hand and antiquarian books about coins and medals.

Non-book material: coins, decorations, English painting, Islamic art, medals, orders, Oriental art
Services: mail order, special order, search service
Catalogue: annual list; numismatic circular with coins, medals, new and out-of-print books ten times p.a. on subscription
Publications: Spink and Son Ltd London publishes books on numismatics

The Spiritualist Association of Great Britain   *(Hyde Park Corner)*
33 Belgrave Square SW1
235-3351

M–F 10:00–6:00

Buddhism / cookery / inner knowledge / mediums / psychic worlds / spiritualism / vegetarianism / yoga

This is a small shop in the foyer of the Spiritualist Association of Great Britain building, selling new books, booklets, pamphlets, newspapers and magazines on subjects of psychic and spiritualist interest (which here does not include magic and the occult).

Services: mail order, special order (only through publishers the shop stocks)

Tate Gallery Shop   *(Pimlico)*
Millbank SW1
834-5651

M–Sat 10:00–5:00   Sun 2:00–5:30

The Tate Gallery Shop has a selection of fine arts books in subject areas which relate, in some way, to the artists in the gallery and the genres they represent. Also available are reference and exhibition catalogues from the gallery, and a selection of art-related magazines.

Non-book material: calendars, cards, diaries, gifts, prints, slides
Services: mail order
Catalogue: Tate Gallery publications
Publications: The Tate Gallery publishes exhibition catalogues, studies of artists, cards, posters and prints

Ujamaa Centre   *(Oval)*
14 Brixton Road SW9
582-5590

M–F 10:30–5:30 (closed 1:00–2:00)

Africa: fiction and non-fiction / Asia: fiction and non-fiction /
Caribbean: fiction and non-fiction / development / education /
ecology / family / health and food / Latin America: fiction and
non-fiction / Middle East / politics / women's issues

The Ujamaa Centre is one of over 30 organizations in the National
Association of Development Education Centres, each of which is
attempting to provide multi-ethnic education materials for
teachers and parents and to the general public, with more for
adults than previously. Issues touching the Third World, and
global topics of survival are most frequently confronted in the
adult material, while children's learning materials include books
of myths, history, health and basic political and economic issues.
    Also housed at the centre is a reference library for use by
Ujamaa Centre members, and the South London Education
department of Oxfam.

Non-book material: cassettes, crafts, games
Publications: Ujamaa Centre occasionally publishes posters, map
sets and various educational material

Victoria and Albert Museum Shop   *(South Kensington)*
Cromwell Road SW7
589-6371 ext. 244

M–Th 10:00–5:30   Sat 10:00–5:30   Sun 2:30–5:15

architecture / art history / art of the book / ceramics / children's
books / conservation and restoration / design / engravings /
furniture and woodwork / gallery guides / graphics / heraldry /
illustrators / metal work / oriental art / paintings and water-colours /
poster history / print collecting / psychology and art / sculpture /
textiles / theatre / UK villages and gardens

The V & A bookshop carries new titles about aesthetic and
technical aspects of all areas of art. An entire section is devoted to
titles on the art of the book, another has a wide range of books
about the conservation and restoration of antiques and art work,

while all the titles, even in more traditional areas for a museum shop, seem to be chosen with great care. Adjoining the bookshop is an impressive gift and crafts shop.

Non-book material: cards, crafts, gifts, posters, prints, reproductions, slides
Services: mail order, special order (when possible)
Publications: The V & A publishes books with a variety of commercial publishers and has its own imprint

The Well Bookshop   *(Victoria)*
2 Eccleston Place SW1
730-7303

M–F 10:00–6:00

bible stories and characters / bibles / biography and testimony / children's books / Christianity / church history / death / family relations / healing / life and lifestyle / prayer / sickness / song books

This small Christian bookshop (entrance in Elizabeth Street) is on a mezzanine floor overlooking a lovely new café, restaurant and giftshop complex. The shop has an increasing stock and carries the most popular new Christian titles in subjects from church history to coping with death.

Non-book material: cards, gifts
Services: mail order, special order

Westminster Abbey Bookshop   *(Westminster)*
20 Dean's Yard
Westminster Abbey SW1
222-5565

M–Sat 9:30–5:00

art / bibles / biography / British literature / cookery / history / London / Penguin / poetry / religion

About 50% of The Abbey Bookshop's stock is bibles or books about religion. The rest of the books are stocked with the tourist in mind and include books (both paperback and hardcover) on the history and architecture of the abbey, the Royal Family, English history and classics of English literature.

Non-book material: calendars, gifts, prints, records of the Abbey Choir, slides
Publications: The Abbey Bookshop has published a book about the abbey, *A House of Kings*

Westminster Cathedral Bookshop   *(Victoria)*
42 Morpeth Terrace SW1
828-5582

M–Sat 9:30–5:00

bibles / biography / breviaries / cathechisms / education / liturgy / missals / moral theology / scriptures / spirituality / theology

This small bookshop concentrates on books of worship and literature about the Catholic faith. Some titles concerning other faiths are also stocked.

Non-book material: cassettes, Christmas cards, diaries, hymn books, registers, records, *Catholic Herald* and *Tablet* newspapers
Services: mail order, special order when possible

Whitcoulls Ltd (New Zealand)   *(Piccadilly Circus)*
6 Royal Opera Arcade SW1
930-4587

M–F 9:00–5:00   Sat 9:30–12:00

biography / culture / fiction / history / lifestyle / literature / New Zealand Government publications / poetry / travel guides

This is both a book and gift shop specializing in the history and culture of New Zealand. Most of the books are imported, all are new, and there are a few New Zealand magazines. It is situated in a very pretty arcade leading up from Pall Mall between the Haymarket and Lower Regent Street.

Non-book material: art, cards, crafts, gift items, records, slides, tapes
Services: mail order, special order
Catalogue: complete list of stock annually
Publications: Whitcoulls Publishers Ltd publishes literature and fiction by New Zealand writers

Wimbledon Evangelical Book Centre   *(Wimbledon)*
2 Queen's Road SW19
947-2982

M–Sat 10:00–5:00   W 10:00–1:00

apologetics / bible stories / biography / children's books / Christian life / Christian service / Christology / church history / commentaries / cults and deviations / doctrine / ethics / evangelism / healing / last days / missionary / non-Christian religions / persecution / religion and science / revival and renewal / sermons and talks / youth

With a speciality in the general area of Christian books, the Wimbledon Evangelical Centre concentrates particularly on titles relevant to evangelism in the modern world. Books approach the subject from a variety of practical, theoretical and academic perspectives. The shop also has a large section of educational and enjoyable children's books. Each August, the Centre organizes the Mustard Seed outreach programme on Wimbledon Common, in an effort to communicate with children in the area.

Non-book material: cards, gift items, posters, records
Services: special order

Camille Wolff   *(Sloane Square)*
12a Lawrence Street SW3
352-7725

M–Sun 10:00–5:00 (telephone advisable first)

Camille Wolff has an excellent stock of books covering both criminology and detective fiction. Who wrote it, as much as whodunit, is certain to be known here. Hardback fiction, all of it in good condition and frequently with dust-jackets, ranges from well-known authors such as John Dickson Carr to the many lesser-known from all periods. (Detective fiction is becoming increasingly collected, one dealer recently paying £2000 for a first edition of Ian Fleming's *Casino Royale* at an auction.) The true crime books range from the Notable British Trials series and the works of William Roughead to studies of forensic work and criminology.

Services: mail order
Catalogue: catalogue issued regularly

Zamana Gallery Bookshop *(South Kensington)*
Ismaili Centre
1 Cromwell Gardens SW7
584-6612/3 ext. 46

Tue–Sat 10:00–5:30 Sun 12:00–5:30

The bookshop attached to the Zamana Gallery reflects the areas covered by exhibitions in the gallery and specializes in art, architecture and textiles of the Third and Islamic World. They also stock a selection of magazines, including *Mimar*, an architectural magazine from Singapore and an associated venture.

Non-book material: cassettes, postcards and posters from the gallery, records
Services: international mail order, library supply
Catalogue: catalogues are available for the exhibitions
Publications: exhibition catalogues

Antiquarian and Second-hand Bookshops

Alpha Book Exchange   *(Streatham – British Rail)*
193 Streatham High Street SW16
677-3740

M–Sat 10:00–7:00

biography / crime / detective fiction / historical fiction / humour /
non-fiction / romance / science fiction / study aids / technical /
thrillers / war / westerns

Alpha carries general second-hand paperbacks and magazines a
selection of new Mills and Boon romances, a few hardcover
non-fiction and fiction titles, out-of-print and 'hard-to-find' titles
and various back numbers of magazines. The shop offers to
exchange books bought there for 50% credit toward the next
purchase and the owner is helpful and cordial both buying and
selling.

Non-book material: see above

Joanna Booth   *(Sloane Square)*
247 King's Road SW3
352-8998

M–Sat 10:00–6:00

18th-century French literature and decorative antiquarian English
books comprise part of the stock of this antique shop near the
Chelsea Antique Market.

Non-book material: antiques, Old Master drawings
Services: mail order
Catalogue: selected list

Cavendish Rare Books Ltd   *(Piccadilly Circus)*
2-4 Prince's Arcade, SW1
734-3840

M–F 10:00–6:00   Sat 9:30–1:30

Americas / Asia / English social history / exploration / Far East / fine bindings / foreign military campaigns / literature / maritime / merchant shipping / mountaineering / naval / North and South Poles / travel accounts

At the head of this attractive arcade leading southwards off Piccadilly is Cavendish Rare Books. It specializes in rare and antiquarian first-hand travel and exploration accounts, maritime and naval history and English social history. The shop is small, but packed with fascinating rare accounts by world travellers.

Non-book material: printed ephemera
Services: mail order, search service in field
Catalogue: specialized lists three or four times a year

Chelsea Rare Books   *(Sloane Square)*
313 King's Road SW3
351-0950

M–Sat 10:00–6:00

ground floor:
biography / children's books / drama / fiction / literary criticism / literature / London history and guides / natural history / poetry / topography / travel accounts and guides / UK guides

basement:
antiques / archaeology / architecture / biography / collecting / Continental art / furniture / galleries and museums / interior design / music

Firmly rooted in the ambiance of Chelsea (and surviving when other bookshops in the area have closed their doors), this second-hand and antiquarian shop is particularly strong in the areas of literature (17th through 20th centuries), early travel accounts, art and children's books. Downstairs is a gallery with prints, engravings, watercolours and maps, as well as books on the arts.

Non-book material: see above
Services: mail order, search service
Catalogue: general catalogue two or three times annually, occasional specialized lists

The Constant Reader   *(Fulham Broadway)*
627 Fulham Road SW6
731-0218

M–Sat 10:30–6:30 (times may vary)

art / archaeology / children's books / crime and detective fiction / fiction / film / food and drink / history / humour / illustrated journalism / literature / military and naval / music / natural history / philosophy / pocket editions / poetry / politics / reference / religion / science fiction / sport / theatre / topography / travel

This excellent second-hand shop has two floors of good general stock with a certain emphasis on titles (in all categories) dealing with oriental topics. The stock here is considerably cheaper than in many shops (the reviser of this guide, for example, found a volume of Locke at less than a sixth of the list-price). A boon to the neighbourhood, The Constant Reader is well worth making a detour for.

Services: mail order

The Gloucester Road   *(South Kensington/Gloucester Road)*
Bookshop
123 Gloucester Road SW7
370-3503

M–F 8:30a.m.–10:30p.m.   Sat–Sun 10:30–6:30

antiques / archaeology / architecture / art / biography / cinema / classics / cookery / crafts / detective fiction / fiction / film / gardening / health / history / humour / literature / music / natural history / nostalgia / philosophy / photography / plays / poetry / politics / reference / science / science fiction / travel guides / women

The old bookseller in *The Human Factor* could remember the days when people would queue for a new World's Classic; it is likely that queues will form outside this shop, owned by the Greene family, which, together with Waterstone's, appears to be pioneering book-buying as the best evening's entertainment in the area. This is a second-hand bookshop and a high level of stock is maintained – it is the sort of shop one had always hoped would open in the area.

Non-book material: postcards, prints
Services: special order
Catalogue: several catalogues

Harrington Bros   *(Sloane Square)*
Chelsea Antique Market
253 King's Road SW3
352-5689

M–Sat 10:00–6:00

Illustrated and decorated books on voyages, travel and natural history, bound literary sets, children's books, atlases and colour plate books are the speciality of this strictly antiquarian bookshop. Located on the ground and first floors of the Chelsea Antique Market, Harrington carries books that are as beautiful as they are interesting, most of which are from the 18th and 19th centuries.

Non-book material: prints and maps
Services: mail order, wants lists accepted

Il Libro   *(Sloane Square)*
Chenil Art Galleries C89
183 King's Road SW3
352-9041

M–Sat 10:00–6:00

botany / fine bindings / history / literature / natural history / ornithology / sport / theatre / travel

This lovely-looking market shop is owned by an elegant Italian whose civilized tastes are evident upon browsing through the shop. Its books, mainly 18th- and 19th-century English titles on botany and ornithology, are important documents in the development of natural history, and their fine condition and lovely bindings make them attractive aesthetic objects in themselves.

Non-book material: maps

Jennings Bookshop   *(Streatham Common – British Rail)*
556 Streatham High Road SW16
764-8135

Th–Sat 9:00–5:45

art / biography / cinema / collecting / cookery / drama / fiction / history / literature / military history and equipment / music / natural history / photography / sports / technical / transport / travel guides

Jennings carries new and second-hand books in a variety of subjects. Most of the titles (about 70%) are second-hand, including low-priced paperbacks and moderately-priced hardcover titles.

Non-book material: second-hand sheet music
Services: special order (limited to publishers in stock)

Christopher Mendez   *(Green Park)*
58 Jermyn Street SW1
491-0015

M–F 10:00–5:30

This is primarily an antiquarian print shop, but bound volumes of 16th- through 18th-century Continental prints and engravings are sold. A few new books about prints and print making are also available.

Services: mail order
Catalogue: prints and occasional books

National Schizophrenia Fellowship   *(Wimbledon)*
Bookshop
5 Victoria Crescent SW19
542-2665

M–Sat 10:00–4:00

This is a charity bookshop, run entirely by voluntary workers and relying on donations to maintain its large stock of second-hand books. The prices are very reasonable and the range of books is quite extensive.

333

Michael Phelps
19 Chelverton Road SW15
785-6766

(Putney – British Rail)

By appointment

Mr Phelps operates from private premises – this is not a bookshop but enquiries are welcome. An excellent range of titles covering the history of medicine as well as of natural, pure and applied science can be found here, in all languages, and ranging from antiquarian to more recent titles. Topics such as baking and nutrition sometimes surface among the more specialized subjects.

Services: mail order
Catalogue: a catalogue is issued of the more expensive titles, together with lists of cheaper ones on science and medicine as well as supplementary lists of various topics

Pickering & Chatto
17 Pall Mall SW1
930-2515

(Piccadilly Circus)

M–F 9:30–5:30

economics / English literature / fine bindings / history / medicine / social sciences / science and technology

This excellent antiquarian shop was formerly part of the Dawson group of companies. It tends to receive more mentions in newspapers than many shops do, journalists being fascinated by the involvement of Sir William Rees-Mogg, a former editor of *The Times*. Working in this shop must certainly be more congenial than editing a national newspaper: its stock, with considerable emphasis on English literature from 1660 to 1800, is the sort that could tempt customers to the point of bankruptcy should they stay long. It has an interesting, growing section of volumes of drama, and has sets of authors in modern editions such as the Davis Swift and the Chapman Jane Austen.

Non-book material: broadsides and song-sheets, autographs and manuscripts
Services: mail order, search service
Catalogue: three major catalogues yearly plus 15 lists
Publications: Pickering & Chatto (Publishers) Ltd are at the same address and produce a series of scholarly collected editions of major authors

Popular Book Centre   *(Victoria)*
87 Rochester Row SW1
834-3534

M–Sat 10:00–1:15   1:45–5:15

This bookshop has a general stock of second-hand books, both fiction and non-fiction. There is also a selection of comics, periodicals and magazines. A second branch in Lavender Hill has a larger stock along the same lines.

Popular Book Centre   *(Clapham Junction – British Rail)*
143 Lavender Hill SW11

M–Sat 10:00–5:00 (hours are flexible)

This shop has a general range of second-hand fiction and non-fiction and a variety of comics, periodicals and magazines. There is no telephone here, so any enquiries should be made at the sister shop in Rochester Row.

Sims, Reed and Fogg   *(Piccadilly Circus)*
58 Jermyn Street SW1
493-5660/0952

M–F 10:00–6:00

Antiquarian, out-of-print and finely illustrated books on fine and applied arts are the speciality of Sims, Reed and Fogg. Most of their books are concerned with painting, architecture, jewellery, glass and silver, and the stock is well displayed.

Services: mail order, search service in field
Catalogue: catalogues on various subjects issued from six to eight times a year

Barbara Stone   *(Sloane Square)*
Antiquarius Antique Market
15 Flood Street SW3
351-0963

M–Sat 10:30–5:30

Barbara Stone is a specialist in antiquarian children's books and illustrated books. Her stock includes some second-hand art books, all in extremely good condition. She can be found at stall J6.

Services: special order
Catalogue: catalogue is issued three times a year and concentrates on the illustrated and children's books (home and abroad)

John Thornton   *(Fulham Broadway)*
634 King's Road SW6
634-6181

M–Sat 10:00–5:30

biography / Catholic theology / fiction / history / leisure / sport / topography

A second-hand and antiquarian bookshop with a general range and a special interest in Catholic theology. Theology in general makes up a large section of the shop, but Catholic theology is the predominant subject in both the second-hand and antiquarian stock.

Services: special order

Trocchi Rare Books Ltd   *(Sloane Square)*
Antiquarius Antique Market
15 Flood Street SW3
351-3820   624-1214 (home)

M–Sat 10:00–6:00

This is a stall in the antique market with an interesting general stock of out-of-print and antiquarian books. The range includes English literature, children's books, illustrated books and a comprehensive section on travel.

Services: mail order

Vandeleur Antiquarian Books   *(Mortlake – British Rail)*
69 Sheen Lane SW14
878-6837   393-7752

M–Sat 1:00–7:30 (hours may vary; telephone advisable first)

This small shop close to Mortlake Station has a large stock, specializing in travel and exploration, British topography, Baedekers and mountaineering. A further speciality is sport and games, especially cricket, golf and chess. It also has a general range of paperbacks and hardbacks and a number of illustrated books.

Non-book material: maps; prints (especially rowing prints)
Services: mail order, special lists and quotations prepared on request
Catalogue: catalogues issued, occasionally on specific subjects

Willcocks Antiques   *(Sloane Square)*
Chenil Galleries
Stand E3
181-183 King's Road SW3

M–Sat 10:00–6:00

Specialists in children's books and illustrated books published from 1850 to 1930.

Non-book material: antiques, decorative prints 1850–1930

South East London

General Bookshops

The Arcade Bookshop *(Eltham Well Hall – British Rail)*
3 The Arcade
Eltham High Street SE9
850-7803/4950

M–W 9:00–5:30   Th 9:00–1:00   F–Sat 9:00–5:30

art / BBC publications / beauty / biography / biology / chemistry / children's books / cinema / classics / cookery / crafts / drawing and painting / English as a foreign language / fiction / gardening / health and child care / history / horror / literature / mathematics / paranormal / Pelican, Penguin / pet care / photography / plays / poetry / reference / science fiction / sports / travel guides

With bargain books overflowing on to the walk of the arcade, this bookshop carries both new and remaindered titles in general subject areas. The Arcade Bookshop has a wide range of children's books, paperback fiction and books in basic academic subjects (e.g., mathematics, early learning, English as a foreign language, study aids and BBC educational publications). They work closely with schools and run in-school bookshops and parent evening displays.

Services: mail order, special order

Army & Navy Stores Ltd *(Lewisham – British Rail)*
45 High Street SE13
852-4321

M–Th 9:00–5:30   F–Sat 9:00–6:00

The book section in this store is easily accessible on the ground floor. They carry the usual popular range of reference books, with an emphasis on paperback fiction.

Non-book material: department store

The Bookplace   *(Peckham Rye – British Rail)*
13 Peckham High Street SE15
701-1757

M–Sat 10:00–6:00 (closed Th)

adult literacy / black studies and politics / children's books / China / classics / cookery / education / fiction / film and TV / health / history / horror / indoor games / Ireland / literature / local history and culture / music / politics / pregnancy and parenthood / science fiction / sociology / travel guides / women and sexual politics / young adult fiction

The Bookplace is an impressive community-oriented general bookshop, admirably involved with the interests and needs of the neighbourhood. Of great concern to the staff of the shop are the areas of basic education – from infant to adult – including adult literacy and numeracy and multi-cultural children's learning materials. Books are available in these fields, and the shop tries to keep young adults involved with books, reading and learning by providing them with their own section of titles. Another important dimension of the shop is provided by the books about black politics and 'people's' history – titles on Ireland, Africa, China and their very own Peckham – most with a multi-cultural perspective.

The shop functions as an informal counselling centre, with a staff who are almost always on call for help and advice. Publishing, education, writing and local business support groups each use the shop in the evenings for their meetings and every May The Bookplace organizes a local book fair.

Non-book material: cards, photographs
Services: special order
Catalogue: shop bulletin, specialized lists (e.g., children's learning materials)
Publications: Peckham Publishing Project publishes books by local authors and about local history and culture

Books of Blackheath   *(Blackheath – British Rail)*
11 Tranquil Vale SE3
852-8185

M–F 9:30–5:30   Sat 9:30–5:00

ground floor: new books
archaeology / architecture / art / astronomy / aviation / bibles / biography / children's books / classics / cookery / crafts / drama / education / fiction / gardening / geography / history / language teaching / linguistics / London / maritime history / music / mythology / natural sciences / philosophy / photography / poetry / psychology / reference / religion / sociology / sports / topography: foreign and British

first floor: remaindered books
anthropology / archaeology / architecture / art / aviation / biography / children's books / cookery / crafts / education / fiction / gardening / history / industrial history / literature / maritime history / music / natural sciences / philosophy / photography / poetry / sociology / sports / topography: foreign and British

Nestled into a picturesque vale which borders the heath, Books of Blackheath offers two floors of new and remaindered books. The sections of history and philosophy are specially strong, although the stock of hardcover illustrated books, biographical works, literature and books about topography is also considerable. Generally, the shop has useful holdings in all the subjects listed above, with some interesting bargain books that can be found upstairs.

Services: mail order, special order

The Bookshop   *(Lambeth North)*
4 Kennington Road SE1
261-1385

M–F 10:00–5:30

art / business / children's / cookery / education and language / fiction / gardening / leisure / Penguin / philosophy and religion / reference / women's studies

This bookshop stocks new hard and paperbacks in the general areas outlined above. They have a speedy customer order service.

Non-book material: cards
Services: mail order, special order

Chener Books   *(East Dulwich – British Rail)*

14-16 Lordship Lane SE22
299-0771

M–Sat 10:00–6:00

adventure stories / art / biography / children's books / classics /
crime / dance history / drama / espionage / fiction / film / gardening /
health / history / literary biography and criticism / literature /
military history / music / natural history / occult / philosophy /
plays / poetry / politics / science fiction / topography / transport /
travel guides

Chener Books is an orderly, and very appealing, general
bookshop. Half of the one-room shop is lined with tightly packed
shelves of current hardcover and paperback books of and about
literature. The shop tries to stock the complete works of the
authors they carry, so all of Eliot, Hardy, Hemingway or Plath, for
instance, will be available.

The opposite side of the shop consists of second-hand books,
which again are concentrated in the area of literature and literary
criticism. Also featured are new books about local history and
personalities and often the shop will have new and second-hand
copies of the same book.

Services: search service for out-of-print (beginning with late 19th
century), special order, library supply, school supply
Publications: local history books

Dennys Booksellers Ltd   *(Elephant and Castle)*

62-64 Weston St SE1
378-7834

M–F 9:30–6:30

ground floor:
general / medical / scientific / technical
basement:
second-hand medical

This is a branch of Dennys at Carthusian Street. It is a large
bookshop carrying the same subject matter as the latter, but is on
two floors with a vast stock of second-hand medical books
downstairs.

Services: mail order, special order

Deptford Booktraders   *(Deptford – British Rail)*
55 Deptford High Street SE8
691-8339

Tue–Sat 9:30–5:30   Th 9:30–1:30

art / astrology / biography / black fiction and studies / children's books / community publishing / cookery / food / current affairs / drama / gardening / health / history / hobbies / language / literature / Latin America / Middle East / Poland / politics / psychology / reference / religion / science fiction / sociology / sport / travel / women's issues

This wide-ranging shop with some emphasis on current events around the world is a part of the Deptford Literacy Centre, the enthusiastic staff especially keen on literacy among children and adults – regular classes are held, as well as story-reading sessions for children in the shop. The multi-cultural aspect of the shop is reflected throughout its stock which provides an extremely useful general bookshop for the area. Notable, too, is the stock of titles from various community publishing specialists such as Centerprise.

Non-book material: cards, diaries, guides, magazines, pamphlets, posters, wrapping-paper
Services: mail order, special order (and see above)

Dulwich Books   *(West Dulwich – British Rail)*
6 Croxted Road SE21
670-1920

M–Sat 9:30–5:30   W 9:30–12:30

art / children's books / cookery / fiction / health / history / Open University texts / Ordnance Survey maps and guides / travel

This is a light and spacious shop with a good general stock and helpful staff on hand to give assistance.

Services: special order

Gallery Book Shop
(North Dulwich – British Rail)
1d Carlton Avenue SE21
693-2594

M–Sat 9:30–5:30

ground floor:
children's fiction / dictionaries

first floor:
arts / biography / cookery / craft / gardening / health / history /
humour / literature / maps / poetry / science / sport / travel

The Gallery Book Shop is small but well-stocked – a splendid local
bookshop with an emphasis on the humanities and an excellent
children's section. More recent hardbacks, both fiction and
non-fiction, are kept than is usual in such shops and the service is
highly knowledgeable and enthusiastic.

Non-book material: cards, wrapping-paper, bookplates,
bookmarks
Services: mail order, special order, search service

The Greenwich Bookshop
(Greenwich – British Rail)
37 King William Walk SE10
858-5789

M–Sat 10:30–5:30   Sun 11:00–6:00

art / astronomy / biography / classics / cookery / crafts / DIY /
education / fiction / gardening / health / history / letters / literature /
London / natural history / poetry / politics / psychology / reference /
religion / sociology / transport / travel / women's presses and
issues

On the corner of King William Walk and College Approach is the
Greenwich Bookshop, a general bookseller with current
paperback and hardcover books. The shop has a good women's
section, with literature from Virago and books on feminist issues.
Books stocked are new, second-hand, and some remainders.

Non-book material: cards, diaries, gift wrapping-paper, posters
Services: special order
Catalogue: Christmas

Roy Hayes (Booksellers) Ltd   *(Eltham Well Hall – British Rail)*
Chequers Parade
Passey Place SE9
850-4658

M–Sat 9:00–5:30

animals / antiques and collecting / architecture / art / children's
books / classics / cookery / crafts / fiction / gardening / health,
pregnancy and childcare / horror / literature / local history / music /
natural history / plays / poetry / science fiction / topography /
transport / travel

Roy Hayes is a general bookshop, with current paperback and
hardcover titles in a variety of subjects and price ranges.

Services: special order, school and library supply

Kirkdale Bookshop   *(Sydenham – British Rail)*
272 Kirkdale
Sydenham SE26
778-4701

M–Sat 9:30–5:30   W closed

ground floor: new and remaindered books
anthropology / architecture / art / biography / children's books /
classics / cookery / crafts / fiction / film / gardening / health and
child care / history / literature / local history / mathematics / natural
history / natural sciences / Penguin / photography / poetry and
verse / politics / psychology / reference / science fiction / sciences /
sports / travel guides / women

basement: remaindered and second–handbooks
antiques / archaeology / architecture / art / astrology / biography /
British Isles / cookery / crafts / economics / fiction / gardening /
history / language teaching / literary criticism / literature / memoirs /
military history / natural history / occult / Penguin / performing
arts / philosophy / plays / poetry / politics / science / technology /
theology / transport / travel and exploration

How nice to find that a large and comprehensive general
bookshop can be supported outside central London. Two floors of
new, remaindered and second-hand books comprise the Kirkdale

347

Bookshop where the second-hand section downstairs is expanding (and where prices are quite reasonable). In each of the second-hand categories listed above, they have a substantial number of books, especially in second-hand literature, fiction, biography and philosophy. Current fiction and non-fiction, paperback and hardcover, are on the ground floor, along with a selection of remaindered books toward the rear of the shop.

Services: mail order, special order

John Menzies Ltd *(Blackheath – British Rail)*
20 Tranquil Vale SE3
852-0367

M–Sat 7:00–5:30

The main emphasis in the book section here is on reference – dictionaries, encyclopaedias, maps and guides. There is some paperback fiction including an A-Z of famous authors.

Non-book material: stationery

Pages *(West Norwood – British Rail)*
22 Knights Hill SE27
670-2107

M–Sat 9:30–6:30

A recent and welcome arrival in an area that has hitherto had little to offer its reading public – nearest rivals can be found between a mile (Dulwich) and three miles (Brixton) distant. It aims to stock a broad selection of fiction and non-fiction, for adults and children, in hardback and paperback, but expects to rationalise as the area's likes and dislikes become apparent.

Services: special orders with publishers in stock

The Passage Bookshop *(Denmark Hill – British Rail)*
Canning Cross
Grove Lane SE5
274-7606

M–F 10:00–6:00   Sat 10:00–5:00

adventure fiction / anthropology / art / biography / children's books / classics / cookery / crime / feminism / fiction / gardening / health and child care / history / literature / magic / medical texts / music / nursing / Pelican, Penguin / philosophy / poetry / reference / religion / science fiction / sport and hobbies / travel guides / witchcraft

The Passage Bookshop, tucked away at the end of a quiet alley, has the feel of a quiet English village shop. Here there is general fiction and non-fiction, a special section of medical textbooks to fill the needs of the students at the hospital nearby, and a generous selection of children's books, including picture books, fiction, sports and classics.

Non-book material: Camberwell Society cards, maps and prints
Services: special order

Popular Book Centre   *(Ladywell – British Rail)*
284 Lewisham High Street SE13
690-5110

M–Sat 10:00–5:30

A general shop stocking a range of comics, some adult material and many sci-fi books. It is opposite the fire station.

W.H. Smith   *(Elephant and Castle)*
Elephant and Castle Shopping Centre SE1
703-8525

M–Sat 8:45–5:30   Tue 9:30–5:30

There is a good book department in this branch of WHS situated in the modern centre with its concrete, glass and escalators. Staff are helpful and tell me that they do particularly well with science fiction books in addition to stocking the normal range of general titles.

Non-book material: stationery, etc.
Services: mail order, special order
Catalogue: *Bookcase* twice yearly

W.H. Smith   *(London Bridge)*
London Bridge SE1
403-3288

M–F 7:00a.m.–7:30p.m.

The books on London Bridge Station cover the standard range with the emphasis on paperback fiction and a section for new hardback titles.

Non-book material: stationery, cards, paper, news, magazines
Services: special order, tokens
Catalogue: *Bookcase* review of books twice yearly

W.H. Smith   *(Waterloo)*
Main Line Bookstall
Waterloo Station SE1
261-1616

M–F 7:00a.m.–9:30p.m.   Sat 7:00a.m–9:00p.m.

The larger of Waterloo's two bookstalls in the middle of the station concourse stocks the usual range including children's books, maps and guides.

Non-book material: stationery, cards, paper, news, magazines
Services: special order tokens
Catalogue: *Bookcase* review of books twice yearly

W.H. Smith   *(Waterloo)*
Loop Bookstall
Waterloo Station SE1
928-8478

M–F 7:00a.m.–7:30p.m.   Sat (summer only) 8:00–4:00

The smaller bookstall in Waterloo, by platforms 16 and 17, stocks mainly paperback fiction, including the top five bestsellers. There is a very small reference section, some bargain books, and maps and guides.

Non-book material: stationery, cards, paper, news, magazines
Services: tokens
Catalogue: *Bookcase* review of books twice yearly

W.H. Smith   *(Eltham – British Rail)*
92-94 High Street SE9
859-3019

M–F 9:00–5:30   Sat 8:30–5:30

The standard range of books can be found here, including the new hardback titles and a variety of books for children of all ages.

Non-book material: stationery, cards, paper, news, magazines, etc.
Services: special order, post-a-book, tokens
Catalogue: *Bookcase* review of books twice yearly

W.H. Smith   *(Lewisham – British Rail)*
The Lewisham Centre
59 Riverdale SE13
318-1316

M–F 9:00–5:30   Tue 9:30–5:30   Sat 8:30–5:30

This book department has a reasonable stock of all the usual subjects with special displays for the current titles.

Non-book material: stationery, cards, paper, news, magazines, etc.
Services: special order, post-a-book, tokens
Catalogue: *Bookcase* review of books twice yearly

W.H. Smith   *(Woolwich Arsenal – British Rail)*
68-72 Powis Street SE18
854-7108

M–Sat 8:30–5:30

The book department here stocks a comprehensive range and it is particularly strong on fiction, including the new hardback titles, a section of bestsellers and classics.

Non-book material: stationery, cards, paper, news, magazines, etc.
Services: special order, post-a-book, tokens
Catalogue: *Bookcase* review of books twice yearly

W.H. Smith   *(Forest Hill – British Rail)*
Forest Hill Station
Devonshire Road SE23
699-2789

M–Sat 8:30–5:30

Outside Forest Hill station, this branch of W.H. Smith has an upper floor shared by books and records. The book selection is quite wide for a small shop. They have a special table for the new hardback titles.

Non-book material: stationery, cards, paper, news, magazines, etc.
Services: special order, tokens
Catalogue: *Bookcase* review of books twice yearly

W.H. Smith   *(Catford Bridge – British Rail)*
23 Winslade Way SE6
690-1972

M–Sat 8:30–5:30

The book department here stocks a range of fiction, children's books and titles of general interest including music, art, transport and cookery. They have a section for the new hardback titles and paperback fiction.

Non-book material: stationery, cards, paper, news, magazines, etc.
Services: special order, tokens
Catalogue: *Bookcase* review of books twice yearly

Speciality Bookshops

Ambassador Christian Bookshop

(Norwood Junction – British Rail)

Portland Road SE25
656-0189

M–F 9:15–5:00   Sat 9:15–4:00

This is the largest Christian bookshop in South London, housed in an an old Salvation Army Citadel.

Non-book material: bible readings, cards, cassettes, periodicals, posters, prayer cards, records and a wide range of Christian gifts
Services: organize mailings and book agencies for churches; book evenings

The Bookboat

(Greenwich – British Rail)

Cutty Sark Gardens
Greenwich Church Street SE10
853-4383

M–Sun 10:00–5:00 (closed Th)

adventure stories / Asterix / babies' board books / boats, canals and ships / classics / colouring books / dictionaries / Dr Seuss / educational / fairy tales / fiction / films and TV / hobbies / Ladybird / Lion / multicultural titles / mysteries / nursery rhymes / picture books / poetry / Puffin / science fiction / song-books / storybooks / things to do / Winnie the Pooh / Lisbeth Zwerger

Permanently moored alongside the Cutty Sark Gardens is London's only floating bookshop. A 60-foot Humber keel barge (built in Hull and once used to carry coal and steel) has been converted into one of London's few children's bookshops south of the Thames. A wide range of current titles is available for all ages and reading levels.

Creativity has not stopped with The Bookboat either. A double-decker bus has been converted into a mobile children's educational bookshop and mini film theatre. Artists from Puffin and Collins publishers painted the outside of the vehicle.

Non-book material: badges, cards, pens, paints, stickers, wrapping paper
Services: special order in any field, school accounts

Books Plus   *(New Cross)*
23 Lewisham Way SE14
691-2833

M–F 11:00–6:00   Sat 10:00–5:00

anthropology / art and language / black studies / children's / community and social work / education / feminism / health care / history / individual liberties / literature / Marxist studies / minorities / poetry / politics / psychology / religion / sociology / women's fiction / women's issues / women's studies

Books Plus is a feminist, socialist bookshop, selling new hardcover and paperback books as well as a range of feminist and political newspapers and magazines. Most of the books are concerned with social, economic and political issues, but there is a wide range of women's fiction and literature. Women's issues and studies, black studies and individual liberties are particularly interesting sections here. All children's books are non-racist and non-sexist.

Non-book material: badges, cards, posters, jewellery
Services: mail order, special order, library supply
Catalogue: list available

Church Army Resource Centre   *(Blackheath – British Rail)*
Independents Road SE3
318-1226

M–F 9:30–5:00   Sat 10:00–4:00

Located in the Church Army headquarters, the shop specializes in audio-visual material, but there is a wide range of Christian literature which complements the devotional technology.

Non-book material: audio-visual department, geared towards educational needs
Services: mail order, supplies schools and churches
Catalogue: lists of audio-visual material

Church Missionary Society   *(Waterloo)*
157 Waterloo Road SE1
928-8681

M–F 9:00–4:45

There is no longer a public display of the books in the Society's stockroom, so this is not a place for weekend browsing. If you know exactly what you are looking for, they will search for it amongst the stock of books connected with the international Christian mission.

Non-book material: audio-visual aids, cassettes
Services: mail order for the Society's magazine
Catalogue: lists audio-visual aids and a selection of the book stock
Publications: The Society publishes its own quarterly magazine and a newsletter for subscribers

Commissariat,   *(West Dulwich – British Rail)*
Dulwich College
College Road SE21
693-4565

M–F 8:30–12:00   1:00–4:45 during term   9:00–12:00   2:00–4:45 during holidays

This shop is housed within the grounds of Dulwich College, sharing its premises with the school's outfitters and sports equipment, but it is open to the public and the entrance is on Dulwich Common. The books are aimed at children from eight to nineteen years and they include paperback fiction, revision aids and some textbooks which are related to the Dulwich College curriculum.

Non-book material: school uniform, sports equipment, stationery

Daybreak Books   *(Lee – British Rail)*
68 Baring Road Lee SE12
857-118

Tu–Sat 9:00–1:00   2:00–5:30

bibles / biography / children's books / Christianity / church history /
commentaries / cookery / daily life / doctrine / education / faith /
fiction / gardening / healing / literature / music / poetry and verse /
prayer / reference / religion / spirituality

Daybreak Books carries a very limited selection of general titles in
addition to their speciality in Christian books. There are two floors
of books on all aspects of Christianity from scholarly bible
commentaries to accounts of daily Christian life, and the staff are
quite willing to help with anything you don't find on their shelves.

Non-book material: cards, cassettes, posters, records, stationery
Services: mail order, special order
Catalogue: selected lists quarterly
Publications: Daybreak Publications has published two books on
Christianity

Eurocentre Bookshop   *(Lee – British Rail)*
21 Meadow Court Road SE3
318-5633

M–F 9:00–5:00

This bookshop is part of a language school and specializes in EFL
material for students and teachers. The stock includes books
catering for the particular courses in the school and some more
general background titles. The bookshop can be opened on
request at reception outside the official hours.

Non-book material: EFL cassettes

Goldsmiths' College Book   *(New Cross)*
& Stationery Shop
Lewisham Way SE14
692-7171

M–F 9:00–7:00 during term   M–F 9:00–5:00 vacation

art / biology / chemistry / design / education / fiction / French (language) / geography / German (language) / health / history / linguistics / literature / mathematics / music / Open University / philosophy / physics / plays / poetry / politics / psychology / reference / Shakespeare / sociology / technology

Most of the books here are current paperback titles related to the courses given at the college. Each subject area is represented by a good range of titles, and the shop is well labelled and organized.

Non-book material: artists' materials, stationery
Services: mail order, special order
Publications: stock selected publications from the college

Hayward Gallery Bookshop   *(Waterloo)*
South Bank SE1
928-3144

exhibition hours

This small foyer shop carries a selection of titles on contemporary art, art history, exhibition catalogues, books related to current exhibitions and Arts Council publications.

Non-book material: cards, prints, journals
Services: mail order, special order

Holy Cross Catholic Bookshop   *(Catford – British Rail)*
4 Brownhill Road SE6
461-0896

M–Sat 9:30–5:30

The range of books here is catholic in both senses of the word, from geology to philosophy and including lives of the saints, doctrine, church history and scriptural studies. There is a section of children's books and a particular interest in educational material.

Non-book material: audio cassettes, cards, pictures, statues, videos
Services: mail order, educational supply
Catalogue: catalogue available for the book stock only

357

I.S.O. Publications
(Lambeth North)

137 Westminster Bridge Road SE1
261-9588/9179

M–F 9:30–5:30   Sat 11:00–2:00

These are the specialists in military, aviation and naval subjects, with some magazines included in their predominantly hardback stock.

Non-book material: badges, kits, posters
Services: bi-annual mail order list
Catalogue: a forward catalogue and a stock catalogue are avilable
Publications: I.S.O. Pictorial series, *Outlines* series, books published with the Galago publishing company

Imperial War Museum Shop
(Elephant and Castle)

Kennington Road SE1
735-8922

M–Sat 10:00–5:40   Sun 2:00–5:40

This shop inside the war museum specializes in the two World Wars and is particularly geared towards the school children who visit the museum in their thousands.

Non-book material: accessories, BBC archive material and even the popular music of the war years, cassettes and records of military music, education packs, photographic packs, postcards, posters, souvenirs
Services: mail order, educational supply
Catalogue: on sale in the shop for 50p

Kimpton's Medical Bookshop
(London Bridge)

23 St Thomas Street SE1
403-1152

M–F 10:00–5:30

Stock carried is the same as at the other two branches, with the exception of veterinary science and the addition of some popular fiction, non-fiction and general interest books.

Services: mail order; special order; visits to medical meetings and schools of nursing for the display and sale of books; the Teviot subscription agency is able to handle orders for all British and international periodicals and journals
Catalogue: Kimpton's monthly Book News; specialized subject-lists
Publications: Kimpton's and Teviot Scientific publish books in the field of medicine

Labour Party Bookshop   *(Elephant and Castle)*
150 Walworth Road SE17
703-0833

M–F 9:00–5:00

biography / defence / economics / EEC / energy / fiction / history / industry / law / Marxism / philosophy / politics / reference / social issues / socialism / Third World / trade unions / women

Located in the attractive new Labour Party headquarters, the Labour Party Bookshop specializes in books on political, social and economic issues. Pamphlets, booklets, reports and leaflets are in abundance, on topics from socialism to sexism.

Non-book material: badges, balloons, beer mats, gifts, posters, scarves, ties
Services: mail order, special order
Catalogue: quarterly lists
Publications: The Labour Party publishes campaign handbooks, discussion documents, reports and the magazines *Labour Weekly*, *New Socialist* and *Labour Party News*

London City Mission   *(London Bridge)*
175 Tower Bridge Road SE1
407-7585

M–F 9:00–5:00

The stock here is a combination of quite specialized books ordered by the missionaries and a more general range including autobiographies, doctrine, prayer, bibles and bible commentaries. There is limited space for books in the Mission but nevertheless there is a steady turnover of stock.

Non-book material: cassettes of mission recordings, posters
Services: special order
Publications: mission books

Francis Marsden Books for Printers   *(Elephant and Castle)*
London College of Printing
(St George's Road)
Elephant and Castle SE1
735-8570

M–F 10:15–5:30 (term time only)

bookbinding / cinema / colour printing / composing / design / design history / economics / graphic reproduction / graphics / gravure printing / journalism / law / lithographic, screen and flexographic printing / management / photography / print finishing / printing / science / typography

This is a bookstall, just above the foyer in the London College of Printing, which carries new titles related to the printing and design courses given at the college.

Non-book material: artists' and printing material

Mercury Bookshop   *(Woolwich Arsenal – British Rail)*
Thames Polytechnic
Wellington Street SE18
317-0646

M–F 8:45–5:30   W 8:45–5:00

architecture / art / economics / education / engineering: civil, electrical, mechanical / fiction / history / literature / Penguin / plays / poetry / politics / psychology / sociology / surveying

This is a fairly small college bookshop in the foyer of the Thames Polytechnic. All the books are new and the shop caters to the student interests and courses at the polytechnic, though there is a general selection of Penguin paperbacks.

Services: mail order (infrequently), special order

The Motion Picture Bookshop   *(Waterloo)*
National Film Theatre
South Bank SE1
928-3517

M–F 11:30–9:00   Sat–Sun 5:30–9:00

BFI dossier series / biography / cartoons / criticism / documentary /
early cinema / English cinema / genres / history / horror / other
media / science fiction / screenplays / screenwriting / TV

As the bookshop of the NFT, The Motion Picture Bookshop
specializes in new titles about film, TV and video. Many of the
books concern the British cinema and film history, but they carry a
range of titles often on foreign, international film, directors, stars
and film theory. Technical aspects of the cinema, including the
subject of writing for the screen, also feature in the shop's stock.
Major cinema journals are available as well as the British Film
Institute's publications. A small selection of second-hand books is
available.

Non-book material: cards, posters, magazines, badges
Services: mail order, special order, search service
Catalogue: monthly booklist

Museum of Garden History   *(Victoria/Waterloo)*
St Mary-at-Lambeth
Lambeth Palace Road SE1
261-1891

M–F 11:00–3:00   Sun 10:30–5:00 (March to December only)

This museum is run by the Tradescant Trust and centred in the
much restored church of St Mary-at-Lambeth. It is a delightful
place to visit for those interested in plants and part of the
churchyard has been designed as a replica of a 17th-century
garden, containing only plants grown by the Tradescants and
other plants of that period. The shop sells a wide variety of gifts
with flower and garden themes and among these is a small section
of books on the same subject.

Non-book material: see above

National Theatre Bookshop   *(Waterloo/Embankment)*
National Theatre
South Bank SE1
928-2033

M–Sat 10:00a.m.–11:00p.m.

autobiography / biography / children's books / criticism / film / humour / memoirs / plays and play texts / Shakespeare / stage history / theatre skills

The National Theatre contains one main bookshop, specially designed and set in the foyer of the Lyttleton theatre, and two bookstalls in the foyers of the Olivier and Cottesloe theatres. The latter are open performance hours only. The main shop contains a large cross-section of play texts (including those at present being staged by the National Theatre), together with a huge range of critical and historical books on all aspects of the theatre. There are also small sections of poetry, fiction, general arts titles and children's books.

Non-book material: cassettes, magazines, National Theatre gifts, posters, records, T-shirts

121 Bookshop   *(Brixton)*
121 Railton Road SE24
274-6655

Summer M–Sat 2:00–6:00   Winter M–Sat 12:00–4:00

The 121 Bookshop is an anarchist and feminist shop oriented toward the needs of the Brixton community. Political issues take precedence among the subject areas, with books on race relations, civil liberties and international and revolutionary politics in stock. The feminist section includes titles about sexual politics, children, gay liberation and health. Most of the books are in the area of non-fiction (including self-help titles on, for instance, plumbing and printing), though a bit of anarchist fiction is available. Books on black studies and specific problems in the Third World are less plentiful at 121 because Sabarr Books, a black community bookshop, is just up the road.

121 also carries a range of political and community magazines and newspapers. The shop sponsors community meetings and discussion groups and is open on Sunday afternoon for Brixton Squatters Aid.

Non-book material: badges, cards, posters, T-shirts
Services: mail order, special order in fields of anarchy and feminism, squatters aid, women's café
Catalogue: comprehensive list
Publications: a poetry and an anarchist magazine are published by the shop

Parks Bookshop   *(Elephant and Castle)*
18 London Road SE1
928-5378

M–F 9:30–6:30   Sat 9:30–1:00

accountancy / biology / business / chemistry / computing / economics / education / engineering / food science / law / management / marketing / mathematics and statistics / nursing / physics / politics / printing / psychology / social administration / sociology / taxation / women's studies

This is the sister branch to Parks in Holborn. Their stock consists of academic and professional titles in the areas outlined above. They are next to the London Polytechnic.

Services: mail order, special order
Catalogue: Parks business catalogue

Sherratt & Hughes at the   *(Waterloo)*
South Bank Centre
The Royal Festival Hall
South Bank SE1
633-9323

M–Sun 10:00a.m.–11:00p.m.

art / classical music / cooking / design / fiction / fine art / gardening

The newest addition to W. H. Smith's 'other' retail chain has taken over what used to be the Festival Hall Bookshop, extended the area further into the foyer and expanded the stock. Although classical music, fine art and design still feature large, other subjects, such as cooking, gardening and some upmarket fiction have crept in, all carefully chosen to appeal to the South Bank supporting public. Sheet music is no longer stocked.

Non-book material: periodicals
Services: special orders, mailing to Friends of the South Bank

Anthony J. Simmonds – Maritime Books

(Greenwich – British Rail)

15 The Market
Greenwich SE10
853-1727

M–Sat 10:00–6:00 (Sun open in summer)

Simmonds sells new, second-hand and antiquarian books about the sea, though its focus is less oceanographic than on the literature of exploration, travel, trading, yachting, sailing and naval and maritime history. Although the business is primarily mail order, the shop is open to the public and books from the catalogue can be seen and bought. New books come from publishers around the world, including a few private press publications from the USA. There are a limited number of remaindered books available as well.

Non-book material: ephemera, models
Services: mail order, special order, search service
Catalogue: one major catalogue per year with additional shortlists approximately every three months

Soma Books

(Kennington)

38 Kennington Lane SE11
735-2101

M–F 10:00–5:30

Africa / art / Buddhism / Caribbean / children's books / comparative literature / crafts / decorative arts / education / ethics / fiction / history / India / Islam / language / literature / meditation / mythology / philosophy / poetry / politics / reference / religion / sociology / Sufism / women / yoga

Soma was initially a mail order business but has had a retail bookshop for the past few years. The shop's books are about India, Africa and the Caribbean, with an enormous variety of publications in English as well as Gujarati, Bengali, Hindi, Urdu and Punjabi. Titles on politics, art, history, literature, mythology and religion are stocked, but the shop's real speciality is in the area of children's learning materials. The Indian and West Indian staff are active in the field of multiracial education and are both knowledgeable and helpful. Soma is a black bookshop making a great effort to reach the white population of Britain.

Non-book material: cards, charts on mythology, hand-made stationery, miniatures
Services: mail order, special order
Catalogue: children's books and learning materials, subject lists

South London Christian Bookshop   *(East Dulwich)*
15–19 Lordship Lane
East Dulwich SE22
693-7969

M–Sat 9:00–5:30 (closed Th)

The Christian Bookshop specializes in books on evangelism and evangelist education. The scope of their titles is, however, interdenominational, with a good selection of books on bible and gospel commentary.

Non-book material: Christian cards, records, cassettes and video, handicrafts
Services: coffee bar, mail order

The Spurgeon's   *(Norwood Junction – British Rail)*
Book Room
Spurgeon's College
189 South Norwood Hill SE25
653-3640

M–F 9:30–5:00   7:00–9:00 (closed Wednesdays)

This is the bookshop for students training for the ministry at Spurgeon's bible college but the general public are welcome. It stocks all the recommended texts and more popular works for a wider audience. The range includes bible commentaries, studies of the Old and New Testaments, church history, biographies and books on family and personal life.

Non-book material: cards, cassettes of religious music and Christian rock music, stationery
Services: special order
Catalogue: a catalogue is planned for 1987

Antiquarian and Second-hand Bookshops

The Bookshop, Blackheath Ltd   *(Blackheath – British Rail)*
74 Tranquil Vale SE3
852-4786

M–Sat 9:30–5:00 (closed Th)

animal biology / architecture / art history / artists / Asia / biography / British topography / chemistry / children's books / classics / collecting / commercial art / cookery / essays / Europe / fiction: 19th and 20th centuries / gardening / health / history / literature / London and local history / maritime history / mathematics / military history / modern first editions / natural history / plays / poetry / sports / theatre / theology / translations / travel

The Bookshop, which faces the edge of Blackheath, is a meticulously organized second-hand and antiquarian shop. Every inch of space in the shop is used, with children's books, first editions, modern and 19th-century fiction and titles on natural history standing out as particularly strong sections. A few new and remaindered titles creep onto the shelves but the majority of the stock is second-hand books.

Non-book material: prints of local topography
Publications: *Blackheath Village and Environs*, 2 vols by Neil Rhind

Bookshop Crystal Palace   *(Crystal Palace – British Rail)*
77 Church Road SE19
Telephone not available at publication

M–Sat 9:30–5:30

art / astronomy / biography / cookery / education / fiction / geology / history / humour / language teaching / literature / local history / maritime history / mathematics / military history / music / natural history / ornithology / palaeontology / poetry / romance / sciences / sports / travel and exploration / travel guides

With substantial holdings of books in the sciences, this general bookshop carries second-hand, remaindered and new books. Natural history, geology, ornithology, palaeontology and education theory are particularly large sections here, but second-hand Pelicans, cookery books, sporting guides and titles on European, African and Asian history are also available, as well as books on other general subjects.

Services: mail order by request only

The Camberwell Bookshop   *(Denmark Hill – British Rail)*
28a Camberwell Grove SE5
701-1839

Tue–Sat 10:00–6:00   closed 2:00–3:00

caricature / cartoons / design / fine and applied art / modern architecture

A second-hand and antiquarian bookshop, concentrating on arts subjects in the second-hand department. There is also a general range of antiquarian books and a sideline in magazines and periodicals.

Non-book material: prints

Check Books   *(Blackheath – British Rail)*
1 Tranquil Passage SE3
318-9884

Tue–Sat 10:30–6:00

Three floors of second-hand and antiquarian books provide a large general stock, with a particularly good selection of art and literature. The sister shop in Bloomsbury specializes in Middle Eastern and foreign travel.

Services: mailing list

Coffeehouse Bookshop   *(Greenwich – British Rail)*
139 Greenwich South Street SE10
692-3885

M–Sat 10:00–5:30 (closed 1:00–2:00)   closed Thursdays

A large selection of second-hand books, particularly paperbacks, with a good literature section.

Non-book material: bric-a-brac, jewellery, records

Jane Gibberd   *(Waterloo)*
20 Lower Marsh SE1
633-9562

W–F 11:00–7:00

In the Cut Market close to Waterloo Station and to the Old Vic is this shop which although it has a medium-sized stock, has a high turnover, about a quarter of its stock each week. Its stock of remainders and second-hand books is general, always of a good quality and with both the hardbacks and paperbacks confined to the humanities.

Greenwich Book Place   *(Greenwich – British Rail)*
258 Creek Road SE10
(near Creek Bridge)
No telephone

M–Sun 12:00–6:00

This business is run from a converted Edwardian pub in open ground near Creek Bridge. It used to be an enormous bookstore, but now the front of the shop is a picture gallery and framing business, while the rear of the ground floor and the basement are used to store the owner's considerable stock of second-hand and out-of-print titles in the fields of biography, foreign languages, general fiction and social sciences. These are sold primarily through mail order, but customers are always welcome to call.

Non-book material: see above
Services: mail order
Catalogue: occasional selected lists in the subjects mentioned above

Hillyers   *(Lower Sydenham – British Rail)*
301 Sydenham Road SE26
778-6361

M–F 8:30–4:30   Sat 8:30–2:00   W closed

Opening early and not closing for lunch, Mr Hillyer keeps a small general stock of books among his antiques and furniture. The books are not necessarily related to these but depend very much upon what happens to arrive from week to week.

Non-book material: see above
Services: mail order

Magpie   *(Greenwich – British Rail)*
87 Blackheath Road SE10
692-2807

Tue–F 2:00–8:00   Sat 11:00–9:00

This second-hand bookshop has a general stock and a particular interest in early sport and transport, usually pre-war. The opening hours are flexible, tending towards very late evening hours, so a perfect place for the weary commuter from Charing Cross in search of a distraction during those endless delays outside London Bridge.

Non-book material: bric-a-brac, ephemera, old furniture

Marcet Books   *(Greenwich – British Rail)*
The Passageway
4a Nelson Road SE10
853-5408   858-724

Tu–Sun 10:30–5:30

architecture / art / biography / children's books / crime, detective / encyclopaedias / Everyman's Library / fiction / history / literature / Penguin / pocket editions / poetry / Reprint Society / theatre / World's Classics

A welcome addition to the thriving Greenwich bookshops is this general second-hand shop to be found along the alleyway at the side of the Coach and Horses. The wide-ranging stock contains a number of first editions, antiquarian titles as well as collections of out-of-print Penguins and other well-known, useful imprints in pocket-sizes such as Nelson's Library, together with sets of standard authors.

Non-book material: magazines, pamphlets, postcards
Services: mail order
Catalogue: yes

369

Observatory Bookshop   *(Greenwich – British Rail)*
141 Trafalgar Road SE10
858-8411

M–F 9:30–3:00 (hours are flexible)

This is a small collection of second-hand paperbacks, mainly fiction, on the premises of a printing company in Greenwich.

Plus Books   *(Tulse Hill – British Rail)*
224 Norwood Road SE27
670-8707

M–Sat 9:30–6:00

Plus Books provides a general range of second-hand books to buy or exchange and, although there are no specialist sections, the emphasis is on fiction. They also stock a wide variety of magazines.

Rogers Turner Books Ltd   *(Greenwich – British Rail)*
22 Nelson Road SE10
853-5271

M–F 10:00–6:00   Th 10:00–2:00   Sat 10:00–5:30   Sun 10:00–dusk

art / biography / geography / history / horology / language / literature / natural history / naval and military / philosophy / religion / science / travel

This shop contains an excellent range of antiquarian, old and out-of-print books, with some emphasis on academic works. All languages are covered (an office is kept in Paris which makes the European service especially good), the prices are reasonable, service friendly and highly knowledgeable – all making this shop well worth a visit.

Non-book material: ephemera, a few pamphlets, magazines
Services: mail order; special order for books throughout Europe and the world; commissions for all major auctions in Europe; appraisal, search service
Catalogue: eight issued a year on history, history of science, horology, linguistics, etc.

The Spread Eagle

(Greenwich – British Rail)

8 Nevada Street SE10
692-1618

M–Sat 10:00–5:30

art / biography / cinema / cookery / fiction / gardening / history / illustrated children's books / literature / modern first editions / music / natural history / poetry / theatre / topography / travel

Opposite the Greenwich Theatre and the Rose and Crown is this shop in part of the last coach-house on the route between Kent and London. A large number of books, antiquarian and second-hand, is kept among a general stock of antiques. The stock, which is especially strong on travel and topography, is regularly changing so that it is difficult to say exactly what will be found at any time; certainly it is reasonably priced and worth visiting along with the other Greenwich shops. Some of the rarer, large art books are kept in the shop's other branch next to Rogers Turner.

Non-book material: see above, general antiques, postcards, ephemera, magazines
Services: mail order

Stone Trough Books

(Denmark Hill – British Rail)

59 Camberwell Grove SE5
708-0612

Tu–Sat 10:00–6:00

archaeology / art / biography / cathedrals and monuments / cookery / crime / fiction / history / literary criticism / literature / medical books / modern first editions / opera / plays / poetry

Stone Trough is a second-hand bookshop specializing in literature, art books, modern first editions and travel books, mostly concerned with Europe. The shop is small, uncluttered and very welcoming, with a stock which reflects the personal interests of the owner. Only 25 authors' works are permitted in the modern first editions section, including Evelyn Waugh, Aldous Huxley, T. S. Eliot, Christopher Isherwood and Graham Greene. Prices are about one-third less than those for similar titles in central London, and to make the trip even more worthwhile, there is a landmark tavern across the road which serves good pub fare.

Services: mail order, search service
Catalogue: modern first editions list annually

Studio Books   *(Blackheath – British Rail)*
2 Montpelier Vale SE3
318-9666

Tue–Sat 11:00–6:00

economics / literature / natural history / politics / sociology / sport / technology

Go through the archway and forty yards along the mews to find this first-floor bookshop at the back of the building, specializing in nineteenth- and twentieth-century out-of-print books. There is a wide range of subjects covered by the stock and 6,000 of the 15,000 books are kept in storage elsewhere. There is a small antiquarian section which concentrates on English literature and a selection of pamphlet material and theatre programmes. The opening hours are flexible and if you ring up in advance the owner is prepared to open the shop for you outside the official hours.

Services: special order

Swan's Bookstall   *(Deptford – British Rail/Tooting Broadway)*
29 Deptford Market SE8
691-3705

T–W   F–Sat 9:30–3:30

espionage / fiction / horror / romance / science fiction / thrillers / war / westerns

Swan's is a second-hand paperback bookstall with mostly science fiction and western adventure novels, though they also carry a substantial number of Mills and Boon romance titles.

Note: Swan's Bookstall has another branch at:
5 Tooting Market SW17
672-4980
M–F 9:00–5:30   W closed

Index   Bookshops by Speciality

Alphabetical Index

Modern Book Co. (W2), 214-15
Morgans & Co. Ltd (N20), 142
Mothers' Union Bookshop (SW1), 315
Motion Picture Bookshop (SE1), 361
Motor Books (WC2), 60
Mowbray's Bookshop (W1), 215
Museum Bookshop (WC1), 60-1
Museum of Garden History (SE1), 361
Museum of London Bookshop (EC2), 110-11
Music Book Centre (W1), 245
Muslim Bookshop (N4), 153
Mustard Seed (NW1), 188
Muswell Hill Bookshop (N10), 142-3
Mysteries (WC2), 61

National Army Museum Bookshop (SW3), 315-16
National Poetry Centre Bookshop (SW5), 316
National Portrait Gallery Bookshop (WC2), 61-2
National Schizophrenia Fellowship Bookshop (SW19), 333
National Theatre Bookshop (SE1), 362
Natural History Museum Bookshop (SW7), 316-17
Neal Street East (WC2), 62
New Beacon Bookshop (N4), 153-4
New City Bookshop (EC3), 100
New Ear Books (N4), 154
Newham Parents' Centre (E13), 127
Nihon Token (WC1), 62-3
Notting Hill Books (W8), 268

Oak Hill College Bookroom (N14), 155
Observatory Bookshop (SE10), 370
O'Callaghan, John (W1), 245
OCS Bookshop (WC1), 188
Odyssey Bookshop (WC1), 63
Offstage Theatre Shop and Gallery (NW1), 189
121 Bookshop (SE24), 362-3
Open Book (W11), 246
Open Way Books (N16), 162
Operation Headstart Books and Crafts (N15), 155
Oppenheim & Co. Ltd (SW7), 287-8
Orbis Books (London) Ltd (SW5), 317

Owl Bookshop (NW5), 172
Oxfam Books (W1), 268
Oxford University Press Bookshop (Zwemmer's, WC2), 79
Oxford University Press Music & Books (Zwemmer's, WC2), 79
Paddington & Friends (W1), 246
Padre Pio Bookshop Centre (SW1), 317-18
Page One Books (E15), 127-8
Pages (SE27), 348
Pages of Fun (SW1), 288
Pan Bookshop (SW10), 288-9
Paperback Centre (SW9), 289
Paperbacks Centre (E13), 120-1
Paperbacks Centre (W1), 216
Paperchase (SW3), 318
Paperchase (WC1), 63
Paraphernalia (NW3), 172-3
Parks Bookshop (SE1), 363
Parks Bookshop (WC1), 64
Passage Bookshop (SE5), 348-9
Penguin at Liberty's (W1), 216
Penguin Bookshop (NW1), 173
Penguin Bookshop (SW3), 289-90
Penguin Bookshop (Collet's, WC2), 45-6
Penguin Bookshop (Covent Garden, WC2), 27-8
Peters Music Shop (W1), 246-7
Le Petit Prince Bookshop (SW7), 318
Phase One Books (NW3), 197
Phelps, Michael (SW15), 334
Photographer's Gallery Bookshop (WC2), 64-5
Pickering & Chatto (SW1), 334
Pilot Software Ltd (W1), 247
Pipeline Bookshop (WC1), 28
Planning Bookshop (SW1), 319
Pleasures of Past Times (WC2), 88
Plus Books (SE27), 370
Plus Books (SW19), 290
Poland Street Publications Ltd (W1), 247-8
Pollock's Toy Museum (W1), 248
Polonez (W12), 248-9
Popular Book Centre (SE13), 349
Popular Book Centre (SW1), 335
Popular Book Centre (SW11), 335
Popular Book Centre (W1), 268
Pordes, Henry (WC2), 88
Port, Raymond (E17), 128
Potter, J.D. (EC3), 111